the northwest herb lover's handbook

A Guide to
Growing Herbs for
Cooking, Crafts, and
Home Remedies

the
northwest herb
lover's
handbook

MARY PREUS

SASQUATCH BOOKS
SEATTLE

To herb lovers of all times and places,

whose fascination, study, and passion for

these remarkable plants carries on a

living tradition.

Printed in the United States of America
Distributed in Canada by Raincoast Books, Ltd.
04 03 02 01 00   5 4 3 2 1

Cover and interior design: Karen Schober
Cover and interior photographs: Mary Preus
Copy editor: Sigrid Asmus
Proofreader: Miriam Bulmer

Library of Congress Cataloging in Publication Data
Preus, Mary.
   The Northwest herb lover's handbook : a guide to growing herbs
for cooking, crafts, and home remedies / by Mary Preus.
     p. cm.
   Includes index.
   ISBN 1-57061-172-6 (alk. paper)
1. Herb gardening—Northwest, Pacific. 2. Herbs—Utilization. 3. Cookery (Herbs)
I. Title.
SB351H5P7382000
635'.7'09795—dc21
99-047198

Sasquatch Books
615 Second Avenue
Seattle, Washington 98104
(206) 467-4300
www.SasquatchBooks.com
books@SasquatchBooks.com

contents

acknowledgments

Many people helped me as I wrote this book, and to them I'd like to express my appreciation herbally, with an imaginary tussie mussie (or nosegay) of herbs and flowers, each carrying a special message of thanks and affection.

First and foremost, a fragrant rose for love to Bob Crew, for being a great husband and for his loving support that never wavered. Heartsease and happy thoughts to Miriam and Eve Preus and Geoff and Tinker Crew for being family. Sage for long and healthy life to my mom, Marie DeGroot, who in many ways made my Silver Bay Herb Farm adventure possible; my dad, Paul Preus, for his ready wit and wisdom; and Aunt Louise Luce, who has always believed in me. Fennel to Jean Galbreath, my right-hand woman at Silver Bay, who is worthy of all praise. Clove gillyflowers (pinks) to signify affection to all my other friends for keeping my life in balance.

Sweet marjoram for joy to all the people at Sasquatch Books, especially Gary Luke, who first suggested expanding my little green book, *Growing Herbs*, and patiently did what it took to set it in motion; Novella Carpenter, who combines personal charm with excellent editorial assistance; and Karen Schober, for getting excited about my photographs. Coriander for hidden worth to the others on the staff who helped to make this book a reality.

Sweet basil for good wishes to Jane Chapin, Phyllis Cleven, Jean Galbreath, Frankie Graham, Diana Isaiou, Ricki Johnson, Caprial and John Pence, Barbara Stedman, Karen Story, James Walsh, and Steve Whippo, who generously shared their recipes. Mint for warmth of feeling to Karen Triplett, the Medicinal Herb Garden at the University of Washington, and Susan Dearth and Marilyn Hepner at Gardenscapes for welcoming me to photograph their gardens, and to Sandy and Jack Livingstone of Sunshine Herb Farm, for keeping me current on the latest herb varieties.

Here's lavender for luck to John Kimble, Head Gardener at Freeway Park in Seattle for help with the tricky Latin names and for good companionship; David McDonald, Resource Conservation Planner at Seattle Public Utilities for his valuable comments on composting and worm bins; and to Ken Plante of Molbak's, for being there to answer all manner of gardening questions.

I'll tuck in rosemary for remembrance to the many authors listed in the bibliography, whose works provided a wealth of information, inspiration, and enjoyment. Lastly, forget-me-nots to my customers at Silver Bay Herb Farm, for all the questions, ideas, recipes, conversations, and most of all for the happy times that linger as precious memories in my heart.

—*Mary Preus*

introduction

"The life of man in this world is but a thraldom,
when the Sences are not pleased; and what rarer object can
there be on earth, (the motions of the Celestial bodies
excepted) then a beautifull and Odiferous Garden plat
Artificially composed, where he may read and contemplate
on the wonderfull works of the great Creator, in Plants and
Flowers; for if he observeth with a judicial eye, and a serious judgement their variety of Colours, Sents, Beauty,
Shapes, Interlacing, Enamiling, Mixture, Turnings,
Windings, Embosments, Operations and Vertues, it is most
admirable to behold, and meditate upon the same. But now
to my Garden of Flowers and sweet Hearbs..."

—THOMAS HYLL, *The Gardeners Labyrinth*, 1568

My adventures
in the richly varied
world of herbs began
when I rooted six
rosemary cuttings
in a clay pot.

Once introduced, I soon fell in love with herbs— their forms, their scents, their powers and properties, their history and their quaint descriptions written hundreds of years ago. What began as a hobby became a passion, and blossomed into a business called Silver Bay Herb Farm, located on the shores of Puget Sound. For more than twenty years, I lived and breathed herbs, learning everything I could about these fascinating plants and sharing my knowledge and enthusiasm with customers at the farm.

In response to my customers' often-voiced questions about how to grow and use herbs I wrote a concise, practical book called *Growing Herbs,* published by Sasquatch Books in 1994. It was a distillation of my experience, written especially for Northwest gardeners. With *Growing Herbs* I hoped to open the door to the world of herbs, and provided detailed information on how to grow, harvest, and use twenty-four herbs with culinary and ornamental value. That small book was well received, and I've treasured the comments of native Northwesterners and people who are new to our unique region who tell me that it's their herb bible, the easiest to use and most informative book on the subject.

Since *Growing Herbs* was published, herbs have entered the mainstream and begun to change our lives in their quiet, unassuming ways. Look around, and you'll see them everywhere. In newspapers and magazines, they are the subject of feature articles. In the grocery store, herbal teas take their place right alongside more conventional brews. In the drugstore, herbal medicines once regarded skeptically as folk remedies are offered as "phytomedicines" with curative effects so well documented by scientific research that even the medical establishment is taking note. In public parks and home gardens, herbs are flourishing in all manner of pots, plots, and landscape designs as their ornamental and drought-resistant qualities become more widely known. Not only have more and more Northwesterners discovered the world of herbs, but many have become very knowledgeable about it.

Still, people keep asking me questions. It's only natural that the original big question, "How do I get started growing herbs?" leads to the next, "What do I do with the herbs I'm growing?" Or to put it differently, for every customer who wonders, "How do I pinch back my basil?" there's another who's asking, "Would borage flowers be good with an anise hyssop punch?" or "Should I strain the roots out of my homemade echinacea tincture?" or "Do I harvest the leaves of my lemon verbena before taking it indoors for the winter?"

The world of herbs is so huge and diverse that it can never be completely known. That's one thing that keeps it interesting. It includes more than 2,000 useful plants that belong to scores of botanical families, from ground-hugging Corsican mint to pesky weeds like dandelion, garden flowers like nasturtium, vining hops, and tall bay trees. Although *Growing Herbs* did cover the basics, as part of the Cascadia Gardening Series it was very compressed, and there are far more than twenty-four herbs worth knowing. So, with the encouragement of Gary Luke at Sasquatch, I decided to expand that slim volume into a larger work that will guide you further, deeper into the world of herbs.

The Northwest Herb Lover's Handbook contains more than twice as much information as *Growing Herbs*, all within the Northwest context. You'll find comprehensive descriptions of fifty herbs that thrive in our region, including some that grow wild for the picking. You'll learn how to bring these herbs into your life to enhance the food you eat, your surroundings, and your general well-being on an everyday basis. I've included recipes, formulas, and directions for practical ways to use herbs that are also quick and easy for people with demanding schedules.

For experienced gardeners and would-be gardeners alike, *The Northwest Herb Lover's Handbook* contains twelve garden plans, plus in-depth gardening information to help you succeed, whether your goal is to grow one plant indoors, a few pots on the deck, or a full-size herb garden. There are detailed instructions on how to grow and propagate each herb, build and prepare your soil, select tools, extend the gardening season, and much more, plus beautiful color photos.

I have to admit it—I'm an opinionated gardener, and I've always been committed to organic methods. Many herbs are marvelously tough, adaptable, and pest resistant, but there are some exceptions. For example, basil is notoriously attractive to insects, sage and monarda are susceptible to mildew, garlic and valerian are among the herbs that do best when well fertilized. Yet why use dangerous chemicals on plants grown to nourish our bodies or restore us to health, or deplete the soil by relying on a quick chemical fertilizer fix, or risk fertilizer and pesticide runoff in our waters? Rich, fertile soil is practically an obsession with me, and I believe that building and maintaining healthy soil results in healthy, disease-resistant plants and, ultimately, a healthy planet. As far as I'm concerned, sustainable organic agriculture is the way to go.

Then there is the matter of choosing which herbs to include in this book. It was not easy to narrow down the list of hundreds of valuable herbs that thrive in the Northwest's hospitable environment. I tried to select plants that are easy to grow in the region, are widely adaptable, and have a variety of uses. All the basic culinary herbs are included, plus tea herbs, ornamentals, and medicinals. There are many more herbs of merit, but there simply wasn't room for them all. Far from exhaustive, this book is more like a map that can help you to get your bearings in the world of herbs and begin exploring some of its intriguing paths on your own.

I've always been charmed by the language of old herbals, but as I delved into them while working on this book my sense of connection to the herbalists of the past grew stronger. They were fascinated by the same plants, studied their ways, and shared their secrets with the herbalists of the future. The authors of many fine contemporary herb books have also been a source of information and inspiration. I offer this book as a link in the chain that connects the herbal past to an exciting future.

Am I an herbalist? What is an herbalist, anyway? According to my American Heritage dictionary, an herbalist is "One who grows, collects, or specializes in the use of herbs, especially medicinal herbs." This definition is so broad that almost anyone could qualify, and indeed the term covers a wide spectrum. There are graduates of universities, respected herbal schools, and correspondence courses that have high standards, all with letters after their names. Then there are herb business owners, medicine makers, writers, growers,

professional wildcrafters, green witches, and wise women who don't trouble themselves too much about science. Many prominent herbalists in this country have gained a remarkable body of knowledge without formal schooling, through reading, gardening, wildcrafting, and learning from others. Without set standards, how much confidence can you have in herbalists? I think this has to depend on the depth of their knowledge and experience of a variety of herbal applications. Confidence is something that has to be earned, and I hope to earn your confidence as an herbalist myself as you use this book.

Becoming an herb lover, on the other hand, is easy to do. It involves nothing more than falling for the charms and attractions of herbs. My instructions and advice will help you become successful in growing and using herbs, but nothing can substitute for hands-on experience. Start with the basics, build on your knowledge and experience, and gradually you will become intimately familiar with the flavors, scents, growth habits, and properties of many herbs. Then your life, like mine, will be so entwined with these remarkable plants that using them is second nature. Their riches will be yours, and you will surely be an herb lover, at home in the world of herbs.

garden

basics

I: Herb-Growing Basics

Herbs are among the easiest and least demanding plants to grow. Gardeners are sometimes astonished by their success with these plants. "The mint just went wild," they tell me.

"The cilantro keeps popping up everywhere, and there's a massive fennel plant in my backyard!" Many popular herbs such as chives, lovage, oregano, and sage are perennials that can be harvested for months or years with little more than an occasional glance their way. If you choose only a few of the easy-to-grow stalwarts and follow the growing tips in this book, you will have plenty of herbs for home use, many of them rarely available in grocery stores. Most will reward minimal effort with an abundant harvest of beauty, fragrance, and flavor.

As you learn about the climate, soil, fertilizer, water, light, and pest-management needs of individual herbs, your success and pleasure in growing them will increase. The information in this chapter is general enough to apply to most herbs. Chapter 5 offers complete details for the planting and cultivation of fifty specific herbs.

Considering Climate

Herb gardeners become very attuned to the special weather conditions of their particular corner of the Pacific Northwest. Ours is a magnificent region of variety and contrasts, ranging in altitude from sea level to nearly 15,000 feet, dominated by the Pacific Ocean and coastal and inland mountain ranges, interspersed with rich valleys and fertile inland plains. Along with this varied topography, the Northwest encompasses several climatic zones, microclimates within those zones, and changeable weather conditions. Add to this the variety of soils, and the result is considerable variation in growing conditions.

Fortunately, most herbs are very adaptable, and overall the Northwest provides growing conditions in which they can thrive. Each climatic zone presents certain challenges to gardeners, but part of the fun is getting to know what to expect and how to use various techniques to expand possibilities, extend the season, and produce maximum harvests.

Sunset magazine divides our region into climatic zones 1 through 6. This zone scheme is based on high and low temperatures, humidity and rainfall patterns, and length of the growing season. Zone 1 is characterized by extremely cold winter temperatures, often at high altitudes.

Zones 2 and 3, which include Washington's Columbia Basin, British Columbia's Osoyoos Valley, and the Snake River plain of Idaho, had average minimum temperatures of 13° to -34°F over a twenty-year period. During the growing season, which lasts four to seven months, there is plenty of heat and sunshine.

East of the Cascade Mountains, the marvel of large-scale irrigation has transformed the arid inland plains and basins of zones 2 and 3 from vast tracts of sagebrush and tumbleweed to productive orchards, farms, and vineyards. Herbs are among the other crops produced on a large scale; the area supplies much of the world's hops and peppermint, and in British Columbia a major ginseng-growing industry is emerging under acres of black shade-cloth. Echinacea and other medicinal herbs are produced commercially in southeastern Washington and the Grants Pass area of Oregon. In this area, spring may come early or late, and the last frost date is sometime around mid-May. During the cold months, snow is predictable and may linger on the ground for weeks or months, protecting plants with an insulating blanket. Drying winds are often more of a problem than cold temperatures, since they can desiccate plants in frozen soil. Wind protection, mulching, shade, and careful late-autumn watering may be necessary to get the most from your plants.

Western Washington and southern British Columbia's zone 4 sustains colder winter temperatures and a shorter growing season than neighboring zone 5. Victoria and Vancouver, the San Juan Islands, the Skagit Valley, and the areas bordering the Olympics and the Cascades are included in this zone. These locations experience winter low temperatures of 19° to -7°F. Some are more rainy than zone 5, while others are sometimes drier, due to the "rain shadow" effect. This occurs as moisture-laden clouds coming in from the ocean drop their rain as they rise over the mountains, leaving the rain-shadow areas to the east drier and sunnier.

Zone 5 describes the populous maritime Northwest, stretching along the Pacific Coast and Puget Sound. Ocean air moderates temperatures both summer and winter, with the twenty-year lows ranging from 28° to 1°F. Except in the rain shadow of the Olympic Mountains and the Vancouver Island Range, rainfall in this area averages 40 to 50 inches annually. During maritime Northwest winters, moisture-carrying air moves in from the Pacific and meets the coastal ranges, producing a cloudy, rainy season that can extend from September through June. One winter might be so mild that calendula plants survive; another winter can begin with a snowstorm at Thanksgiving that kills off dozens of herbs and just gets worse. Rainstorms can blow in from the Pacific (El Niño, La Niña, and the Pineapple Express) and frigid fronts move down the Fraser Valley or along the Columbia River, wreaking havoc on plants.

Portland and the Willamette Valley are in zone 6, which has warmer summers than zone 5, and equally mild winters. This fertile area, which extends from Longview, Washington, to Roseville, Oregon, has cooler summers and warmer winters than zones east of the Cascades, although ice storms howling into Portland along the Columbia from cold eastern areas can devastate plants.

Most of the annual herbs described in this book can be grown throughout the region except in zone 1. Many perennial herbs such as angelica, chives, elder, fennel, hops, lemon balm, lovage, mint, oregano, sage, winter savory, sweet cicely, and most thymes are winter hardy. With good drainage, garlic, most lavenders, and tarragon will survive our coldest weather. Large, upright rosemary plants can be protected from low temperatures by covering them with fir boughs or blankets. Bay trees, lemon verbena, scented geraniums, and small and trailing rosemary must be wintered indoors to ensure their survival. See the individual plant descriptions in Chapter 5 for more information.

Gardening Tools and Equipment

Hand tools are like an extension of a gardener's body, and consequently quite personal. Well-chosen tools and equipment can make the work far easier and more efficient. Buy the best you can afford, and with proper care they will serve you well for years. Experienced gardeners develop their own list of favorites. Here is mine.

Hand fork
Hoe, one or two types
Garden journal
Garden fork
Garden spade
Gloves
Hoses, standard and soaker types
Pruning shears, clip-on holster
Raffia, twine
Rake
Spun-bonded polyester row-cover material
Sprinkler or hose nozzle
Stakes, markers
Trowel
Watering can
Wheelbarrow

Soil Preparation

Perfect soil—dark, crumbly, high in organic matter, well drained, and fertile—seldom occurs naturally in the maritime Northwest. Soils here are often shallow and rocky with hardpan underneath; even the best alluvial soils may be acidic and lack major nutrients. Luckily herbs are among the most tolerant and forgiving of plants, and will grow well in a wide range of soil types and conditions.

To give your herb garden the best start, ready your soil for cultivation with compost, worm castings, or with the fertilizer and soil-mix formulas found throughout this chapter.

Compost

Nothing is wasted in nature. Through a process of growth and decay as old as creation, every living thing born of the earth is returned to it. In the forests, fallen leaves and plant parts are gradually transformed into rich soil from which new generations spring. In the garden, we can manage the process, recycling plant "wastes" into the dark, sweet-smelling, crumbly organic material we know as compost.

The compost pile has been called the heart of the organic garden. In a sense it epitomizes the organic gardener's stewardship of the land, and the commitment to return to the soil more than has been taken from it. Compost builds the soil by improving structure, increasing fertility, and contributing soil organisms that play a critical part in soil health and plant growth. Plants fertilized with compost tend to be vigorous and resist disease.

Well-made compost is rich in humus, a complex and dynamic brownish black substance containing decayed and decaying plant material, combined with the substances produced by soil microorganisms. Humus improves soil structure by gluing soil particles together into aggregates or crumbs that give soil that friable texture called tilth. Pore spaces between the aggregates can hold water or allow it to pass through gradually, improving both water retention and drainage. These spaces also allow room for roots and root hairs to penetrate in search of nutrients. Thus compost can lighten a clay soil, improve the moisture-holding capacity of sandy or poor soil, and help to make nutrients more available to plants in any soil.

Compost contains the top three essentials for plants—nitrogen, phosphorous, and potassium (N, P, K)—plus trace minerals, such as iron, manganese, copper, and zinc. In compost, the nutrients are held in the soil particles and released slowly through decomposition by soil bacteria and enzymes from plant roots. Compost acts like a slow-release fertilizer, making particular nutrients available as plants need them.

Is composting for you? The answer depends on your situation and goals. If you're a city dweller growing herbs in containers, it might be best to put your clean green yard waste out for pickup like other recyclables. There are other fine soil-building products on the market these days, including organic compost, earthworm castings, and mushroom compost. But if you have a lawn and garden, you have all the plant material needed right at hand.

It's good to remember that home composting can be simple or elaborate. Are you looking for an easy way to get rid of garden waste in an ecological manner? Make a simple pile and wait for nature to take its course. Compost just happens. Do you want to kill all the weed seeds in a hot compost pile? You'll need to do more work, turning and monitoring the pile for best results. Are you in a hurry to get compost and work it into your garden right away? Maybe you'd be interested in a tumbling drum, claimed to produce ripe compost in fourteen days. There's a composting method for just about everyone, and the choice is yours.

How to Make Compost

Get started at a time when abundant plant material is available, such as in autumn when leaves are falling. Select your site, considering proximity to the garden and kitchen, screening for aesthetics, and being mindful of the prevailing wind in case of unexpected odors. A shady spot is best for keeping the pile adequately moist in summer. Mark out a square at least 3 feet by 3 feet. Begin with an aeration layer of brushy material that will rot down slowly—for example, the stalks of angelica, fennel, and sunflowers; or rosemary and lavender trimmings. Spread 1 inch of soil over the aeration layer. Add a 6- to 8-inch layer of brown (carbon-rich) material such as chopped dry leaves, straw, or shredded paper. Be sure to add water as you layer, so that materials are as moist as a squeezed out sponge. Follow this with 3 to 4 inches of green (nitrogen-rich) material such as young weeds free of seed heads and persistent roots, fresh seaweed, nettle or comfrey leaves (no seeds or pieces of root!), and spent hops. Raw fruit and vegetable scraps, which may attract animals, should be layered in the middle of the pile or not used. Lawn clippings (herbicide free) are a great nitrogen source but tend to mat if layers are too thick. If you have access to fresh animal manure (not from pets or humans) add a layer of that. Next spread a layer of garden soil or finished compost on top to inoculate the pile with soil microorganisms. If materials are dry, moisten each layer to the consistency of a squeezed-out sponge. Fresh human urine, which is sterile and high in nitrogen, jump-starts decomposition when added straight or diluted 5:1 to prevent odors; this is definitely not for everyone (maybe hardly anyone), but good to know. Keep layering materials until the pile is at least 3 feet high, sloping the sides very gradually toward the top. End with a 2-to 3-inch layer of soil to trap escaping gases, then cover it with a plastic tarp, a piece of old carpet, or a sheet of plywood and let it sit.

Composting is a three-stage process. The first is the "breakdown" of carbon and nitrogen (carbohydrates and proteins) by millions and millions of microorganisms, which do most of the work. As bacteria begin to consume the organic material in the pile, they produce energy in the form of heat and carbon dioxide. Typically, a freshly made pile heats up noticeably within a few days, sometimes giving off steam.

In the "conversion" stage, the pile cools. Fungus and fungus-bacteria organisms take over and keep the process going. Humus is built during this stage, when bacterial secretions and filaments wrap themselves around soil particles, binding them together. When they finish their work, the compost is "raw." (It can be put on the garden, but decomposition will continue, tying up some nitrogen.)

After this, "curing" begins. Larger organisms, including worms, beetles, springtails, millipedes, slugs, and sowbugs, make their way into the pile. Chewing, digesting, excreting, and tunneling, they continue to break down woody stuff and expose more surface area for bacteria to work on. The pile continues to decay until it is dark and fluffy, smells fresh and earthy, and has just a few large pieces left. At this point, the compost has cured and is ready to be used.

You can leave the pile until it rots down to about half its original size, or keep tossing on material as it becomes available. This is passive composting, which can take a year or longer. To speed up decomposition, turn the pile with a fork, moving materials from the outside of the pile to the inside, where breakdown occurs most rapidly. Turning will also provide oxygen to optimize bacterial activity, and reduce the risk of smelly anaerobic bacteria taking over.

You can tell when compost is done curing by its dark color, crumbly texture, and clean smell. Most of the organic matter will be broken down and unrecognizable, although there may be small pieces of eggshell, corncobs, and other tough materials. Some people like to sift compost through a screen before adding it to the garden.

There are many types of compost bins and structures on the market. An illustrated source list, along with plans for various compost structures, is available from the King County Solid Waste Division at (800) 833-6388.

For more composting information, see *Let It Rot* by Stu Campbell, one of the classics on the subject, or Rodale's current encyclopedic tome. If you'd like to become a Master Composter, sign up for a class series sponsored by your County Extension Office.

Compost makes a great mulch around plants, helping to hold in moisture while gradually releasing nutrients. Put a handful in the planting hole with each transplant. It will provide nutrients without burning the roots. Steep 1 cup compost in 4 cups water for a strong compost tea to give indoor and garden plants a boost, or dilute it in up to 2 gallons of water for seedlings.

Worm Composting Systems

It is strange how a gardener's perceptions of certain things can change with deepening involvement in gardening. I used to regard worms as ugly wriggling things, but I've come to appreciate these biological garbage disposal units and the rich fertilizer they produce right on my premises. We've become allies in the pursuit of holistic gardening.

These remarkable creatures, sometimes called the intestines of the soil, break down organic matter by digesting it. As worms pass organic material through their bodies they enrich it with digestive secretions and the diverse bacteria in their gut, producing castings rich in humus, bacteria, enzymes, and minerals. The castings contain more than five times as much nitrogen, phosphorous, and potassium as ordinary soil. Worms also mix and aerate the soil, and secrete calcium carbonate, which has pH-balancing properties.

Eisenia foetida, also called "red wigglers," "redworms," and "composting worms," are voracious eaters of concentrated organic materials. They reproduce rapidly in confined spaces and are not suited for survival in ordinary garden conditions. Red wigglers are available from mail-order worm sellers and through contacts with the Master Composters.

It took some initial convincing by my friend Jean Galbreath, but finally I set up a worm bin and put red wigglers to work. They quietly clean up my kitchen scraps and I'm pleased with the results. The blackish, clean-smelling worm castings and vermicompost (worm castings plus undigested organic material) look like rich compost and are fabulous plant food.

Establishing a worm composting system is not complicated. Basically, you choose a suitable container; put in some dampened bedding material; and add worms, a handful of dirt, and kitchen wastes. Then you put the lid on and let nature take its course. There is a bit more to it, but mastering the finer points is an ongoing process. I'll hit some of the high-lights of vermicomposting.

It's best to locate a worm bin out back in a spot protected from direct summer sun and winter cold. It should be handy to the kitchen but far enough away that occasional odors and fruit flies won't be a problem. It can be so inconspicuous that next-door neighbors in the city never even notice it's there. Some people keep their worm bins in a garage or basement, or bring some worms indoors in the winter to keep them from freezing. The comfort zone of *Eisenia foetida* is between 55° and 77°F, though they can survive temperatures from freezing to 84°F. Mine have survived year-round inside the bin with no special protection.

Bedding material is important! It holds moisture, helps prevent odors, and provides good living conditions for the worms. It is usually cellulose in some form, such as recycled newspapers, shredded paper, egg cartons, or corrugated cardboard. Leaf mold, animal manure, and coconut fiber also make good bedding material. Bedding material should contain about the same amount of moisture as a squeezed-out sponge. Eventually the worms eat the bedding material and turn it into castings. If all the bedding gets used up, the castings become compacted and the worms can't tunnel through them. To keep the system healthy, renew the bedding material every two to four months. Add water in the summer if it dries out—remember, worms like it moist.

Most kitchen wastes make ideal food for worms. They especially like soft things such as bread, leftover casseroles, and moldy food from the refrigerator. Crushed eggshells, tea leaves, and coffee grounds (including paper filters) give castings a good texture. Citrus rinds, broccoli stems, and other pithy materials take a while to break down. Mango, avocado, and soft-fruit pits may sprout in the process if you choose to include them. Avoid meat scraps, bones, and greasy food, and peel off those brand-name stickers on purchased produce so they won't end up in your garden.

For a well-functioning worm compost system, you must maintain a balance between the amounts of worms, bedding materials, food wastes, and moisture. Vermicomposting books recommend allowing 2 pounds of worms and 1 square foot of space per pound of scraps per week. I have never measured these things and probably never will. If you add kitchen scraps sparingly when you first get your bin going, the supply of worms builds up gradually to the proper level. Check conditions as you bury the week's food scraps. If the bedding looks dry, sprinkle on some water. If it's getting too wet, toss on a few handfuls of dry peat moss or work in dry newspaper strips. I usually line my indoor collection bucket with torn-up newspapers or egg cartons, adding some bedding material to the bin right along with the food wastes.

Once established, it takes only a few minutes a week to maintain your worm bin. As long as conditions are right, the worms do most of the work. About every four months, move all the vermicompost to one side of the bin. Put fresh, moist bedding material on the other side and add kitchen scraps. The worms will migrate to the food zone within a day or two, and you can harvest the coarse-textured worm compost and dense castings left behind.

Fertilizing your plants with nutrient-rich castings

completes the worm composting cycle. Vermicompost can be used just like regular compost from a pile, but castings are more concentrated. Mineral salt levels can be too high for seed starting and potting. Instead, use castings to make Potting Mix with Worm Castings and Castings Tea (see recipes below). In the garden, top-dress plants by spreading a thin layer of castings around the base of the stems. Line furrows with worm castings when sowing seeds of herbs such as cilantro and dill. Add a handful to planting holes when transplanting basil and other herbs. Watering will wash diluted nutrients into the soil around the plants, promoting lush growth.

Vermiculture is an ecologically sound method of transforming kitchen food wastes into a top-quality, low-cost soil amendment. Try it, and *Eisenia foetida* might just worm its way into your organic gardening system. For more information, consult *Worms Eat My Garbage*, by Mary Appelhof.

POTTING MIX WITH WORM CASTINGS

1 part worm castings

1 part peat moss

1 part perlite

Mix well in a 5-gallon plastic bucket or other container. Use as a potting mix for seed starting, potted plants, and general use.

CASTINGS TEA

1 cup worm castings

4 cups water

This tea is great for indoor and garden plants alike. Steep castings for 24 hours, then apply to plants.

Preparing Herb Beds

To prepare individual herb gardens, you can rototill to remove weeds and make a crumbly, even soil texture, and then line out herbs in rows separated by paths. Raised beds, however, are a more efficient use of garden space. Although they require greater initial effort, they produce high yields with low maintenance, improve drainage, and can be started earlier in the season.

Beds 4 feet wide by 6 feet long can be weeded and harvested easily from the sides and have room for a good supply of plants. Mark out beds with stakes and twine, shovel on soil from the path area around the bed (remember, a lowered path equals a raised bed), then heap on soil amendments (compost, manure, and fertilizer) as needed. Turn and mix the soil with a garden fork, rake the bed smooth, and you are ready to plant.

Adding Compost

At my farm, we worked a 2-inch layer of compost into the beds as we prepared to plant annuals in spring—two 5-gallon buckets per square yard. We also spread a similar amount around perennials, scratching it in with a hand fork. To prepare a bed that held salad greens or other short-lived annuals for a second crop, I again sprinkled on a 2-inch layer of compost and incorporated it into the soil. When the compost supply ran out, I substituted organic fertilizers.

Using Green Manures

In the nitrogen cycle, nature's way of maintaining soil fertility, grasses and other plants return nutrients and organic materials to the earth as they decompose. Gardeners can use a similar method by sowing *green manure,* cover crops that are turned under while tender. Green manures protect the soil structure from rain damage, prevent nutrient leaching, and help choke out weeds.

Crimson clover, hairy vetch, winter rye, Austrian field peas, and small-seeded fava beans are all good choices for green manure. Crimson clover has beautiful blossoms; if it survives the winter, I let some of it bloom in spring, to the delight of garden visitors. Winter rye, a very hardy annual, produces a tremendous root system and has the advantage of germinating in cool temperatures.

Sow these crops as the herb beds finish producing. The green manure plants should be about 2 inches tall before cold weather arrives. Turn them under before they become tall, woody, and produce seeds. Wait at least three weeks before planting in the bed; decaying plants tie up nitrogen in the soil.

My success with green manures has been mixed. Wild birds, especially crows, assume I am feeding them and gobble up the seeds or mow down tender growth. Hiding the seeds among basil and other annual herbs helps, and covering the seeds with spunbonded polyester row covers works, too. The cover allows light and moisture in, but keeps pests out.

Working with Mulch

Mulch keeps weeds down, conserves water, and adds organic matter to the soil as it decays during the growing season. It also keeps soil temperatures cool and provides hiding places for slugs and snails, so wait until the weather is dry and warm, usually late June to early July, before you mulch. Grass clippings, hay, clean straw, shredded leaves, and newspaper all make good mulch. Black plastic, though it's not really biodegradable, and black garden paper also can be used.

Fertilizing

In addition to amending the soil, I fertilize my garden before sowing seeds and at various times as plants grow. A basic formula for all-purpose fertilizer can be varied according to the ingredients at hand. I use a combination of fish meal or crab meal; bonemeal, greensand, and rock phosphate; and kelp meal (see recipe page 12). Besides the all-purpose fertilizer, I use two strengths of fish emulsion: one for new seedlings and one for maintaining maturing herbs.

My organic All-Purpose Fertilizer Mix contains balanced amounts of nitrogen, phosphorous, and potassium, plus trace minerals. Nitrogen is essential for all green, leafy growth, and is present in animal products such as fish, crab, and blood meal; animal manures; and oil-seed meals, particularly cottonseed. Phosphorous, which is often lacking in maritime Northwest soils, promotes strong growth, healthy root systems, and earlier and better harvests. Phosphorous is available as ground or powdered rock phosphate, bonemeal, and, in smaller amounts, in fish and cottonseed meal. Potassium helps plants form sturdy stems, resist disease, and overcome adverse weather and soil conditions. It also regulates the intake of nitrogen. Greensand and kelp meal are important sources of potassium, and wood ash supplies it in lesser amounts.

Sprinkle the fertilizer over your soil and dig it in, or, to sidedress rows, make a shallow furrow and apply 1 pound (1¼ cups) per 20 feet. For thickly sown beds of cilantro, for example, sprinkle the fertilizer evenly beside the furrow. Give individual plants such as mature basil about ⅛ cup per plant, then cover the fertilizer with soil. Water well. To give your herbs an extra boost, repeat this application midway through the plants' growing season.

I regularly use liquid fish fertilizer in my gardens to give plants a quick nitrogen boost. Every two or three weeks, use ¼ cup of Regular Solution Fish Fertilizer for each plant in containers or beds (see the recipe below).

Many gardeners prefer to mix and apply a lighter solution of fish fertilizer every three to seven days, especially for seedlings. See the Light Solution Fish Fertilizer recipe below. Combine two tasks at once by mixing up the solution in a watering can and fertilizing while you water. You can also irrigate tiny seedlings with a turkey baster. Fish solutions smell bad if aged, so use up any extra to fertilize elsewhere in your garden.

All-Purpose Fertilizer Mix

One batch of this mix weighs a little more than 5 pounds and is enough to fertilize 100 square feet, about the size of four 4- by 6-foot beds. If your soil is too acid and you have not amended it yet, add 1¼ pounds (1⅝ cups) of lime to the following recipe. The recommended materials are often sold by weight and vary considerably in density. For example, 1 cup of cottonseed meal weighs about 5 ounces, while 1

cup of dolomite lime weighs 12 ounces. Weight also varies with moisture content and texture, so the amounts given are therefore approximate. If you do not have a precise scale, use the cup measurements given in parentheses. This is not rocket science.

> 2 pounds (5 cups) fish meal or crab meal
> ½ pound (¾ cup) greensand
> ½ pound (1 cup) steamed bonemeal
> 1 pound (1½ cups) rock phosphate
> 1 pound (2¼ cups) kelp meal

Combine all of the ingredients and mix well.

Regular Solution Fish Fertilizer

Fertilize each plant every two to three weeks with ¼ cup of this fertilizer, using a watering can or turkey baster.

> 1 tablespoon (3 capfuls of a gallon-size container) liquid fish fertilizer
> 1 gallon water

Shake fertilizer concentrate, dilute with water, and apply. One gallon will fertilize about eighty 4-inch pots or six-packs.

Light Solution Fish Fertilizer

Fertilize and water seedlings with this solution every three to seven days. Use approximately ¼ cup per pot.

> 1 tablespoon (3 capfuls of a gallon-size container) fish fertilizer
> 2 gallons water

Shake fertilizer concentrate, dilute with water, and apply. One gallon will fertilize about eighty 4-inch pots or six-packs.

SEED STARTING MIX

Derived from the Cornell University "Peat Lite" formulas, this soilless mix is good for seed germination and container growing of spring-bedding plants. Its components are lightweight, readily available, and require no sterilization. One batch of this mix fills about twenty six-packs (5½ inches long by 3¼ inches wide by 2½ inches tall).

> *4 quarts sphagnum peat moss*
> *4 quarts fine-grade perlite (puffed pumice)*
> *1 tablespoon ground dolomitic limestone*

Mix the ingredients in a 5-gallon plastic utility bucket and add enough water to make the soil workable. Make sure the peat moss is well dampened during mixing.

Watering

Sometimes it is said that poor soil and dry conditions produce the highest-quality herbs, because their flavor and medicinal constituents are concentrated. There may be some truth to this, especially with herbs that are to be used medicinally and are well adapted to an arid climate, but most herbs require a steady supply of water throughout the growing season to really thrive. Tender arugula and watercress are so good in salads, basil and sorrel leaves on sandwiches, fresh cilantro lavished in salsas, parsley and dill with new potatoes, yet without abundant moisture these pungent herbs would be far too tough. Since nature does not always provide all the water they need to put forth lush yet sturdy growth, some form of irrigation is almost always necessary.

The questions of when, how, and how much to water do not have simple answers. Plants have different requirements at different times and stages of growth, soils vary, and then of course there's the weather. For example, lavender seedlings may need to be watered two or three times a day in hot weather, but only once if the day is cloudy; mature lavender plants in the garden may survive nicely without any irrigation at all.

Watering Indoors

Decisions about watering are always judgment calls, and they are especially important indoors where irrigation is a given. Sal Gilbertie, a major East Coast grower of herb plants, considers watering to be the most critical job in his greenhouses. Most herbs need good drainage, and too much water can kill them off as easily as too little. Generally speaking, it's best to let potted plants dry out somewhat, then water thoroughly, rather than sprinkling lightly every day. Don't wait until they are drooping or turning yellow, because this stresses them. Check the moisture level below the surface of the soil by scratching with your fingertip. It can be tricky—sometimes I've found potted plants that seemed moist at the surface but are bone dry at root level. Give plants a good soaking with a watering can or hose, or set pots in a tray of water to allow the plants to take it up slowly. Herbs in window boxes and hanging baskets may need watering every day, and regular fertilizing to replace any nutrients that leach out.

Watering Outdoors

Conventional wisdom holds that if it rains less than an inch a week, it's time to irrigate. Test the soil to be sure, and water if the top layer has dried out to a depth of 3 to 4 inches. Plants' uptake of nutrients is most efficient when the soil around the plants is moist to a depth of at least 12 inches. An inch of rain moistens the ground to about 12 inches in sandy soil, 7 inches in loam, and 4 to 5 inches in clay. The time of day is also a consideration. I try to get my watering done early in the morning, before transpiration and evaporation get under way. This gives the leaves a chance to dry out quickly, avoiding sunscald and prolonged damp conditions that favor the growth of disease. Watering in the evening is advisable only in hot, dry weather when plants are flagging. Seedbeds need to be kept moist until the seeds germinate, so water them daily with a watering can or garden hose, or soak a burlap bag and place it over the bed to hold in moisture.

Much human ingenuity has gone into developing irrigation equipment and techniques, and every gardener and garden writer seems to have a different opinion about what system is best. Some people enjoy the simplicity of standing in the garden with a watering can or hose and spray nozzle, communing with their plants as they bestow water directly on them. This method might be all right for a small area as long as the ground is well soaked, but it's inefficient.

Overhead watering with sprinklers facilitates deep irrigation, and many models are available, with various styles of applying water. Check on their relative merits by asking questions at a reputable nursery, or read up on them in general gardening books. On the downside, sprinklers distribute water unevenly and tend to waste water through evaporation and careless

use. Water is a finite resource to be respected and stewarded, especially as the Northwest's growing population increases demand. Some water-saving innovations include water-holding polymers that are mixed into the soil, and recyclable black-paper mulches that hold in moisture and decompose to enrich the soil.

As one who has carried water in 5-gallon buckets to thirsty plants, I know from experience that water-wise methods become very appealing when water is rationed and wells run dry. One such method is drip irrigation, a very flexible watering system based on low water use and low water pressure. It involves soaker hoses gone high tech: drip tubing with holes drilled by lasers, single- and double-walled soaker tubing, plus micro-sprinkler heads, mini-sprinklers, and foggers, which all give maximum irrigation benefits from minimum amounts of water. I was intrigued by the drip irrigation system at Taylors Herb Garden, near Mesa, Arizona. Thyme and other herbs were planted in shallow depressions. On a hose that lined each row, one emitter per plant dripped water at a slow, constant rate. Only the area around each plant received water, and little was wasted through evaporation.

Drip irrigation kits for home gardens are available at nurseries and garden stores, and require no special equipment to install. Besides conserving water, these systems can save a lot of work. You can loop the hoses around your herb garden, training emitters on rosebushes or moisture-loving herbs. They are ideal for plantings that require frequent watering, such as window boxes and hanging baskets. How about setting them on timers, leaning back in a comfy lawn chair, and enjoying your garden?

Light

Fortunate is the herb gardener who has a growing area in full sun. Most herbs do best with at least nine hours of direct sunlight; where it is too shady, they simply will not flourish. Don't despair if your growing area gets only morning or afternoon sun, is shaded by conifers or other trees, or has dry soil. Just choose from the herbs for special conditions listed in Chapter 2.

Propagation

Part of the pleasure of growing herbs is learning how to propagate them. It's very rewarding to start plants from seed, or multiply them by cuttings and division. All it takes is some basic knowledge, simple equipment, a little time, and careful attention. You can easily produce plenty of plants to set out in your garden, share with friends, or maybe even sell at a profit to fund your herb habit. Besides, in observing and assisting the miracles of germination and rooting you are working closely with the life force. It is a marvel to see how tiny seeds, bare sticks, and bits of root grow into healthy, full-size plants, and infinitely renewing to be part of the process.

There is such variety in the world of herbs that there are really no hard-and-fast rules for the would-be propagator, only general methods and guidelines. Plant propagation is an art as well as a science, one that calls for judgment and nurturing. With experience you get a feel for it and develop your own favorite meth-

ods. Some plants present a challenge, but with many it is necessary only to help things along a little, making sure that conditions are right.

EQUIPMENT FOR STARTING SEEDS

Soil-mixing tub

Gloves

Trowel

Pots, trays

Dibble

Watering can, mister

Potting soil or soilless mix

Plastic wrap or panes of glass

Waterproof marker

Labels

Light source

Starting Seeds

Especially for easily transplanted annuals, starting your own plants from seed is gratifying and inexpensive. All herb seeds can be sown directly in the garden, but to get an earlier start and have greater control over watering and spacing, sow seeds indoors. With a sunny window or indoor lights, you can significantly extend the season of productivity. For example, by sowing basil indoors at three-week intervals beginning in mid-March, you can be harvesting in June.

To get started, assemble your equipment (see above). Lots of nifty equipment is available for sowing and transplanting seeds. Peruse the accessories section of any large seed or greenhouse supply catalog for ideas, and you may soon find grandiose gardening dreams forming in your mind. I'll stick to the basics; you can take it from there.

My favorite soil-mixing containers are galvanized tubs of the sort used for laundry or watering livestock. They are a good height, lightweight, and practically indestructible. Plastic dishpans, storage bins, and buckets work fine, and wheelbarrows, old sinks, and similar containers do too.

Gloves will keep your hands looking presentable in polite company. A lot of times I use plastic gloves, the type sold to prevent dishpan hands, available in grocery stores or by the six-pack in discount warehouses. The close-fitting rubber Wonder or Ultimate Gloves, available in garden centers or by mail allow you to do fine work, even pick up seeds. Goatskin gloves are wonderfully supple and long-lasting if you don't lose them!

A good trowel is worth the investment. I like a heavy-duty aluminum trowel with a plastic-coated handle that can be left in the garden for months without rusting or rotting (go ahead, ask me how I know). I also use a set of small aluminum tools that look a bit like silverware. Some gardeners do in fact use silverware. A narrow trowel designed for transplanting comes in handy but is not strictly necessary.

Plant pots and flats are made of plastic, clay, or fiber. Each material has its advantages: plastic is lightweight and holds moisture; clay is natural and aesthetically pleasing; fiber is lightweight and biodegradable. Fiber pots, including peat pots, are especially good for plants with root systems that resent transplanting, since they can be set right in the ground. Just remember to gently tear the pots apart when you plant, so the roots can spread out easily.

Plastic pots come in an incredible number of sizes and styles, although some sizes are fairly standard. Most gardeners have favorites for various purposes. Patio packs, whether undivided or divided into compartments (usually four or six) are a convenient size. For transplanting tiny seedlings of basil and other herbs, I like 2-inch-square pots without bottoms. Despite their appearance, they really do hold soil and plants. At Silver Bay seedlings were transplanted from 2-inch pots to 3½-inch-square pots, or directly to the garden. The sizes of pots and flats I mention all fit nicely into the familiar nursery trays, which are 10½ inches wide by 21 inches long by 2½ inches deep. These trays are usually crosshatched in a diamond pattern on the bottom, but they are also available in a leakproof model to allow for watering and fertilizing pots from the bottom. Although used tofu trays don't fit into the trays as well, they are a handy size. I punch drainage holes in the bottom with a nail.

For growing larger quantities of seedlings, many market gardeners use sturdy plastic *plug flats*. These are divided into tapering cells of various sizes. The model with fifty cells per tray, each about 2 inches wide and 2¼ inches deep, is a general-purpose size for herbs. When seedlings are large enough to transplant, lift them gently out of the cells by their leaves. Sometimes you have to squeeze the bottom of the cell with one hand to pop the seedling out. Humidity domes that fit over the top of the flat and hold in moisture like a mini-greenhouse are also available. Plug flats and trays are advertised in the accessories section of larger seed and garden supply catalogs, or look for them at your local nursery. With reasonable care, plastic pots, flats, and trays will last for years. Sterilize them with 1 teaspoon bleach per gallon of water before reuse to prevent the spread of plant disease.

An ingenious device worth trying is the handheld "soil blocker," which eliminates the need for pots. With this device, you mold blocks of dampened seed starting mix, sow seeds in them, and later set the blocks directly into the garden with minimal root disturbance.

A dibble (also dibbler or dibber) is a pointed implement for poking planting holes and making furrows. These are available commercially or can be fashioned out of dowels, fruitwood prunings, or similar materials. A pencil works well too. Dibbles save wear and tear on the fingers, which are of course the original garden tools.

An ordinary watering can is okay for seedlings, but it's really nice to have specialized equipment that provides a gentle spray, like a Fogg It haze nozzle or a watering can with fine holes that direct the spray upward.

Make your own seed starting mix (see page 13) or use a commercial mix to save time and effort. Expect an 8-quart bag to fill about one flat of 3½-inch pots. The advantage of a sterile mixture is that it does not carry weed seeds or disease organisms; however, since it contains no nutrients, the seedlings need to be fertilized regularly after they germinate.

Measure the ingredients for your seed starting mix (or pour purchased mix) into the mixing container, removing any large bits of peat or stones. Sprinkle with water and mix well. Test the consistency by squeezing a handful of the mix in your hand (the squeeze test). It should hold its shape, then crumble when you tap it.

Fill your pots or trays almost to the top with the mix. Don't skimp on the corners, since the soil level will drop gradually as the plants are watered. Sow the seeds evenly in rows marked out with a dibble or your finger, or scatter them across the soil surface. If you wish to transplant directly from the pot to the garden, leave plenty of growing space between the seeds—otherwise, you will need to move the seedlings into larger pots as they grow. Carefully cover the seeds with seedling mix to a depth approximately two and a half times the length of the seeds. Leave tiny seeds uncovered, but press them into the surface of the mix. Firm the soil lightly, and mist the soil surface. Cover the pot with plastic wrap or glass to hold in moisture until the seeds germinate, or place a germination dome over the tray. After germination, a pair of seedling leaves (cotyledons) appears, followed by sets of true leaves that more closely resemble the mature plant. Remove the plastic at this point.

Oh, and don't forget to *label* those seeds as you sow them. I've used everything from metal labels to cut-up yogurt cartons to Popsicle sticks, but keep going back to the white plastic labels available at most nurseries. Black grease pencil lasts just about forever; pencils work well too. I've also neglected to label things, quite sure I would remember what I sowed or recognize the seedlings, later to find more mystery plants on my hands. While you're at it, why not jot down the variety, seed source, date, and other pertinent planting information in your three-year gardening journal? You'll be glad you did.

Some seeds require special handling for successful germination. Angelica and sweet cicely seeds, for example, do not remain viable for long and should be planted when they are as fresh as possible, or stored in the freezer. Nasturtium seeds sprout more readily after being soaked in water for an hour or so. Seeds of echinacea require stratification, a period of chilling in moist conditions, before breaking dormancy. Details on these and other special requirements are described under the individual herbs in Chapter 5.

Seedlings at this tender stage, like all babies, need regular and careful attention. Check them daily to be sure that they don't dry out. The surface of the planting mix should look damp but not soggy; if the soil pulls away from the edges of the pot like a cake from the baking pan, it's getting too dry. Overwatering prevents root aeration and increases the possibility of fungus gnat infestation and *damping off*. Fungus gnats are tiny black flies that live in the soil and may be vectors for disease. Damping off is a fungus disease that favors warm temperatures, high humidity, and poor air circulation, and causes mass destruction as the seedlings' stems become so spindly at the base that they can't support the plants, which keel over and die. To prevent damping off, use vigorous seeds, sterilized potting soil and equipment, and provide good air circulation with a fan or open window. It is possible, though more difficult, to grow healthy plants in a nonsterile starting mix: lower temperatures and peat moss help to inhibit the growth of damaging organisms.

Good light is crucial in producing young seedlings that are stocky and robust. The ambient light of gray winter days just won't do it. As seedlings stretch toward the light, their stems become long and weak. Various lighting kits on the market will provide the light they need, but inexpensive fluorescent lights, or grow lights that screw into a regular lamp fixture, work fine too. Keep the light within a few inches of the seed tray, raising it gradually as the seedlings grow.

Water your seedling with Light Solution Fish Fertilizer (page 12) every three to seven days. Fill a watering can with warm water and swish it back and forth over the plants to make a gentle shower. If possible, avoid using a hose connected to an outdoor faucet; even with a flaring rose nozzle, a cold, forceful spray can check the seedlings' growth. Within a few weeks you will have nice, healthy seedlings with two or three sets of leaves, ready for transplanting.

When the weather warms, usually in mid-April, get your herbs used to outdoor conditions by hardening them off gradually. Put them outside in direct light for two hours the first day, then bring them in. Repeat this routine for about five days, exposing them to natural conditions for a little longer each day, and finally leave them out overnight before transplanting to the garden. Without this step the temperature change can stress the plants, or the tender leaves can become sunburned, especially with basil seedlings. For transplanting, wait for cloudy weather if possible. Transpiration (plant breathing) is faster on breezy, sunny days, causing plants to give off water faster than their roots can absorb it. This can shock and weaken vulnerable seedlings.

There are many sources of additional information on starting herbs from seed. Some seed catalogs provide thorough instructions on how to start individual plants. Rodale's *Encyclopedia of Herbs* contains hard-to-find information on starting unusual herbs from seed, and *The Seed Starters Handbook*, by Nancy Bubel, is a classic. Or ask the knowledgeable staff at your favorite herb farm or nursery for good advice for conditions in your particular growing area.

Vegetative Propagation

Some herbs, such as oregano and thyme, do not "come true" from seed, while others, such as French tarragon, don't produce seed at all. Plants like this are propagated by their vegetative or asexual parts, that is, the stems, roots, or leaves.

Cuttings

When I began writing this section, these words came to me: "A cutting is any part of the parent plant which, when severed from the plant and placed in favorable conditions, produces an independent plant, usually identical to the parent." I memorized them in Clarence Muhlick's plant propagation class at the University of Washington, sitting on creaky folding chairs in a small greenhouse tucked behind Parrington Hall. I loved that class because being among plants and breathing the air of green living things was a wonderful break from more abstract studies, and Mr. Muhlick brought coffee and doughnuts whenever he had to give us a test. Many a time I've dug out my notes to glean more from his wealth of knowledge, and I can't say that for many other college classes.

Softwood Cuttings

Most commercial propagation of perennial herbs is done by rooting cuttings of the current year's growth of the stems, called *softwood cuttings*. One stock plant can produce numerous offspring with this method, which is fairly easy and can provide many plants within a short time, usually four to six weeks.

SOFTWOOD CUTTING EQUIPMENT LIST

Sharp knife or pruning shears
Rubbing alcohol
Sterilized pots or trays
Standard Propagating Mix
Resealable plastic bag
Damp paper towel
Cooler (if needed)

You can keep your equipment list simple if you're rooting just a few cuttings. A pair of sharp pruning shears or a sharp knife is essential, whether it's your favorite paring knife, pocket knife, an X-acto knife, or a budding knife. Wipe the blade with rubbing alcohol before you get started, and repeat this precaution often as you proceed. Assemble your sterilized pots or trays, which should be at least 4 inches deep, and fill them with moistened propagating mix. Have your other equipment at hand so that all is in readiness for the cuttings.

Keeping in mind that plants, conditions, and specific details on propagation vary widely, here are some general guidelines for rooting softwood cuttings. Take cuttings in the early morning or on a cool, cloudy day while the stems are turgid (full of water), before they begin to lose moisture by transpiration as air temperatures rise. The best time for taking soft-wood cuttings is early summer, when new growth has firmed up somewhat. Select healthy material from the top or sides of the parent plant. Rosemary is an ideal herb for a beginning propagator because it is easy to tell when the wood is at the right stage for cuttings.

Pick a rosemary stem 4 to 6 inches long and bend it between your fingers. If it wobbles back and forth it's too soft, and if it doesn't want to bend it's too old. It should break off cleanly with a little snap. Strip the leaves from the bottom 2 inches of the stem, taking care not to touch the end of the stem with your fin-ger, which may contain substances that retard root-ing. Place the cutting in a resealable plastic bag lined with a damp paper towel, and place it in rooting medium as soon as possible.

Follow these basic steps to propagate lavender, sage, mint, oregano, and many other herbs. Because softwood cuttings have leaves but no roots, they dry out easily through transpiration. It is very important to keep them out of the sun. Prevent moisture loss with the plastic bag and paper towel method, or, if it's going to be a while, keep them in a portable cooler. Don't let them stand in water. With reasonable care, cuttings can remain viable for several hours, even days. I've transported cuttings of choice herbs thousands of miles on an airplane and rooted them successfully.

To increase the number of cuttings from one plant, cut the stems in pieces with a very sharp, clean knife before inserting them into the propagating mix. It's not necessary to have a growing tip on each cutting, but make sure that there are two or more nodes—the bumps on the stem where the leaves attach. Make the cut at the base just under a node, straight across or at a slant. It's okay to put cuttings from different kinds of herbs together in the rooting medium.

STANDARD PROPAGATING MIX

1 part builders' sand
1 part perlite

A good medium for softwood cuttings must have a light texture to promote root growth. Builders' sand is sometimes used alone, but a sterile mixture of half sand and half perlite seems to suit more plants. This contains no nutrients, so cuttings must be removed or fertilized as soon as rooting begins. Propagating mix should not be reused unless it is resterilized, but it makes a great addition to your compost pile as long as the pile gets hot enough to kill disease pathogens.

Generally speaking, it's best to stick your cuttings into a propagating medium as soon as possible, though there are exceptions to this rule. There are various methods of *sticking cuttings*, but the main thing is to see that the base of each stem is in firm contact with the mix. I like to poke a hole in the mix with a dibble, set the cutting in the hole, and firm the mix to release air pockets. Of course, you can poke the hole with your finger, too. Poking cuttings directly into the propagating mix could damage the base of the cutting. Water the cuttings in with a gentle spray.

70°F is a good temperature for speedy rooting, though some plants prefer cooler conditions. *Bottom heat* really helps, too. You can provide this by setting your pots or trays on a wooden box that has a 25-watt bulb underneath it. High humidity prevents excess water loss through the leaves, so make a mini-greenhouse by bending lengths of wire (coat hangers work well) into arches over the pot, then covering it with a plastic bag; fasten that plastic tightly with a rubber band. If it's a small pot, you can simply invert a wide-mouthed jar over the top. If you want to get more serious about this, buy a commercial heating mat or make a propagating bed by laying a heating cable under propagating mix in a cold frame.

Check on your cuttings regularly. Water them if they need it, remove the covering if the leaves look too wet, and notice when new growth begins to sprout. To test whether plants are rooted, tug gently on their leaves. If they resist, loosen the cutting from underneath with a trowel or an old spoon and give the roots a visual inspection. Once cuttings have rooted, begin fertilizing them or move them to pots or the garden.

Herbaceous Cuttings

Plants that have succulent stems, such as scented geraniums, are propagated by herbaceous cuttings. This method of propagation is similar to working with softwood cuttings, but the timing is different, since herbaceous cuttings are generally taken in the fall. Select healthy plant material, preferably from stocky plants that are growing in full sun. Take cuttings 3 to 5 inches long, making the cut at an angle, just below a node. Allow geranium cuttings to dry for a few hours to seal off, then strip off all but two or three leaves and place the cuttings in a standard propagating mix with bottom heat. Test cuttings for roots as with softwood cuttings, and repot or plant them out when they have rooted.

Hardwood Cuttings

Rooting hardwood cuttings is one of the easiest and least expensive methods of vegetative propagation. This method is used for deciduous woody plants, such as elderberry and rose (as well as grapes and fruit trees), and cuttings are taken in the dormant season before leaf buds begin to swell. From healthy, moderately vigorous plants growing in full sun, cut 6- to 8-inch pieces of wood from the previous year's growth. Cuttings should include at least two nodes, with the lower cut just below a node and the top cut $\frac{1}{2}$ to 1 inch above a node. Central and side growth makes the best cuttings; the tips are usually cut off because they don't contain enough stored food. It's wise to make a slanting cut on the bottom, so you can distinguish it from the top later on.

Bundle your cuttings together with all the tops going in one direction and bury them horizontally or upside down in dampened sandy soil, sand, or sawdust until spring. In areas with sub-zero winters, store in similar materials in a root cellar or other protected area where they will not dry out. Or you can pack the cuttings in damp peat moss and store them in the refrigerator. During storage, the cuttings develop a callus, or hardened tissue layer, from which the first roots often emerge.

In spring, plant the cuttings outside with the bottom ends down. You can set them out directly in the garden, preferably in a special propagating bed. As long as they are kept adequately moist they will probably root fine. Or make a simple propagating frame by knocking the bottom out of a wooden box 8 or 9 inches deep. Set this right on the ground and fill it with propagating mix, then insert your cuttings. A piece of glass placed over the top will help keep the cuttings from drying out, but watch for molds. Test cuttings for roots as with softwood cuttings, and plant them out when they have rooted.

Layering

Rosemary, sage, and other perennial herbs often propagate themselves by layering. Where a low branch lies touching the ground, roots may develop on the stem. These are called *adventitious* roots, meaning "not in the usual place." The parent plant provides nourishment until the new roots are large enough to take over the job. Then you can sever the connection with the mother plant, using a sharp knife or hand pruners, and voilà! there's a good-sized new plant. It may be a little lopsided, but gradual pruning will take care of that. To encourage layering, scrape off a little of the bark where the branch will touch the ground, then cover the branch with soil and pin it down with a bent wire at least 8 inches long, a rock, or a brick. To increase your stock of thyme and certain other plants, you can mound dirt up at the base of the plant to encourage root formation along the buried stems. Check back in two months or so, and proceed as directed above. This is known as mound or stool layering.

Suckering

Anyone familiar with the ways of raspberry plants knows how suckers connected to the parent plant underground can pop up around it. Elder, bay, and other herbal trees may send up suckers, too. Digging these up and replanting them elsewhere is pretty straightforward. Just make sure they have a sturdy root system, use a sharp spade or hand pruners to cut them from the parent, and keep them watered until they are growing well on their own. You'll usually have the best results when you transplant suckers in spring or fall.

Root Cuttings

Herbs such as comfrey and horseradish are easily propagated by cutting pieces of root, usually in late winter before spring growth begins, and placing them in soil until they produce new roots. The most important thing to remember is to put them right side up. See the individual herbs listed in Chapter 5 for plant-specific details.

Root Division

Many perennials grow outward from the *crown*, that is, the base of the plant that remains even if its leafy tops die down. The center of the crown becomes tough and woody and eventually dies away. On closer inspection, what looks like one big clump is actually a cluster of independent plants that have formed around the edges of the crown, usually connected by a tangle of roots. By separating these roots you can divide the one plant into several.

Many perennial herbs have tough, dense root systems. These you can tear apart, separate with a knife or hand pruners, or slice into clumps with a sharp spade. Others require more careful handling. Some beginning gardeners cringe at the thought of taking a knife to a plant or tearing it apart, but actually it is beneficial to the plant. Crowded roots and stems compete for nutrients and light, so for optimum growth and flowering most perennials need to be divided every three years.

If you are hesitant to begin chopping up your plants lest they die on you, ease into it. Practice with a chive plant, even one from the produce section of the grocery store that's been forced into early growth. Rinse the dirt off with a hose or swish the plant in a bucket of water, then lay it out on a table covered with a plastic sheet or on the ground. Look at the roots closely to see how the individual plants that make up the clump are formed, each like a miniature green onion with roots. Then take the clump of roots in your hands and tear it in half, exerting pressure downward and outward from the crown. There! Two chive plants. Tear each of these in half again, and you'll have four small plants of a good size to set out in a planter or in your garden. Actually, chive plants that have been forced for the market don't usually have enough energy left to make strong plants, but this was just for practice. If you have a big chive plant in the garden, use a sharp spade to slice it in half while it's right in the ground. Then slice it into smaller clumps and plant them out.

Lemon balm is a good one to try next. Dig up a plant in early spring, before the stems grow more than 4 inches tall. It will be easy to tell the new growth from the old, dark brown wood in the center of the crown. Tear or clip rooted sections of new growth from around the edges, and there are your new plants. Easy.

A mint plant, with its long, creeping rootstocks, has a different appearance. You'll see how thin rootlets grow from each rootstock, connected in turn to an aboveground stem. Separate the rootstocks and replant them, or clip off rooted pieces and bury each one in a moist spot. Soon you'll have all the mint you need.

From this you can progress to tarragon, which is more complex. If you dig up a tarragon plant in February or March, you'll see the upper parts of the roots with their pinkish buds and pale shoots poking out, and their rootlets growing downward, all connected to the bundle of large twisting roots lower down. It's less obvious where one plant ends and the next begins, and the buds and shoots are very brittle, so be gentle as you clip the larger rooted pieces and tease them apart.

Offsets

Certain plants, including lovage, horseradish, and others with thick, fleshy roots, form small plants on the outer edges of the crowns. If you examine these closely, you'll see that they are small but complete, having a root, leaves, and a growing tip. Slice them off the main root and plant them out, and they will soon develop into full-size herbs. Some other herbs develop "eyes" or growing points from the roots. Use a sharp, clean knife to cut these off, leaving a chunk of root attached, and plant the whole thing.

The individual herb listings in Chapter 5 of this book contain directions for propagating your plants. For more detailed and specific information, consult a good book on the subject, such as *Plant Propagation: Principles and Practices*, by Hartman and Kester, first published in 1959 and most recently revised in 1997.

Organic Pest and Disease Management

One of the benefits of growing herbs is that most are resistant to insect pests and diseases. Exceptions exist, however, and they include some garden favorites. Over the years I have experimented with various organic methods to keep destructive insects away from prized plants. Organic gardening requires building healthy soil that grows strong plants and using nontoxic methods for prevention and control, beginning with cultural practices and resorting to strong commercial products only when all else fails.

Following is a brief rundown of the most common pests in the Northwest and methods for controlling them. Look for more information on pests and diseases under individual herb descriptions found in Chapter 5.

Herb Pests

Aphids: Both green and black aphids are fond of dill, fennel, scented geraniums, nasturtiums, and other herbs. They can be a serious problem in the greenhouse and quite an annoyance outdoors.

Garlic repels aphids if planted among your herbs and edible flowers. Some gardeners report success with a spray made from garlic and hot pepper whirled with water in the blender. A commercial product called Garlic Barrier is also available. For severe infestations I use insecticidal soap, according to package directions, in both my greenhouse and garden. This contact insecticide, based on natural fatty acids, quickly breaks down and leaves no residue.

Flea beetles: These tiny, black, hard-bodied insects hop from place to place, leaving small shotlike holes in the leaves of herbs such as basil and arugula, and many vegetables. They live on weeds in and around the garden, so clean cultivation is one of the best ways to keep them in check.

Try covering herbs susceptible to flea beetles with floating row covers immediately after seeding or transplanting. These miracle blankets, made of spun-bonded polyester, let in light and trap heat and moisture while keeping out insects. As a last resort for really troublesome infestations, rotenone dust, made of ground plant roots, is the best organic control measure I have found. But use it with care; this broad-spectrum insecticide is harmful to beneficial insects too. For best results, apply rotenone when the air is still, according to package directions. Rotenone biodegrades within five to ten days.

Slugs and snails: The bane of maritime Northwest gardeners, these pests adore basil, tender tarragon shoots, and various salad greens. I have even seen them attacking thyme plants. My neighbor complains that if you kill one slug, six more come to its funeral.

Again and again, people have asked me how to deal with these many-toothed monsters: there *are* ways to diminish the problem. Slugs and snails lurk in shade, so it is imperative to remove their hiding places. Clear away boards, boxes, piles of weed stalks, and other debris around your garden. Keep weeds down, particularly around the bases of perennials or shrubs. Keep your compost heap contained if possible. Mow the grass around the edge of your garden. These measures really help to reduce the number of slugs and snails.

Beyond the above cultural suggestions, I use several other tactics. Learn to recognize slug eggs, which look like small translucent beads, and squash them on sight. Go on search-and-destroy missions on cool, damp mornings and rainy days. In the evening, have beer parties for your slugs. Outline your herb beds with wood ashes or diatomaceous earth (composed of sharp, dustlike skeletons of prehistoric algae). Use nasty poisons if you must. Try anything, and good luck.

Garden webworms and tomato fruitworms: Both of these pests are recent arrivals in my garden. Webworms twist the leaves of lemon balm, mint, and other herbs around themselves to make hideouts while they devour plants; fruitworms eat basil as fast as it can grow. The bacterium *Bacillus thuringiensis* (Bt) provides specific control for caterpillars when sprayed on plants in the evening according to package directions. It kills caterpillars when they ingest it, but leaves no toxic residue and is harmless to earthworms and other beneficial organisms.

About Diseases

Herbs generally are disease resistant, but specific herbs have occasional problems. Some mints are susceptible to rust infection; garlic may suffer from mold and rot. Check the listing of individual herbs in Chapter 5 for descriptions of diseases.

herb

**II: Planning and Building
Twelve Herb Gardens**

gardens

From ground-hugging thymes to 25-foot bay trees, herbs encompass "any plants useful for flavor, fragrance, or physic," according to the Herb Society of America.

Countless herbs are used in different ways around the world. But in my experience a few dozen of these are the consistent favorites of cooks, gardeners, and medicine makers who save money and have better-quality herbs by growing their own.

Choosing Your Herbs

Before you ever buy a packet of seeds or lift a spade, consider whether you want to grow herbs for seasonings, fragrance, beauty in the garden, medicine, or a combination of uses. Begin to familiarize yourself with the appearance, growth habits, and ideal growing conditions of the plants you are considering. Visit gardens where you can see them firsthand (see Resources). Decide if you need annuals, which complete their life cycle in a single season; biennials, which will live two years; or perennials, which could remain in the same spot for several years, growing gradually larger.

The character of an herb garden is partly determined by the size, aspect, and soil of the site. A sunny area with moderately fertile, well-drained soil is ideal for growing the greatest variety of herbs, but you can work with a dry hillside, a parking strip, a shady backyard, a damp area, or gravelly spots. At least some herbs will grow in almost any garden conditions. If you have room only for planters, you can still have success with herbs. See the ideas for container gardens in this chapter, and the lists of herbs that thrive in special growing conditions.

To compensate for the periodic stresses of drought, seasonally low rainfall, and water restrictions experienced from northern California to Vancouver, British Columbia, incorporate water-thrifty herbs, such as lavender, rose geraniums, oregano, sage, or common thyme. For a postage stamp size–garden, perhaps in a city, choose from herbs with compact habits such as parsley, winter savory, rosemary, lavenders, and certain scented geraniums.

In some garden areas you may depend on evergreen herbs such as rosemary, sage, thyme, and winter savory as constants in your landscape design as well as in your cooking repertoire. Or perhaps you are looking for a ground cover to enhance ornamentals or complete a planting. Consider herbs that spread madly, such as perky nasturtiums or pretty creeping thymes in shades of green, gold, and gray. Also, many annual herbs can fill your garden with short-term color while perennials become established. You can find the right herbs for almost any situation.

Placing Your Herbs

Once you have selected your herbs and learned about the conditions they prefer, decide whether you will grow them in containers, your yard or vegetable patch, or in a separate herb garden.

Container Gardens

Many herbs are excellent choices for container gardening, especially when space is limited. This rewarding method of growing herbs also saves you the effort of maintaining a large garden. You can place your containers within easy reach of the kitchen and even make them portable. You can also control the soil mixture, watering, and fertilizing of individual herbs or of groupings with similar cultural requirements.

Most of the attractive containers available in garden stores and nurseries are suitable for growing herbs. I have grown herbs in old wheelbarrows, old watering cans, and recycled tires, too.

For organic growing, choose a quality commercial blend of organic materials and nutrients, or mix your own Basic Potting Soil, using the following recipe.

BASIC POTTING SOIL

Potting mixes containing soil or compost hold their texture and fertility longer than soilless mixes, but do produce some weeds unless sterilized. Avoid using garden soil alone, as it tends to be heavy and poorly aerated, and hardens after watering.

In this formula, the compost or earthworm castings contribute good soil structure and nutrients, peat moss holds water and nutrients, perlite (puffed pumice) lightens the mix and provides aeration, and sand improves drainage.

> 8 *quarts compost, earthworm castings, and/or*
> *composted chicken or steer manure*
> 4 *quarts sphagnum peat moss*
> 4 *quarts coarse perlite*
> 4 *quarts builders sand*
> 1 *cup All-Purpose Fertilizer Mix (page 12)*
> 3 *tablespoons ground dolomitic limestone*

Mix all ingredients thoroughly in a 5-gallon plastic bucket with enough water to moisten well. Peat moss absorbs water slowly; if possible, allow the potting mix to stand overnight so moisture is evenly distributed.

To ensure good drainage, line the bottom of the container with broken clay pot shards or gravel. I have also used plastic packaging pellets in the bottom of deep containers, covering them with a plastic sheet punched with drainage holes.

Nearly all the herbs in this book are suitable for growing in containers, with a few caveats. Oregano and lemon balm tend to take over if combined with other herbs. Mints should be planted separately and the roots trimmed back often. Lovage and fennel grow tall but can be appropriate for large-scale container gardens. Plant lists and directions for six specialty herb containers are given later in this chapter.

Existing Gardens

The easiest way to begin growing herbs is to tuck them into open spots in the yard. As long as their requirements for sun, soil, and moisture are met, they will usually thrive.

You could plant mint beside a water faucet; sweet woodruff under rhododendrons; sweet basil and marjoram in tubs on the deck where they will get lots of sun; sweet cicely in the shade of an old apple tree; lavender beside your gate; and creeping thyme along your path. What, no path, no gate? No matter. Plant your lovage at the back of your flower bed, the garlic around the roses, your tarragon next to the salvias, and edge the whole thing with 'Spicy Globe' basil for a gorgeous effect. There are endless possibilities for these adaptable plants.

Vegetable Gardens

Herbs can be incorporated into a section of your vegetable garden. For most home gardeners, one bed 4 feet wide by 6 feet long provides ample space for annual herbs and allows for convenient harvesting. You might plant one quarter of the bed with herbs such as arugula, cilantro, and baby dill, which can be sown in succession anytime from mid-March through mid-September, perhaps in combination with salad greens. Group slower-growing nasturtiums, savory, and sweet marjoram, sown or set out in May and harvested until frost, in another quarter of the bed. Sweet basil—an herb to grow and use in quantity— might fill the remaining half.

Perennial herbs will outlive your vegetables, and without some forethought you could end up with a sage plant here, a rampant mint there, and other herbs to work around in future seasons. Place all your perennial herbs in one bed, or around the edge of the garden in a decorative fashion—and, hey, you have an herb garden!

Herb Gardens

Herb gardens lend themselves to countless themes and variations. They can be almost any shape, whether rigidly geometric or softly contoured. Consult books on garden design for planting schemes (see Resources), but keep in mind that decisions you make now can always be changed. Half the fun of gardening is rearranging plants according to fresh inspiration.

Aesthetically, your garden will be most successful if you visualize how the mature plants will look throughout the seasons. As your experience grows, you will see that certain garden arrangements are more convenient for harvesting and maintenance, that some plants do best in a specific part of the garden, and that great beauty comes from particular combinations and juxtapositions of plants.

With their fresh scents and varied foliage, herbs can lend a delightful ambience to an area used for outdoor meals or conversation. Their subtle and restful colors are perfect for small havens that refresh and calm the senses. Place an ornamental herb garden where it can be viewed from the living room; position a kitchen garden close to the back door. If the garden will do double duty as a play area, sturdy herbs such as fennel, mint, nasturtiums, rosemary, sage, and thyme can stand up to occasional abuse from children and pets.

By concentrating herbs in one area, you will be more likely to use and care for them. When you go out to pick a sprig of rosemary for your minestrone, you might harvest a few nasturtium blossoms to brighten up your salad. Perhaps you will notice that the sage is beginning to bloom, that a slug is attacking your basil, or that a bit of quack grass is creeping into the chives. Fifteen minutes later, the situation is all squared away—for now, at least.

Twelve Creative Theme Plantings

Herbs bring romance to a garden as few other plants can, and link us to faraway people, places, and times. Even ordinary herbs like parsley possess dimensions of history, lore, and symbolism. Grouping them together according to theme offers creative opportunities that engage the mind as well as the senses.

I have seen gardens built around herbs of the Bible, Shakespeare, the Shakers, the pioneers, the Zodiac, and various color schemes, to name a few. Herbs can star in bee and butterfly gardens, dye plant gardens, formal knot gardens, meditation gardens, and low-allergen gardens—as you can imagine, there is no end to the possibilities. For starters, here are the outlines for twelve herbal theme gardens, from a simple garden in a basket to a medicinal herb border bursting with flowers and foliage.

HOT AND DRY AREAS	FULL SHADE	PARTIAL SHADE	MOIST AREAS
Bay tree	Chervil	Arugula	Chervil
Echinacea	Sweet woodruff	Borage	Catnip
Lemon balm	Watercress	Catnip	Comfrey
Monarda	Wild ginger	Comfrey	Elder
Rose, rugosa		Elder	Lovage
St. John's wort		Feverfew	Mints
		Horseradish	Monarda
		Nasturtium	Nettle
		Nettle	Parsley
		Salad burnet	Sorrel
		Sorrel	Sweet woodruff
		Valerian	Valerian
		Viola	Viola
		Watercress	Watercress
			Wild ginger

Preparing Herb Planters

You can create many variations on the planter theme, following these general directions and then using the herbs and containers of your choice.

Begin by placing at least 2 inches of broken clay pots, sharp gravel, or other drainage material in the bottom of your container. Then fill it almost to the top with Basic Potting Soil. Scoop or dig out planting holes and set plants in place. Add soil to the top of the container, firming plants in well. Seeds of quick-growing annuals can be sown directly into containers—cover them with about ½ inch of soil, and press down lightly. Soak well with Regular Solution Fish Fertilizer (page 12). Drench the roots completely and fertilize steadily about once a week.

Herb Garden in a Basket

2 basil
1 chive
1 sweet marjoram
2 trailing nasturtium
1 parsley
1 thyme
1 basket (12 inches by 12 inches by 4 inches deep)

This live herb garden makes a lovely gift for Easter, Mother's Day, or any special occasion. Choose common herbs from the list, or jazz it up by using more unusual varieties such as 'Purple Ruffles' basil, garlic chives, Italian parsley, and lemon thyme. Prepare the soil, add the plants, fertilize, and it's ready to grow.

Edible Flower Planter

1 calendula
1 chive
1 lavender
1 rose geranium
3 compact nasturtium, 3 trailing nasturtium
1 rectangular wooden planter box (1 foot wide by
    4 feet long by 8 inches deep)

The renewed interest in cooking with flowers inspired this planter that includes many of the best-tasting edible flowers. Grouped together in a rectangular wooden planter, they make a pretty sight and are easy to pick for the table.

Fill and fertilize your container according to the directions for preparing herb planters.

Create a row with the calendula, chive, lavender, and rose geranium equidistant from one another. The calendula and rose geranium are the quickest-growing of these taller plants. Intersperse the nasturtiums between them, with the trailing ones nearest the edges. Place compact nasturtiums in front. The annual calendula and nasturtiums will need to be replaced each season, and the rose geranium moved indoors for the winter, but the other plants can remain in the planter year-round.

Italian Herb Planter Barrel

2 sweet basil
1 sweet marjoram
1 oregano (optional)
1 Italian parsley
1 upright rosemary
1 thyme

1 half whiskey barrel (15 inches deep, 23 inches in
  diameter)

2 cubic feet (about 28 quarts) Basic Potting Soil

24 quarts plastic packaging pellets

Nearly everyone loves the flavors of Italian herbs, and the five chosen for this easy garden are suitable for terra-cotta pots, window boxes, wooden half whiskey barrels, or even a sunny garden spot. Add oregano to the list, by all means, but watch out for its spreading roots.

Fill the bottom of the half whiskey barrel 5 inches deep (one third full) with plastic packaging pellets. Punch drainage holes in a sheet of plastic and lay it on top. Add 2 cubic feet (about 28 dry quarts) of potting soil (Basic Potting Soil recipe page 30, or purchased). Plant the herbs and fertilize according to the directions for preparing herb planters. When you set in the plants, remember that the basil and parsley will be the fastest growers. Give this barrel a sunny spot, and it will reward you with an abundance of flavorful herbs.

HERBES DE PROVENCE PLANTER

2 basil

1 lavender (dwarf variety such as 'Munstead')

2 sweet marjoram

2 rosemary

1 summer savory

2 thyme

For a continental flavor, choose a weathered terra-cotta pot or a classically styled concrete planter that holds about 5 gallons. Fill the container with soil. Now plant with herbs of southern France. Center the lavender in the middle of the pot; arrange the other herbs

around it in a pleasing pattern. Fertilize according to the directions for preparing herb planters.

Place this planter in full sun and watch the bees and butterflies enjoy it. The lavender, rosemary, and thyme are perennial; the others are annual.

PACIFIC RIM PLANTER

1 sweet basil

1 Thai basil

1 packet cilantro seeds

1 garlic chive

6 garlic plants

1 gingerroot (Zingiber officinale) or hot pepper
  plant (optional)

1 lemongrass (optional)

1 spearmint

This herb garden reflects the diverse populations of the maritime Northwest, incorporating plants of Japanese, Chinese, Vietnamese, and other Pacific Rim cultures. A lovely glazed pot from an Asian market or an old sake tub, if you have the good fortune to find one, would make a great container for this garden.

Fill a 5-gallon container according to the directions for preparing herb planters. Set the sweet basil, lemongrass, or the hot pepper plant in the center, as they will grow tallest, and surround them with the other plants. Look at farmers' markets in late spring for already started garlic plants, which will mature with the other herbs. To keep the spearmint under control, you may wish to use a separate pot. Leave a 6-inch circle for the cilantro, and sow half the seed packet close together in it; sow the remaining seeds in about a month for a continuous supply of leaves.

Fertilize according to container planting directions earlier in this chapter.

If you find a sprouting gingerroot in the grocery store, tuck it in among the other plants. Hot peppers such as 'Super Cayenne' or 'Riot' are excellent container plants with lots of color. They keep producing until Christmas if brought into a cool greenhouse.

In this garden, cilantro, basil, and garlic are annuals; lemongrass a tender perennial; and garlic chives and mint perennials.

CULINARY HERBS IN A STRAWBERRY POT
Choose from:

Basils	Dwarf sage
Dwarf Greek oregano	Garlic chives
Bay tree	Common thyme
Curled or Italian parsley	Lemon thyme
Chervil	Silver thyme
Trailing rosemary	Lavender, 'Munstead'
Chives	Sweet marjoram
Summer or winter savory	Nasturtiums, 'Alaska'
Cilantro	Viola

You can grow a veritable garden of culinary herbs in one attractive terra-cotta strawberry pot, and position it for maximum convenience outside your kitchen door or on the deck beside the barbecue. For the greatest variety of herbs, choose a large pot with eight to ten pockets.

Place a layer of gravel or broken crockery in the bottom of the pot. To facilitate deep watering, insert a length of perforated drainage pipe (or even a length of old hose pipe punched with holes). To keep it in position, heap gravel around its base, and hold the pipe upright as you fill the pot with a potting mix of compost, perlite, and sand, mixed with a cup of All-Purpose Fertilizer Mix.

Select the herbs you use most from the list above, keeping in mind that basil, chervil, cilantro, sweet marjoram, nasturtiums, and violas are annuals. In the large opening at the top, plant a bay leaf tree, 'Munstead' lavender, or three to five basil plants. Tuck the other herbs in the pockets as desired. Place the container in a sunny location. Fertilize the plants every two weeks with Light Solution Fish Fertilizer or Compost Tea.

Kitchen Garden Plots
If you have the room and time to plant, consider creating a garden plot. Below are two gardens for 16 and 24 square feet, respectively.

TWELVE-HERB KITCHEN GARDEN

6 sweet basil	2 parsley
1 bay tree (optional)	1 upright rosemary
2 chives	1 sage
1 packet cilantro seeds	1 spearmint
1 packet dill seeds	1 tarragon
2 oregano	2 thyme

All the herbs recommended in this book are suitable for a kitchen garden, but I consider these to be the most basic. This pretty group would be perfect in a sunny area just outside the door. By the end of summer, it will be bursting with herbs, and by the following spring, you will have fairly substantial perennials and divisions of mint to give away. The bay tree is an extra that adds a charming focal point when it's sizable.

Make this garden 4 feet long on each side, nicely edged with bricks or stones. In mid-April, dig over the whole plot, working in 4 cubic feet of compost, to improve soil texture, and about 1 pound (2 cups) of All-Purpose Fertilizer Mix (page 12). Rake it smooth enough for a seedbed.

Put your bay tree in the center, in a sunken pot or directly in the ground, remembering that you will probably take it indoors for the winter. Divide the remainder of the plot into four sections, each 4 square feet in area. Sow a 3-inch-wide band of cilantro around the perimeter of one bed, and one of dill around a second. About a month later, you can make a second sowing of these herbs around the remaining two beds. Save the center of the first square for six basil plants, to be set out in early May (protect them from cold with plastic milk cartons with bottoms cut away until nights are warm). In the second square, plant one upright rosemary ('Arp' is hardiest), one sage, and two thyme plants. These three herbs have a similar tolerance for dry soil. In the third square, plant two chive plants, two parsley starts, and one tarragon. These herbs do best in a richer, moister soil. That leaves the fourth square for the spreaders, oregano and mint. Set the oregano nearest the bay tree, and either keep the mint in a pot and sink it into the ground or be prepared to keep slicing the roots with a shovel to keep it under control.

INSTANT TWENTY-FOUR HERB GARDEN

Janice Peltier of Herban Renewal in Seattle introduced me to a quick and easy way to make gardens. She successfully uses her No-Till, Sheet-Mulch

Method for many gardens around her urban lot. When a neighbor moved away and bequeathed me her compost heap, I tried this method for a wedge-shaped garden that went together in less than a day.

Arugula	Marjoram
Basil	Mint
Bay tree	Nasturtium
Calendula	Oregano
Chives	Parsley
Cilantro	Rose geranium
Dill	Rosemary
Fennel	Sage
Garlic	Savory (winter and summer)
Lavender	Sweet cicely
Lemon balm	Tarragon
Lovage	Thyme

The varying heights of herbs in this garden make it a good candidate for a perennial border–type arrangement. When the plants are mature, the tall bay tree, fennel, and lovage dominate the background; at medium height are calendula, dill, rose geraniums, lavender, lemon balm, mint, oregano, rosemary, and sweet cicely; basil, sage, and summer savory fill in the middle; and low-growing arugula, chives, cilantro, garlic, nasturtium, parsley, tarragon, thyme, and winter savory are out in front.

This selection of herbs capitalizes on an interesting variety of leaf shapes and textures, flower colors, and fragrances. Annuals, such as basil, calendula, cilantro, dill, nasturtiums, and summer savory, are interspersed with perennials and placed for easy access. As an added bonus, the flowers of many of these herbs, including basil, cilantro, dill, lavender, lemon balm, lovage, marjoram, oregano, rosemary, summer savory, and thyme, attract bees to the garden. Fennel is an important butterfly plant. Put the mint (sunk in pots to avoid invasiveness) and sweet cicely in a shady corner.

To plant, choose an area 4 feet wide by 6 feet long, perhaps along the south or west side of a fence or garage. Stake out the perimeter of the garden, and edge it with a sharp spade to kill grass roots. Dig out pernicious weeds such as dandelions and horsetail. Sprinkle a thin layer of compost or manure on the ground, and blanket it with two or three layers of flattened brown cardboard boxes, making sure the entire area is evenly covered (soak the boxes for easier handling). Then shovel on as much organic material as available: garden soil, worm castings, compost, kitchen waste, manure, shredded leaves. Build up mounds for varying heights of 1 to 3 feet if you like. Spread with 3 cups of All-Purpose Fertilizer Mix (page 12) and top it off with a thick layer of finished compost. Sow and plant your herbs directly into the bed and water them well. Within a very short time, your "instant" garden will fill in and look great.

GRAY GARDEN FOR A PLANTING STRIP

3 lavender: 1 'Hidcote,' 1 'Provence,' 1 'Silver Frost'
3 sage: 1 'Berggarten,' 1 pineapple, 1 purple
2 scented geraniums: 1 'Gray Lady Plymouth,'
*   1 'Snowflake Rose'*
1 sweet cicely
12 thyme: 3 silver, 3 white creeping, 6 woolly
1 variegated pineapple mint
3 borage

Optional herbs not included in this book:

1 artemesia, 'Silver Mound'
2 baby's breath, 'Bristol Fairy'
2 santolina, dwarf gray
1 southernwood
3 woolly lamb's ears
2 yarrow, 'Moonbeam'

For a city planting strip, sturdy herbs able to withstand dry conditions and a degree of neglect are ideal. This narrow garden, about 3 feet wide and 15 to 20 feet long, is densely planted with herbs in shades of gray that do well in full sun. Here they are used as ornamentals rather than culinary herbs, so there's no need to fret about things like dogs and car exhaust. If you want all low-maintenance perennials, choose substitutes for the frost-tender scented geraniums from the optional list.

Position the lavenders, sages, scented geraniums, and sweet cicely in a zigzag pattern along the planting strip. Fill in with the thymes and borage, and the pineapple mint, sunk in a container in the ground to prevent rampant growth. If herbs from the optional list are included rather than the scented geraniums, remember that baby's breath, southernwood, and yarrow grow tall; santolina and 'Silver Mound' artemesia are rounded, and woolly lamb's ears are lower-growing ground covers.

HERBAL BEVERAGE GARDEN

This garden will provide a generous supply of herbal teas to enjoy either fresh or dried. The wide variety of flavors becomes practically limitless if you choose to experiment with blending two or more herbs.

Anise hyssop
Basil
Borage
Chamomile, Roman
Dill
Hops (optional)
Lavender
Lemon balm
Lemon verbena
Monarda
Parsley
Rose, rugosa, sweetbriar, or Charles de Mills
   (optional)
Rose geranium
Rosemary
Sages (pineapple, tricolor, golden)
Common and lemon thyme
And the rampant spreaders, contained:
   Mints: orange mint, peppermint, spearmint
   Sweet woodruff
Chamomile, peppermint, lemon balm, lemon verbena, rose hips, monarda, lemon thyme, and anise hyssop are well known as delicious tea herbs. Many culinary herbs, such as basil, parsley, sage, spearmint, common thyme and lemon thyme, make surprisingly good-tasting teas with nutritive and medicinal qualities as a bonus. Dill is included for its flavorful seeds, which improve digestion. Lavender, pineapple sage, and rose geranium are also very pleasant.

Mint, rose petals, and lemon balm are used in liqueurs, borage in claret cup and punch, sweet woodruff in May wine, lovage in cordials, and hops, of course, in beer.

The garden is circular, with the rose bush (or hop vine) at its center surrounded by four kidney-shaped beds about 4 feet wide and 4 feet long with paths in between. Rosemary, lemon verbena, monarda, and lavender grow relatively large, so plant these in the centers of the beds. Plant the three sages alongside the rosemary. With monarda, plant parsley, basil, borage, and mints. Roman chamomile, anise hyssop, dill, and lemon balm share the bed with the lemon verbena, and the thymes, along with sweet woodruff and rose geranium, surround the lavender.

Experienced gardeners may wonder how this combination of hardy and tender perennials, heat-loving annuals, and rampant spreaders can possibly work in a smallish garden. The answer: sunken pots. Protect potted lemon verbena, pineapple sage, and rose geranium indoors from cold weather, then sink them along with basil starts among the hardier plants after danger of frost. Control mints and sweet woodruff in pots, but lift them every spring, cut them apart, and repot in fresh soil.

MEDIEVAL MONASTERY GARDEN

It is fascinating to read accounts of ancient monastic gardens, where many of the herbs we grow today were tended with surprising sophistication. Parsley, chervil, coriander, dill, poppy, savory, and lovage were among the eighty-nine species of plants listed for inclusion in the imperial gardens by Charlemagne in A.D. 812. When society fell apart during the Dark Ages in medieval Europe, the knowledge of growing and utilizing herbs was preserved in monastery gardens. This garden honors those who passed on this legacy to us.

The Monastery Garden's ancient and practical design features parallel rows of raised rectangular beds. It is a kind of mix-and-match design that allows the flexibility to accommodate the needs and characteristics of many individual plants. The directions below serve as guidelines for choices within this framework rather than a strict design plan.

Bay tree	*Sage*
Borage	*Salad burnet*
Chervil	*Summer and winter*
Comfrey	*savory*
Coriander	*Sorrel*
Dill	*Spearmint*
Horseradish	*Sweet basil*
Lavender	*Sweet cicely*
Lovage	*Sweet marjoram*
Parsley	*Sweet woodruff*
Peppermint	*Tarragon*
Rose (Apothecary's	*Thyme*
rose, Damask rose)	*Viola*
Rosemary	

The herbs for this garden were selected from a list of more than 250 medieval plants in the gardens of The Cloisters, a division of the Metropolitan Museum of Art in New York City. I have grouped them according to their growth habits and preferences as to light and soil conditions. Alternatively, they could be arranged according to their use, color, or other characteristics.

Let's say that this garden site has average soil with good drainage and areas of full sun, partial shade, and full shade. Prepare as many 3-foot by 5-foot beds as desired and edge them with bricks or pressure treated 2-by-4 boards sunk into the ground. Amend the soil in each bed as necessary, referring to the Planting information and cultural directions for individual herbs in Chapter 5.

Prepare a bed that receives full sun, enrich the soil with plenty of organic matter and fertilizer, and plant it with sun-loving annuals, two crosswise rows of each. Choose from these herbs, listed in ascending order according to height: sweet marjoram, coriander, summer savory, sweet basil, borage, and dill.

Enrich the soil of a bed that gets plenty of sun and plant it with perennial herbs. Choose from Apothecary's rose, Damask rose, bay tree, parsley, salad burnet, sorrel, and tarragon.

In a drier soil that is not amended, plant drought-tolerant herbs such as rosemary, thyme, sage, lavender, and winter savory.

Rampant spreaders can be successfully confined in individual beds. Comfrey, horseradish, peppermint, spearmint, and sweet woodruff are all suitable for semishaded beds with enriched soil. You can combine single specimens of these take-over types in one bed while they are young, but you will probably end up digging most of them out later.

For a shaded bed, enrich the soil and choose from low-growing chervil and violas, and taller sweet cicely and lovage.

An extensive model of this style of garden is the Medicinal Herb Garden at the University of Washington in Seattle. A garden ornament such as a sundial or a statue of St. Francis or St. Fiacre (the patron saint of gardeners) would be in keeping with the simplicity of this garden and its monastic theme.

MEDICINAL HERB BORDER

Because medicinal herbs come in a variety of shapes and sizes and favor different growing conditions, it is a challenge to grow them side by side. Some of the healing herbs described in this book are good-sized bushes, vines, or even trees; others are invasive and hard to control once established. The plants listed below are relatively well-behaved and can get along together in a long border.

1 angelica

3 calendula

1 catnip

1 chamomile

1 echinacea

1 elder (if space permits)

1 fennel

1 feverfew

6-12 garlic

1 hop, variety of choice

1 lemon balm

1 parsley

2 roses (1 rugosa, 1 old red rose of choice)

1 rosemary

1 sage

2 thyme

1 valerian

Prepare a border that is 20 feet long and 5 feet wide. It should be situated in a sunny location with average soil, ideally against a wall or fence. The border design is anchored by the larger specimens in the back, with the rosemary and two roses in the center and the lower-growing herbs interspersed in front.

Erect a tall wooden pole or tepee at one end of the bed and plant the hops beside it. Space angelica, one rose, rosemary, the second rose, valerian, and fennel about 4 feet apart in a row. Position the two roses toward the front, the rosemary between them and farther back, in line with the taller plants on each side. Tuck the garlic plants around the roses. Plant the sage between the hop and the angelica but toward the front, and continue with the catnip, echinacea, feverfew, calendula, and lemon balm in an undulating row toward the front. Plant chamomile, parsley, and thyme at the edge of the bed. If space permits, plant the elder at the end of the garden opposite the hops. The hop vine could also be trained over an arbor or along the fence. When fully mature, this will be a garden full of exuberant herbs with a variety of textures.

Note: For medicinal use, it is generally best to plant herb varieties with *officinalis* in their Latin name. All the herbs in this garden except the roses, rosemary, sage, and thymes will die back in the winter. A garden design similar to the Medieval Monastery Garden, featuring rectangular beds, would also work well for these plants. Some of the more aggressive herbs, such as comfrey, horseradish, and St. John's wort, could be included.

preserving

III: Harvesting, Preserving, and Wildcrafting Herbs

harvesting

Summer has arrived,
and your herbs are growing
beautifully. Now what? Many
people succeed in starting an herb
garden but are at a loss when it
comes to harvesting and storing
what they have grown.

Following are some general guidelines. For more ideas, check the harvesting and preserving sections included in the individual herb listings in Chapter 5.

Harvesting

No set formula tells you when to cut herbs and how much to take, but the best time to harvest leaves is just before a plant blooms, when the essential oils containing flavor and fragrance are at their peak. If you become impatient, start by cutting plants sparingly when they are 3 or 4 inches tall, and continue until they flower.

For most leafy herbs, cut the stems back to about 2 inches from the ground. With tougher-stemmed herbs such as sage, snip or pinch back the leafy tops of the plant. *Pinching back* means using your thumbnails or hand pruners to remove plant tips, usually severing the stem just above a leaf node and taking less than a quarter of the plant's leaves. When harvesting fresh herbs for cooking or home remedies, you will probably cut only as much as you need right then. Snipping and clipping herbs regularly will keep them compact and productive.

If buds begin to form on an herb, harvest most of the plant and use it fresh or preserve it for winter. Afterward the plant will grow a second and sometimes a third crop.

If you don't cut your plants back, they will flower and go to seed; the leaves will toughen and may turn yellow or brown. If it is not too late in the season, say mid-August, cut the plants back and wait for new growth; go ahead and use the leaves as long as they have good flavor and are not too tough. You may also be able to use the flowers or seedpods you have harvested, depending on the plant.

After mid-September, slow down on harvesting

perennials, since they are preparing for dormancy. If you cut too late in the season and stimulate new growth, your plants may not have the reserves needed to make it through a cold winter.

In short, *do* harvest and use your herbs. Nothing can compare with the flavors of herbs fresh from your garden.

Preserving

Drying or freezing herbs and seeds for later use takes only a little time and effort. When the weather is dreadful, fresh herbs are scarce in your garden and expensive at the grocery store. The palette of flavors available from herbs you have grown can really brighten winter meals.

One or more of these popular methods of preservation can be right for each herb.

Drying Herbs

Herbs can be dried using a food dehydrator, a microwave, or air, depending upon time and availability. I do not recommend using an oven, except as specifically noted. General directions follow.

Food dehydrator: This time-saver produces dried herbs with great color and flavor. The usual dehydrator method is to chop the herbs, cutting out large fleshy midribs, or to strip the leaves from their stems, and then dry them at 90° to 110°F for 2 or 3 hours. Cool for a few minutes before testing for doneness—leaves should crumble in your hand.

Microwave: Microwave ovens preserve the color and flavor of herbs beautifully, but can handle only about ¼ cup at a time. Place the herbs in a single layer between paper towels and microwave for 1 minute. Cool 1 minute and check. If they are not quite dry, try additional 30-second intervals.

Air-drying: The simplest way to preserve herbs, air-drying usually takes two to three weeks. Bunch the herbs together with rubber bands, and hang them out of direct sunlight where air circulation is good until the leaves rustle between your fingers and feel brittle. As the stems dry and contract, the rubber bands shrink and hold them tight.

Old-fashioned, collapsible wooden clothes-drying racks work well for herbs and can be tucked unobtrusively into a corner. If herbs take over your life, you may find yourself screwing hooks into the ceiling of an attic or utility room and stringing twine between them. This method is fine for many leafy herbs. When drying seeds used for flavoring, such as coriander, dill, and fennel, cut air holes in a paper bag and tie it around the stalks to catch seeds that drop off as they dry.

The simple "nonmethod": By way of personal confession, one way I frequently air-dry herbs is the "lying around the kitchen" technique. My summers are busy and sometimes I do not get around to doing anything more with certain herbs than spreading them out on a paper plate or a sheet of paper. They blend in with the kitchen clutter until I finally get around to putting them in a jar. Small bunches of herbs also hang from utensil racks, cupboard hooks, and pushpins on the bulletin board until the winter day when I need a few sprigs of whatever for that night's dinner. When the next season's fresh herbs come along, the dried ones go in the compost. While I do not exactly recommend this nonmethod, the flavors of the herbs are still superior to most anything I could buy in a store.

Drying Seeds

Harvest ripe seeds from garden plants when they turn light brown, before they start dropping. Spread seed heads on screens or hang them in bunches over a cloth or inside a paper bag for about two weeks until dry. Rub off the dried seeds and store in an airtight container. Use this method to dry seeds for propagation as well as for cooking.

Storing Dried Herbs

Dried herbs last for one to two years when stored in appropriate airtight containers that protect them from heat, light, and moisture. Opaque glass or pottery jars and metal tins with tight-fitting lids are ideal. Be sure to label containers as you fill them. Do not use plastic; it breathes and allows the herbs to absorb moisture.

Whole leaves keep their flavor longer than ground or crumbled ones, but they also take up more room. To separate leaves from stems, rub a handful of herbs between your palms over a sheet of newspaper or old cloth. Compost the stems or use them for fire starters. Before storage, you may wish to chop the leaves coarsely in a food processor using a steel blade.

Freezing

The delicate flavors of certain herbs are better preserved by freezing than drying. Chives, chervil, cilantro, dill, parsley, and tarragon are among these, and I would not want to face a winter without a good supply of pesto made from my basil crop.

Blanching: This step is often recommended to stop enzyme action, which can compromise the flavor of frozen herbs. After gathering and lightly rinsing your herbs, dip them in boiling water for a few seconds; remove and plunge them in ice water. Drain the herbs on kitchen towels, then dry them with a salad spinner or roll them up in a dish towel.

Next spread the herbs out on a cookie sheet and put them in the coldest part of your freezer, usually near the bottom. The leaves or pieces will freeze quickly and remain separate. Transfer your frozen herbs to a glass jar with a tight-fitting lid and return to the freezer.

Herb cubes: Many people purée herbs with a little water, freeze them in ice cube trays, and transfer the cubes to a glass jar. Use the premeasured herb cubes as needed to enhance your meals.

HERBS FOR DRYING

Angelica (leaves, roots)

Anise hyssop (leaves)

Basil (leaves)

Bay (leaves)

Calendula (flowers)

Catnip (leaves, flowering tops)

Chamomile (flowers)

Chives (flowers for ornament)

Comfrey (leaves, roots)

Dill (young leaves)

Echinacea (flowers, leaves, roots)

Elder (flowers, berries)

Fennel (stalks for stuffing baked fish, French style; seeds)

Feverfew (leaves)
Garlic (cloves)
Hops (strobiles)
Lavender (flowers, leaves)
Lemon balm (leaves)
Lemon verbena (leaves)
Lovage (leaves, root)
Marjoram (leaves)
Mints (flowers, leaves)
Monarda (flowers, leaves)
Nettle
Oregano (flowers, leaves)
Parsley (leaves)
Rose (petals, leaves, hips)
Rose geranium (leaves)
Rosemary (leaves)
Sage (leaves)
St. John's wort (flowering tops)
Savory, summer and winter (leaves)
Tarragon (leaves)
Thyme (flowering tops, leaves)
Valerian (root)

HERBS FOR FREEZING

Certain herbs better retain their flavor when frozen. The following herbs can last for six months in the freezer.

Basil (as pesto, or ground with olive oil)
Chervil (leaves)
Chives (leaves)
Cilantro (leaves)
Dill (chopped leaves or whole unripe seed heads)
Elder (flowers, berries)

Feverfew (leaves)
Garlic (when cloves start to sprout)
Hops (strobiles)
Horseradish (root, whole or ground)
Lovage (leaves)
Nasturtiums (aerial parts)
Nettle (leaves)
Parsley (leaves)
Sorrel (leaves)
Sweet cicely (leaves)

Wildcrafting

Hundreds of healing herbs grow uncultivated in this region. Some are native plants; others are invasive escapees from cultivation, otherwise known as weeds. Dandelion, elder, nettle, St. John's wort, wild rose, and watercress are some of the wild plants described in this book. There are many other wild plants, equally interesting and valuable, that could not be included, such as hawthorn, red clover, yarrow, uva ursi, devil's club, tansy, horsetail, and many more. Purslane, plantain, cleavers, chickweed, pigweed, shepherds purse, dock, and quack grass are among the useful garden weeds. Learning to identify, harvest, and utilize these plants will not only provide you with food and medicines, but also deepen your herbal knowledge and your understanding of the need to preserve wild places.

Gathering wild plants requires knowledge, attentiveness, and timing, but the first requirement of a wildcrafter is an attitude of respect for the plants and responsibility for their continued survival. You don't have to worry about overharvesting dandelions and other garden weeds, but wild plant populations are more fragile and the demand on them is intensifying. In some parts of the country, wild stands of popular medicinal plants such as arnica, goldenseal, American ginseng, and lady's slipper are under tremendous pressure. Harvest herbs from large, healthy plant communities only, and leave at least three quarters of the plants so that they will continue to flourish. It is illegal to harvest plants in national parks and other protected areas.

Obviously, correct identification is crucial. An experienced teacher is invaluable in learning to identify each plant with certainty. Otherwise, get a good field guide and key out the plants, using basic botanical precepts to distinguish small but significant differences in appearance. There are some poisonous plants out there that look a whole lot like herbs. For example, water hemlock could easily be mistaken for sweet cicely, or digitalis for comfrey. Identification is sometimes easier when you know what type of environment or locale is likely to host particular plants. You wouldn't look for St. John's wort in deep, shady woods, and watercress doesn't thrive on dry hillsides. *Flora of the Pacific Northwest,* by Hitchcock and Cronquist, is a treasure trove of botanical information on native plants.

Seek herbs in their season to harvest them in their prime. Each plant has a unique life cycle, emerging, blooming, reproducing, and dying in its own time, within the larger cycle of the changing seasons. It's also important to know which part of the plant to gather for your purpose, whether leaves, flowers, seeds, the entire aerial tops, or roots. Nothing substitutes for direct experience in learning to recognize the peak of perfection for each plant part. Remember, like time and tides, plants wait for no one. A few days can make a big difference in quality.

As I harvest herbs to make healing medicines, I try to clear my mind of extraneous thoughts. When I focus my attention on the plants and the moment, I feel a wordless attunement that nourishes my spirit. Who knows—this intuitive receptivity might increase the healing powers of my herbal medicines. There is surely no harm in cultivating a meditative attitude, and there are many things we do not know about plants.

Once you have harvested your herbs, handle them carefully and tend to them quickly. Methods of preserving and processing them are described in other parts of this book. Please refer to the general sections and the profiles of individual herbs for more specific details.

As expanding interest in medicinal herbs worldwide increases the demand for these plants, sustainable commercial cultivation is beginning to replace wildcrafting of many species. The National Center for the Preservation of Medicinal Herbs recently established by Frontier Natural Products Co-op of Norway, Iowa, is among the organizations taking steps toward this. They are providing a model for home gardeners and commercial growers alike.

cooking

healing

IV: Using Herbs

Herbs are sometimes called "the useful plants," and their enduring appeal arises in part from their remarkable variety of applications.

Using Herbs

Charlemagne's description of herbs as "the friend of the physician and the praise of cooks" still holds true, and that is just the beginning. As you learn their ways, you can find uses for herbs in many aspects of your everyday life. Depending on your preferences and the time you have available, this may mean just a few herbal touches here and there. Or you may come to regard them as friends or allies. Next thing you know, you'll be using them all the time, and living your own personal version of an herb lover's lifestyle.

Cooking with Herbs

The Northwest climate is admirably suited to growing a great variety of herbs that have originated in diverse geographical areas and are an integral part of cuisines around the world.Freshly harvested herbs possess a depth of flavor, intensified by their aromas,

that simply can't be matched by a dried, frozen, or freeze-dried product. Once you learn this truth from experience, you may never again be satisfied with the dried herbs available in little tins and bottles on the supermarket shelves. That's what happened to me.

The recipes and suggestions for cooking with herbs in this book grew out of my experience. Herbs, fresh whenever possible, are staples in these everyday recipes. Like many people with busy schedules, a single mom who is raising kids and running a business does not have much time to cook. Yet good food has always been important to me, so I've developed a repertoire of everyday recipes that are easy and delicious. I'm adventurous by nature, and at Silver Bay herbs surrounded me in abundance. As I delivered fresh-cut herbs every week to intimate restaurants and large hotels, I peeked into the kitchens and talked to the chefs. They gave me great tips on cooking with herbs, and I learned even more when they came to the farm to cook wonderful alfresco meals under our gazebo near the sea.

I've been privileged to work with many creative regional chefs who celebrate the Pacific Northwest's fabulous bounty of fresh ingredients. They have a profound appreciation for the luscious fruits, nuts, and vegetables; splendid fish and seafood; meats and poultry; and, of course, the flavorful herbs of our region. By crediting growers and producers on their menus, they are heightening awareness of and pride in local agriculture. Some of their recipes are included in this book. They encourage us to take a new look at Northwest regional cooking and find ways to enhance those good old standbys with the vibrant flavors of fresh herbs.

Cooking with fresh herbs naturally leads to a greater awareness of the seasons. You want to make some pesto? You get your basil *in season*, when it's plentiful, gorgeous, and cheap. Blend it up, eat it fresh, put your stash in the freezer, and pat yourself on the back as you enjoy it year-round. Fresh chanterelles available at the market? Sauté them with a little olive oil; add some salt, pepper, and fresh tarragon; and have yourself an autumn feast. Even those who don't garden can take advantage of seasonal produce at its best, whether by informed selection in the grocery store, by shopping at a farm stand in the country, or by patronizing local growers at one of the many farmers' markets that have sprung up throughout the Northwest.

With their fresh and varied flavors, herbs are an important part of the healthy cuisine promoted by wellness organizations, including heart and cancer associations and HMOs. Even the United States gov-

ernment is getting into the act, with a new food pyramid and full-color posters that urge us to cut back on salt and fat and to use herbs as seasonings. Medicinal herbs are also gaining respect as science and tradition combine to usher in a new understanding of their properties and actions.

These two trends dovetail in *phytocuisine*, a newly emerging phenomenon that places emphasis on eating plants that have health-promoting or medicinal qualities. In the grocery store we're seeing echinacea in fruit juice and ginseng in chewing gum, and this sort of thing may develop into a huge industry. But is the whole idea really so new? It was an *aha!* experience to realize that in many cases we are rediscovering what the ancients knew intuitively and from experience: herbs, even the trusty culinary standbys we take for granted, can help keep us healthy when we incorporate small amounts into our diets regularly. Peppermint is a proven digestive aid, garlic is antibiotic, and rosemary sharpens the memory, to mention only a few examples. Then there are the wild herbs—elderberry, the cold and flu fighter; nettles, the tonic superfood. Exploring the medicinal attributes of culinary herbs was one of the more interesting aspects of working on this book. Happily, there will always be more to explore in the world of herbs.

Recipes

HIGH SUMMER SANDWICH
During the busy months of August and September at Silver Bay, we never tired of these hearty lunch sandwiches of arugula with fresh garden vegetables.

Cream cheese or light mayonnaise

Sweet brown mustard

Whole wheat sandwich bread such as Ezekiel or wheatberry

Tender arugula leaves

Big, fat, ripe tomatoes, sliced

Yellow cheddar, medium or sharp, sliced

Cool crunchy cucumbers (Sweet Slice is the ultimate in my book), sliced lengthwise

Spread cream cheese or mayo and mustard on the bread. Pile on the arugula leaves, sliced tomatoes, cheese, and cucumber slices. For a deluxe version, use marjoram mayonnaise (page 57).

Summer Pasta Salad

My longtime neighbors at Silver Bay, Phyllis and Lloyd Cleven, serve a variation of this salad at their annual corn-on-the-cob celebration. It is also fine as a main dish.

⅔ cup olive oil

3 tablespoons red wine vinegar

¼ cup chopped fresh basil

1 to 3 cloves of garlic, mashed

2 tablespoons grated Parmesan cheese

¼ teaspoon freshly ground black pepper

16 ounces rotelli, tortellini, or other pasta

1 each red, green, and yellow pepper, sliced in rings, then in half

3 medium tomatoes

2 tablespoons chopped green onion

1 tablespoon chopped fresh oregano (Greek or Italian)

¼ cup pitted black or Greek olives

8 ounces feta, crumbled, or fresh mozzarella, cubed

¼ cup pine nuts, for garnish

4 3-inch sprigs fresh basil (piccolo preferred), for garnish

Combine the oil, vinegar, ¼ cup basil, garlic, Parmesan, and black pepper in a blender and process until smooth. Cook pasta al dente and drain. Combine remaining ingredients, except garnishes, in a salad bowl; toss with pasta and dressing; and garnish with pine nuts and basil sprigs. Serve at room temperature. Keeps in the refrigerator for up to 3 days. Serves 6 to 8.

Chilled Cream of Chive Soup

Chef James Walsh, formerly of the Four Seasons Olympic Hotel and the Stouffer Madison Hotel in Seattle, presented this memorable soup at one of Silver Bay's Northwest Chefs' Picnics.

2 stalks celery

½ pound onions

2 pounds baking potatoes, peeled

4 leeks

2 tablespoons butter

1 bunch chives (about 1 ounce)

2 bunches green onions

1 clove garlic

2 sprigs thyme

1 bay leaf

8 cups chicken or vegetable stock

Fresh cream to taste (½ to 1 cup)

Unsweetened whipped cream, chopped nasturtiums, and chopped chives for garnish

Cut celery, onions, potatoes, and leeks into large dice. Melt butter in an 8-quart saucepan. Add the onion and cook for 3 to 5 minutes. Add leeks, green onions, celery, and garlic, and cook for 5 minutes. Add potatoes, chives, thyme, bay leaf, and stock. Bring to a boil, then lower the heat and simmer until all vegetables are soft. Remove the vegetables from the broth and purée in a blender or food processor with a little stock. Add more stock and fresh cream until the soup is of the desired consistency. Chill and serve with a dollop of whipped cream, chopped nasturtiums, and plenty of chopped chives.

CHICKEN CORIANDER POT PIE

The recipe for this delicious pie comes from my dear friend Jane Chapin, who received it from a friend in Germany more than 20 years ago. You need to plan ahead and allow a couple hours to prepare this dish, but it's worth it. Read through the recipe once to familiarize yourself with the sequence of steps. For a vegetarian version, simply omit the chicken.

2 tablespoons olive oil

2 to 4 tablespoons butter

1¾ pounds skinless, boneless chicken, cut into bite-size pieces

2 onions, chopped fairly small

2 large carrots, cut in rounds

3 heaping tablespoons flour

2¼ cups hard cider or apple juice

Salt and black pepper

4 teaspoons ground coriander seed

3 teaspoon mild French mustard

1 large cooking apple, peeled, cored, and cut in chunks

8 ounces sour cream

¼ pound mushrooms, sliced

Pastry for a 10-inch single-crust pie

1 egg yolk, lightly beaten

Preheat oven to 350°F. Heat the olive oil and butter in a cast iron Dutch oven or ovenproof pot on top of the stove. Stir the chicken, onions, and carrots into the melted fat. Stir in the flour. Heat the cider and stir it into the chicken mixture. Add salt, pepper, coriander, and mustard. Bring to a boil, stirring once or twice, and when the mixture thickens and is simmering, cover the Dutch oven and cook in the center of the 350°F oven for 45 minutes, stirring once during cooking. Take the Dutch oven out of the oven, add the chopped apple, and return to the oven for another 20 minutes, stirring once. Remove from oven and cool. Stir sour cream and mushrooms into the mixture, check for seasoning, and pour into a quiche dish 9 to 10 inches in diameter and 1½ inches deep.

Turn the oven up to 400°F. Roll out the pastry fairly thick, roughly the size and shape of the quiche dish. Dampen the edges of the dish. Roll the pastry back over the rolling pin and out again onto the dish. Trim the pastry so it is very slightly larger than the edge of the dish and then press down lightly. Roll out the scraps of pastry and use to decorate as you like. Glaze crust by brushing all over with egg yolk. Bake in the center of the preheated oven for 20 minutes, or until golden brown. Cool slightly, then spoon out portions. Serves 6 to 8.

CALENDULA TOMATO SALAD

Brilliant color contrasts and rich flavors make this dish spectacular, but it's super-easy.

4 large, juicy-ripe beefsteak tomatoes

Petals from 4 calendula flowers

12 to 20 borage flowers

1 tablespoon chopped basil

1 tablespoon chopped chives

2 tablespoons balsamic vinegar

3 tablespoons fruity olive oil

Slice the tomatoes and arrange them on an attractive platter. Sprinkle the calendula petals, borage flowers, basil, and chives over them. Drizzle with the vinegar and oil and serve. Serves 4.

DILLY BEANS

Barbara Stedman, the honey lady of Silverdale, Washington, gave me this recipe long ago. I've increased the amount of vinegar, in keeping with current Extension Office recommendations.

3 pounds small, tender green beans

4 cups water

4 cups white wine vinegar

4 teaspoons pickling salt

6 fresh dill heads

6 hot red peppers (or 6 teaspoons red pepper flakes)

6 teaspoons pickling spices

6 large cloves garlic

Wash 6 pint jars and heat them in a 200°F oven. Pour boiling water over 6 jar lids and allow to stand. Wash the beans, and trim them to fit into the jars with ½ to ¾ inch to spare.

Combine the water, vinegar, and salt, and bring to a boil. Remove jars from the oven and pack them quickly with beans, dill heads, peppers, spices, and garlic. Pour boiling brine over the contents of the jars to within ¼ inch of the top. Cover with hot lids, screw on rings, and process in a boiling water bath for 10 minutes. Makes 6 pints.

ELDERBLOSSOM FIZZ

This delightful semifermented punch has a bubbly kick similar to that of unpasteurized apple cider. Serve it iced.

5 quarts cold water

3½ cups sugar

12 elderflower heads in full bloom

1 lemon, thinly sliced, seeds removed

¼ cup white wine vinegar

Fresh or frozen elderflowers, for garnish

Bring the water to a boil. Pour into a large, sterilized glass jar and add the sugar, stirring until dissolved. Allow the mixture to cool.

Add the elderflower heads, lemon slices, and vinegar. Cover with cheesecloth or plastic wrap, fasten with a rubber band, and allow to stand at room temperature until fermentation begins, usually in 2 or 3 days. Strain and let it sit for about 6 more days, or until it is nice and bubbly. Serve chilled with ice, garnished with fresh or frozen elder flowers.

FENNEL CHAI

Fennel has been grown in India for centuries, where it flavors meat dishes and pilafs, and sometimes the popular spicy tea known as chai.

1 cup cinnamon chips

⅔ cup fennel seeds

2 tablespoons whole cardamom seeds (without husk)

2 tablespoons black peppercorns

1 teaspoon whole cloves

Combine all ingredients and store tightly covered in a tin or glass jar.

To make a cup of chai, bring ⅔ cup of water plus ⅓ cup of milk to a boil, and add 1 to 2 teaspoons of the spice mixture. Turn off the heat and steep for 10 minutes. Bring to a boil a second time and add 1 teabag or 1 teaspoon of black tea and 1 teaspoon of honey. Steep 5 minutes, then strain into your cup and enjoy.

VERMOUTH ROASTED GARLIC

Vermouth, a refreshing herb-flavored wine, gives this garlic presentation an added dimension of flavor. Substitute broth if you prefer. The olive oil adds richness, but is optional.

6 whole bulbs of garlic, unpeeled

1 cup vermouth or broth

1 tablespoon olive oil (optional)

Wash the garlic bulbs, then slice the tops off horizontally and set them in a ceramic or glass baking dish. Pour the vermouth over them and drizzle with the olive oil. Cover the dish and bake at 350°F for 45 minutes to an hour, until soft. Squeeze the bottom of each clove to pop out the garlic, and spread it on crostini, crackers, or rustic bread.

HORSERADISH MASHED POTATOES

4 cups water

2 pounds russet potatoes

1 to 1½ cups milk

4 tablespoons butter or nonfat sour cream

1 to 2 tablespoons freshly grated horseradish

Bring the water to a boil in a medium saucepan. Peel potatoes and cut them into 1-inch chunks. Add them to the boiling water, cover, and cook over medium heat until they are easily pierced with a knife, 10 to 15 minutes. Meanwhile, warm the milk in a separate saucepan over low heat. Drain the potatoes and mash them with a hand masher or an electric mixer. Mix in the butter or nonfat sour cream and the grated horseradish, then add the warm milk gradually and continue to beat until the potatoes are fluffy. Pile them in a pretty dish and serve them hot. Serves 6.

HERBES DE PROVENCE

You can easily grow every ingredient in this aromatic blend (see Herbes de Provence planter instructions, page 34). Small packets tied with lavender ribbon make wonderful gifts.

¼ cup dried lavender, organic preferred

1 cup dried sweet basil

1 cup dried summer savory

½ cup dried thyme

¼ cup dried fennel seeds

Combine all ingredients and store in glass containers with tight lids. Use about a teaspoon to season 6 portions of meat, cottage cheese, or vegetables. This mixture can also be infused in apple juice as the basis for a savory jelly.

LAVENDER COOLER

I served this refreshing beverage at Silver Bay tea parties. It combines the intriguing flavor of lavender with the zestiness of orange and bergamot. Black tea, if used, adds body.

4 cups boiling water

20 fresh lavender flower heads with stems

2 teaspoons Earl Grey tea (optional)

½ cup light honey

Juice of 2 oranges

Ice

Lavender sprigs and orange slices, for garnish

Pour the boiling water over the lavender blossoms and tea. Steep for 10 minutes. Strain and add honey and orange juice, and chill. Layer ice, lavender sprigs, and orange slices in a pitcher. Add Lavender Cooler and serve.

SPANAKOPITA WITH LOVAGE

Lovage gives a new twist to this Greek favorite, which my family often requests for festive occasions. If lovage is unavailable, substitute parsley.

2 pounds spinach, cleaned and chopped

1 to 3 large cloves garlic, minced

1 cup chopped onion

1 cup chopped leeks, if available

5 tablespoons olive oil

3 eggs, beaten

8 ounces feta, crumbled

¾ cup grated Parmesan cheese

3 tablespoons chopped fresh lovage

Freshly ground black pepper, to taste

2 tablespoons butter, melted

1 package (1 pound) filo dough, thawed

Pine nuts, for garnish

Steam spinach in minimal water until wilted. Sauté garlic, onion, and leek in 3 tablespoons of the olive oil. Combine eggs, cheeses, lovage, and pepper; stir in spinach and onion mixture. Combine remaining 2 tablespoons olive oil with the melted butter. One by one, brush 10 sheets of filo dough lightly with a little of this mixture and lay them in an oiled 11½- by 14-inch baking pan. (Two people working together can do this quickly.) Spread the filo layers with half the filling. Layer with 10 more sheets of oiled filo. Cover with the remaining filling. Finish with 10 more sheets of filo, brushing the top well with the oil. Fold and tuck to fit the pan. Score the top diagonally in diamond shapes with a sharp knife. Sprinkle with pine nuts if desired. Bake at 350°F for 50 minutes.

SWEET MARJORAM MAYONNAISE

Chef and food consultant Diana Isaiou created a superb meal of grilled ahi tuna and roasted onions on bruschetta, slathered with this great mayonnaise.

1 bunch marjoram, chopped

2 egg yolks

Juice of 1 lemon

½ teaspoon salt

½ teaspoon white pepper

1 cup olive oil

In a food processor combine the marjoram, egg yolks, lemon juice, salt, and pepper. While the machine is on, slowly add the oil until the mixture thickens.

SWEET MARJORAM SPAGHETTI SAUCE

My friend Karen Story says she finally got the seasonings in her spaghetti sauce just right. Sweet marjoram is her secret.

1 tablespoon olive oil
1 onion, chopped
1 to 3 cloves garlic, minced
2 cups chopped vegetables, such as carrots, celery, red
    bell peppers, and/or zucchini
6 cups peeled, chopped tomatoes (or two
    28-ounce cans)
1 teaspoon sea salt
2 bay leaves
1 teaspoon each fresh oregano and thyme
1 tablespoon each chopped fresh sweet marjoram,
    parsley, and basil
1 tablespoon each flour and water (if needed to thicken)
Additional sweet marjoram, for garnish

Heat oil in a large saucepan, add onion and garlic, and sauté until translucent. Add dense vegetables (carrots, celery, peppers) and sauté 5 minutes longer. Stir in tomatoes, salt, and bay leaves. Simmer uncovered for 1 hour. Add zucchini (if used), oregano, and thyme. Simmer 30 minutes longer. Add sweet marjoram, parsley, and basil. Mix flour and water if needed, and stir in. Simmer 10 minutes, stirring occasionally or until thickened. Serve over spaghetti or fettuccine, garnished with freshly chopped sweet marjoram. This sauce is also great in lasagne or ricotta-stuffed manicotti.

TABOULI

A Middle Eastern specialty, tabouli refreshes the palate with the flavors of mint, parsley, lemon, and tomatoes. It's an ideal make-ahead dish for summer celebrations, and actually tastes better the second day.

1 cup boiling water
1 cup bulgur
¾ cup chopped parsley
½ cup chopped mint
4 green onions, chopped, including tops
1 cup cooked navy beans
½ cup fresh lemon juice
½ cup fruity olive oil
Freshly ground black pepper to taste
2 large tomatoes, chopped
Whole mint leaves, for garnish

Pour the boiling water over the bulgur and allow to stand 20 minutes to 1 hour. (You can also use cold water, but let it stand 2 hours.) Fluff it with a fork, add all ingredients except tomatoes, and stir well to blend. Add tomatoes and stir lightly. Garnish with mint leaves.

STUFFED NASTURTIUM FLOWERS

4 ounces mild chèvre (goat cheese)
¼ cup chopped walnuts or pecans
¼ cup golden raisins
2 tablespoons chopped nasturtium blossoms
15 to 20 whole nasturtium blossoms

Combine the chèvre, nuts, raisins, and chopped blossoms. Use the mixture to stuff the whole flowers for a sensational appetizer.

Nettle Frittata

Nettles are more nutritious than spinach and can be substituted in almost any recipe with *florentine* in its title. They give this frittata an extra hearty flavor.

2 cups fresh nettle tops

½ cup water

1 tablespoon olive oil

½ cup chopped onion or leek

1 clove garlic, chopped

½ cup chopped red bell pepper

6 eggs, lightly beaten

½ cup crumbled feta cheese

Freshly ground pepper to taste

Bring the water to a boil in a small saucepan, drop in the nettles, cover the pan, and cook over medium heat for 10 to 15 minutes, until the nettles are tender and no longer prickly. Drain, reserving the liquid, and chop them coarsely when they are cool enough to handle.

Heat the olive oil in a medium-size skillet and saute the onion or leek, garlic, and red bell pepper over medium heat until tender, stirring occasionally. Beat the eggs with 2 tablespoons of the reserved cooking liquid from the nettles and pour them into the pan. With a spatula, draw the egg mixture from the sides of the pan toward the center as it begins to set and lift the bottom, allowing the uncooked egg mixture run underneath. When the egg mixture is nearly firm, arranged the drained nettles and crumbled feta on top and grind pepper over all as desired. Set the pan on the top rack of the oven under the broiler for a few minutes until the frittata is set and the cheese is slightly browned. Serve hot with toast or fried potatoes. Serves 4.

Tapenade

Lavish this dark, flavorful spread on crusty bread or crisp crackers for an easy yet elegant appetizer.

3 cloves garlic

2 cups pitted Greek olives

1 can pitted black olives

2 tablespoons olive oil (optional)

10 grinds of fresh black pepper (¹⁄₁₆ teaspoon)

1 tablespoon fresh Greek oregano, coarsely chopped

Juice of ½ lemon (2 tablespoons)

Start the processor and drop in the garlic cloves to mince them. Push them down from the sides and add the remaining ingredients. Process until smooth or slightly chunky.

Green Rice

This recipe appeared in my first published book, *The Leek Cookbook.*

3 cups cooked brown rice

1 medium leek, including green top, chopped

1 cup chopped fresh parsley

1 cup grated cheddar or Swiss cheese

1 clove garlic, minced

2 eggs, separated

1½ cups evaporated milk

¼ cup olive oil

Salt and pepper to taste

Juice and zest of 1 lemon

Paprika

Combine the rice, leek, parsley, cheese, and garlic, and place in an oiled 2-quart baking dish. Beat the egg yolks and combine with the evaporated milk, oil, salt, pepper, and lemon juice and zest. Stir into the rice mixture. Beat the egg whites until they form soft peaks, then fold gently into the casserole. Sprinkle with paprika and bake at 300°F for 45 minutes.

WHITE CHOCOLATE ROSE PETAL CHEESECAKE

Talented pastry chef Stephen Whippo (a.k.a. Mr. Chocolate) earned celebrity status at Silver Bay Herb Farm. Tea party guests were ecstatic when he presented this rich and extravagant dessert. He generously shared his recipe, which can be halved to make a smaller cheesecake (use the shorter baking time). It's best made the day before serving.

FILLING:

2 cups sugar

1 ounce fresh ginger, chopped or grated

Zest of 4 oranges

1 ounce red rose petals, dried

3 pounds cream cheese, softened

12 eggs

1½ pounds white chocolate

2 cups cream

1 tablespoon vanilla

¼ cup Grand Marnier

Place sugar, ginger, and orange zest in a food processor and process until the ginger and zest are finely ground. Grind rose petals separately in a coffee-type grinder and add to the sugar mixture.

Beat cream cheese until smooth and light. Add the sugar mixture and beat until fully mixed, scraping down the sides. Beat in eggs two at a time, scraping down the sides and bottom often, until all are added.

Chop the white chocolate into ³⁄₈-inch pieces. Heat the cream just to a boil, pour it over the chocolate, and stir until the chocolate is completely melted. Add the vanilla and Grand Marnier. Pour the chocolate mixture into the cream cheese mixture and blend until smooth. Strain the batter through a fine sieve for an even smoother texture, if desired.

CHOCOLATE CRUMB CRUST:

½ cup (1 stick) butter, melted

2 cups bittersweet chocolate chips

5 cups cake or cookie crumbs

½ cup brown sugar

5 egg yolks

Preheat oven to 350°F. Melt the butter with the chocolate chips. Grind crumbs and brown sugar in a food processor until fully blended. Add chocolate-butter mix, then the egg yolks. Press into the bottom of a 10-inch springform pan. Bake for 10 minutes. Remove from the oven and allow the pan to cool.

When the pan is no longer too hot to touch, fill it with the cheesecake batter. Bake at 250°F for 45 to 60 minutes. Remove the cheesecake from the oven when it is just set (jiggles slightly), before cracks appear. Cool slowly for at least 1 hour at room temperature.

WHITE CHOCOLATE GLAZE:

10 ounces white chocolate

1 tablespoon corn syrup

5 tablespoons heavy cream

3 tablespoons Grand Marnier

Fresh rose petals, for garnish

Chop the white chocolate and put it in the bowl of a food processor. Heat the corn syrup, cream, and liqueur to a simmer. (If you are using a gas stove, be careful that the mixture does not flame.) Turn on the processor, pour in the liquid, and continue processing until the mixture is smooth. Pour over the cooled cheesecake. Chill in refrigerator until glaze is firm, as long as 3 hours.

STRAWBERRY GARNISH:

1 pint (2 cups) strawberries
¼ cup Grand Marnier

Wash, hull, and slice strawberries lengthwise. Pour Grand Marnier over the strawberries, enough to flavor the berries without covering them completely. Macerate for 30 minutes.

Remove the sides from the springform pan. Arrange the strawberry slices in concentric circles over the cheesecake. Sprinkle a few fresh rose petals over the top if desired. Serves 12 to 16.

VICTORIAN ROSEMARY COOKIES

These excellent cookies are light and slightly chewy and contain no fat except in the egg yolks. Thank you, Frankie Graham of the Bremerton Garden Club, for this treasured recipe.

1 cup sifted flour
1 teaspoon baking powder
½ teaspoon salt
2 eggs
1 cup brown sugar, packed
1 tablespoon chopped fresh rosemary
1 cup golden raisins
1 cup chopped pecans
2 tablespoons chopped orange peel
Confectioner's sugar, for garnish

Sift flour with baking powder and salt. Beat eggs, gradually adding brown sugar, then dry ingredients. Fold in rosemary, raisins, nuts, and orange peel. Spread into a greased 9-inch pan and bake 35 to 40 minutes at 375°F until golden. Cool. Dust with confectioner's sugar and cut into squares. Makes 12 cookies. These travel well and can be stored for a long time.

SAGE CORNMEAL MUFFINS

Cornmeal gives these muffins a slightly crunchy texture, yogurt tenderizes them, and fresh sage makes them irresistibly aromatic.

⅔ cup cornmeal
⅓ cup soy flour
⅔ cup whole wheat flour
1 teaspoon baking soda
1 large egg
⅓ cup honey
1 cup plain yogurt
⅓ cup canola or safflower oil
2 tablespoons minced fresh sage

Preheat oven to 350°F. In a mixing bowl, combine cornmeal, soy flour, whole wheat flour, and baking soda. In a smaller bowl, beat the egg with fork and stir in the honey, yogurt, oil, and sage. Add egg mixture to dry ingredients and stir until just blended. Fill muffin tins ¾ full and bake 25 minutes or until lightly browned on top.

SAGE BUTTER

If you really like sage, spread this butter over Sage Cornmeal Muffins. Or try it on corn on the cob, boiled potatoes, or rustic bread.

1 small garlic clove

4 tablespoons fresh sage, coarsely chopped

¼ pound (1 stick) butter, softened

½ teaspoon celery seeds

¼ teaspoon black pepper

¼ teaspoon grated nutmeg

2 teaspoons fresh lemon juice

Start the blender and drop in the garlic clove. Add the sage and start and stop the blender a few times to chop sage and garlic, pushing down with a rubber spatula. Add the butter, celery seeds, black pepper, nutmeg, and lemon juice, and blend well, pushing down with the spatula as necessary. Transfer to a butter dish and let stand for at least 30 minutes for flavors to mingle. If you have extra, freeze it for winter use.

SALAD BURNET TEA SANDWICHES

Cucumber sandwiches, a standby at fancy tea parties, are more interesting when flavored with salad burnet. The spread is also fine for heartier sandwiches.

1 loaf white or light whole wheat bread

1 cucumber

1 8-ounce package cream cheese, softened

1 tablespoon milk

3 tablespoons salad burnet leaves, chopped

1 tablespoon parsley, chopped

1 teaspoon lemon zest

1 tablespoon lemon juice

5 grinds of black pepper

Salad burnet sprigs, viola flowers,
*   and nasturtiums, for garnish*

Trim the crusts from the bread and cut slices into triangles. Peel and grate the cucumber, then squeeze out excess liquid. Combine cream cheese with milk, herbs, lemon zest and juice, and pepper. Spread on sandwich triangles and serve open faced, garnished with salad burnet sprigs and edible flowers.

SAVORY LENTIL SOUP

Lentils cook quickly and are high in protein. With a green salad and some good bread, this soup makes a satisfying meal.

1 large onion

2 cloves garlic

3 large carrots

2 stalks celery

2 tablespoons olive oil

2 cups red lentils

4 cups tomato juice

4 cups water

2 tablespoons fresh summer savory (or 2 teaspoons dried)

2 bay leaves

3 sprigs fresh thyme

¼ teaspoon red pepper flakes

Salt and fresh pepper to taste

Sauté onion, garlic, carrots, and celery in olive oil until softened, about 10 minutes. Add lentils, tomato juice, water, savory, bay leaves, thyme, and pepper flakes. Bring to a boil, then simmer 20 minutes or until lentils and vegetables are tender, stirring occasionally. Season to taste with salt and pepper.

SWEET CICELY RHUBARB CAKE

Using sweet cicely, the "sugar saver," enabled me to halve the sugar in this version of Grandma Dahl's recipe. The hint of herbal flavor complements the tangy rhubarb nicely.

 2½ cups rhubarb, diced in ½-inch pieces

 1 cup sweet cicely leaves and tender stems, chopped

 1¼ cups sugar

 3 tablespoons butter, softened

 ½ cup canola or safflower oil

 2 eggs

 1½ cups buttermilk

 1 teaspoon vanilla

 3 cups flour

 1½ teaspoons baking soda

 2 teaspoons cinnamon

Mix rhubarb and sweet cicely with ¼ cup sugar and let stand. In a separate bowl, cream 1 cup sugar with butter and oil. Add eggs, buttermilk, and vanilla. Sift flour with baking soda and cinnamon. Alternate adding the buttermilk mixture and the flour mixture to the butter, eggs, and sugar. Fold in the rhubarb and pour the batter into a greased 9- by 13-inch baking pan. Bake 40 minutes at 350°F.

CAPRIAL'S HERB SCONES WITH SMOKED CHICKEN SALAD

Well-known television chef and cookbook author Caprial Pence and her creative chef-husband John presented many delicious meals at Silver Bay Herb Farm. You can sample more wonderful food at Caprial's Bistro, their restaurant located in Milwaukie, Oregon, near Portland. Thanks, Caprial and John.

HERB SCONES:

 1½ cups flour

 1 teaspoon dry mustard

 1 teaspoon chopped garlic

 1½ teaspoon baking powder

 1 tablespoon fresh tarragon, parsley, and/or savory

 ¼ cup (½ stick) unsalted butter, diced

 1 teaspoon salt

 ⅓ cup half-and-half

Place flour, mustard, garlic, baking powder, and herbs in a bowl and blend together. Add butter and mix with your fingers until a crumbly dough forms. Add salt and half-and-half, and mix just until the dough comes together. Let it rest 15 minutes. Roll out to ¼-inch thickness and cut into triangles. Bake at 350°F until golden brown, about 25 minutes. Cool.

SMOKED CHICKEN SALAD:

 2½ cups smoked chicken, shredded

 1 Walla Walla onion, diced

 1 red onion, diced

 2 Granny Smith apples, diced

 ½ cup chopped toasted hazelnuts

 1 teaspoon chopped fresh tarragon

 ⅓ cup Lemon Mayonnaise*

 Fresh arugula leaves

Combine chicken, onion, apples, nuts, and tarragon in a medium-size bowl. Add mayonnaise and mix well. Place on Herb Scones and top generously with fresh arugula leaves.

 *To make Lemon Mayonnaise, follow the directions for Marjoram Mayonnaise, page 57, but omit the marjoram.

SALAD CHAMP SALAD

In a contest for the coveted "Salad Champ" title, I represented the Pike Place Market and won first place with this creation. Salicornia or "sea beans" grow wild in the salt marsh at Silver Bay and are seasonal; the salad is great even without their salty crunch.

1 cup steamed broccoli tips

1 cup steamed baby carrots, sliced diagonally

1½ cups blanched sea beans

½ cup steamed snow peas

1 head of butter lettuce

1 cup spinach

1 cup arugula leaves

1 cup mizuna leaves

6 calendula flowers

6 nasturtium flowers

3 tablespoons walnuts, coarsely broken

LEMON THYME-WALNUT OIL VINAIGRETTE:

1 tablespoon minced shallot

1 teaspoon minced fresh lemon thyme

1 teaspoon minced summer savory

⅛ teaspoon pepper

Pinch of cayenne pepper

2 tablespoons walnut oil

⅓ cup light flavored olive oil

⅓ cup plus 1 tablespoon fresh lemon juice

1 teaspoon honey

Steam the broccoli tips, carrots, sea beans (if used), and snow peas separately until tender-crisp, then plunge into ice water to prevent overcooking. Drain. Wash, spin, and tear the lettuce, spinach, arugula, and mizuna. Combine the ingredients for the vinaigrette in a glass jar, put the lid on, and shake well. Place the vegetables and salad greens in a large salad bowl, add the dressing, and toss well. Garnish with flowers and walnuts. Serves 6.

JEANIE'S WATERCRESS SALAD

Jeanie Topness, my first full-time employee at Silver Bay, is a talented cook and designer who now has her own plant-based business in Mount Vernon, Washington. I get cravings for this unusual salad she used to make for lunch.

1 large bunch of fresh watercress

1 cup fresh bean sprouts

½ cup sliced water chestnuts, drained

DRESSING:

3 tablespoons plain yogurt

2 tablespoons mayonnaise

1 tablespoon dark sesame oil

2 teaspoons soy sauce

Wash and spin or drain the watercress. Break off the tips and tender leaves, discarding any yellowed leaves and thick stems. Blanch the bean sprouts by dipping them in boiling water for a few seconds, plunge them into ice water, and then drain. Combine watercress, bean sprouts, and water chestnuts. Stir the dressing ingredients together in a small bowl, pour over the salad, toss, and serve.

MAI BOWLE

4 to 6 sprigs of sweet woodruff

1 bottle of good Johannisberg Riesling or 1 can of frozen white grape juice

1 quart fresh strawberries

¼ cup honey

¼ cup brandy (optional)

Pick the sweet woodruff and warm in a low oven for 5 minutes to bring out the aroma. Add the sprigs to the wine or fruit juice and stand for 3 to 7 days. About 4 hours before serving, mash 3 cups of the strawberries with the honey, reserving the remaining berries. Stir in the wine or juice and brandy if used. Chill well and serve garnished with the remaining whole strawberries and a few fresh sweet woodruff leaves and flowers. Cheers!

HERBAL VINEGARS

Depending on the intended use and the properties of the ingredients, herbal vinegars may be culinary, medicinal, or cosmetic. Vinegar is a solvent, less efficient than alcohol, that extracts the flavor, color, and some of the beneficial constituents of the herb.

General directions: Harvest and wash a large bunch of fresh herbs, approximately 2 ounces, and place them in a wide-mouth quart canning jar. Add flavorings and spices as desired. Fill almost to the top with white or red wine vinegar, cider vinegar, or rice vinegar, making sure that all of the herbs are submerged. Cover with a double layer of plastic wrap and fasten with a rubber band. Allow to marinate for about a month. Strain and decant into decorative bottles, and seal with corks or other nonmetallic lids.

ROSEMARY VINEGAR

Cosmetic as well as culinary, this vinegar can also be used as a hair rinse to enhance dark hair and balance the pH. Combine 1 cup of rosemary vinegar with 4 cups water and use as a final hair rinse. Or, add a cup to your bathwater for its revivifying effects and to relax aching muscles. Delicious for marinating chicken and adding flavor to fried potatoes.

2 cups rosemary stems, about 4 inches long

3 to 4 cups apple cider vinegar

Follow general directions.

NASTURTIUM AND PEPPERCORN HERBAL VINEGAR

This unusual, delicately flavored vinegar was a favorite of many Silver Bay customers. Put in plenty of red and orange flowers to give it a distinct orange tint. It's delicious with green salads that include fresh nasturtiums, and also for marinated chicken breasts.

1 quart nasturtium flowers, leaves, and stems

1 tablespoon peppercorns, slightly bruised with a pestle

2 plump shallots

Pinch of cayenne

3 to 4 cups white wine vinegar

Rinse the nasturtium blossoms gently and inspect them to make sure they are free of aphids and other bugs. Pack them into a clean 1-quart glass canning jar with rinsed leaves and stems, peppercorns, shallots, and cayenne. Fill the jar with cold vinegar and cover it with plastic wrap fastened with a rubber band. Steep for 4 to 6 weeks. Strain and re-bottle in glass containers with nonmetallic lids. Nasturtium flowers don't hold their shape long in the vinegar, but put a few fresh ones in for decoration if you plan to use it within 2 months.

TARRAGON VINEGAR

Pack a glass canning jar with tarragon sprigs, top it up with white wine vinegar, cover with plastic wrap, and allow to steep for 4 to 6 weeks. For a fresh twist, add basil, garlic, and a few peppercorns or clove buds.

Healing with Herbs

The plants we know as herbs have within their leaves, flowers, bark, and roots the power to heal human ailments. Plants form the foundation of every system of medicine the world has ever known. Over countless centuries, people learned their powers through experience and passed down this knowledge, priest or priestess to acolyte, healer to apprentice, teacher to student, wise woman to daughters, in a living tradition preserved and amplified by successive generations. Eventually the knowledge was codified as systems of medicine and preserved on stone tablets, papyrus scrolls, and in herbals and official pharmacopoeias.

With the development of science and technology in the Western world, however, a new system of medicine emerged and gained dominance. This system was also plant based, but a greater understanding of organic chemistry made it possible to identify and isolate the active constituents in plants, to determine their effects on specific disease organisms and bodily systems, and to synthesize stronger and cheaper chemical substitutes for many, though not all, plant constituents. This system, variously called Western, allopathic, orthodox, modern, or techno medicine, has made marvelous strides in treating diseases, traumas, and even in unlocking the secrets of life itself. Synthetic medicines often produce fast and dramatic relief of physical symptoms, although the underlying causes may remain untreated. Over time, problems with this approach have become evident, such as undesirable side effects, the increasing immunity of disease organisms, and the high cost of medical care and prescription drugs.

Perhaps as a reaction to these problems or perhaps relating to a more fundamental shift of social values, there is currently a tremendous resurgence of popular interest in herbal medicine, not only in North America but around the planet. In a complex and quickly changing world, many things are beyond our control. One thing we can be responsible for is taking care of ourselves with better diet, regular exercise, and other aspects of a healthy lifestyle. Herbal medicine, with its simplicity and accessibility, can play a part in this and also offer a link to traditions of the past. We can take another look at the ancient wisdom and learn for ourselves the healing powers of plants. There is a certain comfort in the connection with herbalists of past centuries, and, on a more basic level, to the plants and the earth itself. What better way to go back to our roots and feel grounded?

It is an exciting time for anyone involved with herbal medicine. Hand in hand with this groundswell of interest in the subject has come a dramatic increase in scientific inquiry into herbs. Old wisdom is being enhanced by the new, as modern research techniques and technology are focused on these herbs, helping us to understand how and why they work. In many cases, scientific evidence validates traditional uses, giving herbal medicine new credibility. But do you have to "believe in it," as one of my customers suggested? In my opinion, there is always a mind-body link involved in healing, and, even more nebulous, a spiritual aspect. As surely as there is a placebo effect with Western medicine, there is well-documented scientific evidence of herbal efficacy.

Much of the research on herbs is being done abroad, with Germany in the forefront. There, traditional herbal remedies have never lost favor, and are prescribed by doctors and sold in pharmacies along with allopathic drugs. The government department commonly known as Commission E, which regulates and researches herbal medicine, has produced at least 380 reports, called Therapeutic Monographs on Medicinal Products for Human Use. These monographs describe identification, constituents, therapeutic value, usage, safety, dosage, and other information and are updated to keep current with new discoveries. They are widely regarded as the world's most accurate and complete information on medicinal herbs. Commission E also oversees standards and labeling of herbal medicines.

The World Health Organization (WHO) has also taken an important role in furthering the understanding and use of medicinal plants. The organization has concluded that the traditional plant-based medicines used by the overwhelming majority of the world's people are often as effective as Western pharmaceuticals, and far less expensive. Consequently, WHO is involved with correct identification, evaluation, preparation, quality control, cultivation and conservation of medicinal plants in order to promote world health.

In the United States, where herbal medicine has been outside the mainstream for about eighty years, renewed interest in the subject has precipitated considerable controversy and confusion. With regard to governmental regulations, herbs exist in a complex legal twilight zone somewhere between food and drugs. Standards are less clear and consistent than in Europe, and labeling laws disallow claims of therapeutic effects. With the regulatory situation in flux, the burgeoning herbal industry is attempting to determine and uphold its own standards, and to resolve labeling, quality control, and safety issues.

One thing is clear: herbal medicine is not going to go away. The Northwest is home to many fine naturopathic physicians, thanks to the presence of Bastyr University, the country's first naturopathic college, located near Seattle; the National College of Naturopathic Medicine in Portland; and the Dominion Herbal College in Burnaby, British Columbia. Doctors of naturopathic medicine complete a rigorous course of study and utilize a holistic approach that stresses preventive medicine, mental and physical well-being, and *Vis medicarix naturae*—the healing power of nature.

What's more, in response to patients' demands and better information about medicinal herbs, the conventional medical profession is changing. More and more M.D.s and other medical practitioners are learning about herbal therapies. The *Physicians' Desk Reference* has published its first edition for herbal medicine. Some health insurance policies now cover naturopathic doctors and medicines.

These may be signals of a new era of balance, in which herbal and allopathic medicines are not regarded as mutually exclusive, but complementary. Perhaps in time a rational and comprehensive regulatory system, based on the German model, will be adopted in the United States. In the meantime, a wealth of information and health-care choices are available to the public.

My philosophy could probably be described as a middle-of-the-road one. For my family's health care, I have turned to trusted doctors, both naturopathic and allopathic, and I keep some of my own herbal medicines on hand too. Our pediatrician vainly attempted to suppress a smile as my daughter listed the herbal remedies I tried before bringing her in to his office, but he treated us with unfailing respect, and, as with any good doctor, his listening skills and compassion were an important part of the healing process.

Herbs have been my passion for more than twenty years. I've gained familiarity with hundreds of plants and their properties through growing and gathering them, researching them, attending classes and workshops, and by listening to my customers. Yet for some years I hesitated to experiment with medicinal herbs.

That changed during a difficult time in my life, when I experienced many simultaneous personal losses, yet had to carry on running my business and raising my children. In gathering woodland plants for memorial-service decorations, my forearm came into contact with poison oak leaves. A severe rash developed within a week, and soon my arm was covered with itching, dripping sores. In my ignorance, I dabbed them with tissue, spreading them up my arm to my chest. Completely miserable, I consulted a dermatologist and took the medicine he prescribed, but with no relief. Then my friend Rhonda Hume, a naturopathic physician, came to the farm to teach a class on medicinal herbs. As she examined my raw,

oozing arm, she questioned me about my life, then commented, "Your arm is weeping. Could it be expressing all the sorrow you are keeping inside?" Rhonda gathered comfrey, blackberry root, and other herbs and gave her students a real-life demonstration of an herbal poultice, applying the mashed herbs to my arm, then wrapping it with muslin and a plastic bag. When I removed the poultice the following morning, the sores were closing up. Healing had begun at last.

This anecdotal but powerful evidence convinced me that herbal medicine was worth exploring. As I learned more about herbs' healing power and safety I applied that knowledge, treating myself and my kids for minor colds, stomach upsets, cuts, burns, and bumps with over-the-counter-type herbs such as rose hips, peppermint, chamomile, and calendula. Gradually, herbal medicines were woven into the fabric of life on the farm.

In the course of business, people have asked me what herbs I would recommend for relief of all sorts of conditions. Whether it was insomnia, acne, or allergies; impotence, hot flashes, or night sweats; abortion, cancer, or cirrhosis of the liver; they hoped that as the owner of an herb farm, I could come up with an herbal cure for most anything.

Disclaimer Statement and Cautions

I am not an expert on medicinal herbs nor a medical practitioner of any description. It is beyond the scope of this book and my expertise to offer anything more than general information and simple formulas. I make no claims as a healer or herbal practitioner, and cannot prescribe medications or address the complexities of dosage. For additional information, please refer to the excellent books listed in the Resources section of this book. And of course, if you have severe or lingering symptoms, consult a qualified M.D. or N.D. for proper diagnosis and treatment.

How Herbs Work on the Body

Studies on humans clearly show that herbs do work. Although they may take longer to do so, their effects are often as successful as popular drugs, without undesirable side effects. For example, German studies have shown valerian to be as effective in promoting sleep as sleeping pills, and St. John's wort to equal popular antidepressants for lifting the spirits.

Much of the current research involves isolating specific constituents and administering standardized dosages in order to affect particular disease organisms or body systems. This approach, which follows the allopathic paradigm, wins greater acceptance of herbs in the science-oriented medical community. However, many herbal practitioners disagree with this reductionist philosophy.

Plants are complex, and many have numerous constituents, some of which may be undiscovered. Herbs do not necessarily work like the synthesized allopathic medicines to which we have become accustomed. They can have a regulating or balancing effect, working in ways that seem contradictory or unrelated. Herbs can also have several actions, both internal and external, affecting different parts of the body in various ways. Their active and inert principles may interact in synergistic ways to promote healing and prevent side effects. As ongoing research brings new factors to light, understanding of the way herbs work keeps changing. Summations of the latest findings of research conclude again and again that it "is not yet fully understood." The way of herbs will probably always retain some element of mystery, and personally, I would mourn its loss.

Herbal medicine has its own lexicon, with lots of colorful words such as fomentation, elixir, carminative, and febrifuge. These words can sum up a process, explain actions on the body, and facilitate clear communication. They are explained as they appear in the text.

Herb Medicine Making

Making your own herbal remedies can be an empowering part of taking care of yourself. Once you master a few basic, time-honored techniques, you can stock your medicine chest with handy natural remedies for relatively little expense. What's more, you will know exactly what has gone into making them, and you can add your loving care to each step in the process of growing, gathering, handling, preserving, and processing them into high-quality preparations.

The herbal medicine preparations described in this book are simple, safe, and effective remedies for common minor ailments. But will they really work? The best way to become convinced is to try them out and see for yourself, as I did with the poison oak rash that wouldn't go away. You will be carrying on the experiential tradition of herbalism that has evolved since humans first discovered plants.

Making herbal medicines can be very satisfying,

but there is a lot to learn in order to do it well. It is as much an art as a science, and can be an absorbing lifetime study. It demands knowledge of the plants and processes involved, and attention to many details. The plants and medicines described in this book are just a beginning.

TEAS

Herbal teas are simple yet effective herbal medicines. Soft or distilled water, the "universal solvent," is used to extract the medicinal properties from fresh or dried herbs. Wash and chop or bruise fresh herbs; break dried herbs into small pieces. Select a container with a tight-fitting cover—a teapot is all right, but allows volatile constituents to escape, so I prefer a cup with a lid or a fruit jar that can be tightly closed. Water is not a preservative, so make small amounts of herbal tea and use them within twenty-four hours. Choose the strength of tea and proceed according to the directions below. For more information, see individual herb descriptions.

Infusions. To make an infusion, pour boiling water over fresh or dried herbs, cover, and allow to steep. The length of time for steeping varies with the herb used. Delicate herbs such as chamomile and lemon balm need only 10 minutes or so; denser leaves may steep 30 minutes or longer. Some herbalists recommend steeping infusions for several hours for a more effective brew. Strain the infusion after steeping.

Macerations or Cold Infusions. This method is recommended for volatile herbs such as valerian, and for mucilaginous herbs. Pour warm or cold water as specified over the fresh or dried herb. Allow to stand for several hours or overnight. Strain before use.

Decoctions. Hard plant materials such as roots and barks are *decocted*, or simmered in water. Place the herbs and water in an enamel, stainless steel, or glass pan. Bring the water slowly to a simmer, and continue to simmer, uncovered, for about 20 minutes. Allow to cool, then strain.

Syrups, Elixirs, and Robs. These preparations are based on the idea that a little bit of sugar, actually a lot of sugar, makes the medicine go down. Syrups are herbal infusions or decoctions, concentrated by simmering, with added sugar or honey. The correct proportions, at least 1 cup sugar or ½ cup honey per 2 cups of tea, must be used in order to prevent fermentation. Stored in the refrigerator, syrups will last about two months. In elixirs, alcohol is added; in robs, the sweetened syrup is cooked down until thickened.

REGULAR TEA

1 teaspoon of dried herb or 1 tablespoon fresh herb per cup of water.

STRONG TEA

1 tablespoon of dried herb or 3 tablespoons fresh herb per cup of water.

MEDICINAL-STRENGTH TEA

1 ounce of dried herb per pint (2 cups) of water.
Standard dose: 1 cup of infusion 3 times a day.

COMPRESSES

Active principles of herbs can be absorbed through the body's largest organ, the skin. To prepare a compress, make a strong tea by infusion or decoction. Dip a cotton cloth in the tea, wring it out enough to avoid dripping, and place it on the affected part. Compresses may be hot, warm, or cold. *Fomentations* are alternating warm and cold compresses.

POULTICES

A poultice is similar to a compress, but with a poultice the herb itself is applied to the skin. Chop the herb coarsely and process in a blender with a bit of boiling water. If you like, rub a little oil on the skin so it's easier to remove the herb later. Place the mashed herb directly on the skin or sandwich it between two pieces of gauze. Cover the gauze with plastic wrap or wax paper, then put a hot water bottle over it to provide moist heat. Leave it on for 20 minutes to 1 hour.

BATHS

There is a branch of alternative medicine called hydrotherapy, which utilizes water itself, in varying temperatures and applications, as a therapeutic agent. Variations on the theme include sitz baths, footbaths, hand baths, and eye baths. Healing herbs in the bath make a combination that is very therapeutic. Begin by making a medicinal-strength tea by infusion or decoction. Strain and add it to the bath.

You can also put the herbs in a muslin bag and run hot water over them, then use the bag as a scrub. Or, instead of herbal tea, add 10 to 20 drops of essential oils to the bath and have a good soak.

TINCTURES

Generally speaking, tinctures are alcohol- and water-based extracts of herbs, although glycerin or vinegar is sometimes used instead of alcohol. They are convenient and remain potent for years. One medicine-dropperful of an herbal tincture contains only a small amount of alcohol, but if this is a concern, add the tincture to a cup of boiling water and the alcohol will quickly evaporate.

Many herbalists consider fresh herbs make the best tinctures, and find that the folk method is perfectly adequate. Fill a sterilized canning jar with the chopped herb, then pour in enough 100 proof (50 percent water) vodka to cover. Screw on the lid and allow the mixture to macerate (cold steep) for about 2 weeks, shaking occasionally. Strain the mixture through a fine cloth (men's cotton handkerchiefs work well), squeezing all the liquid out of the *marc*, which is what the herb is called at this point. Bottle in glass and label immediately with the name of the herb, source, parts used, amounts of herb and solvents, and the date.

Tincture making can get complicated because there are many variables. Different constituents of an herb are extracted by varying ratios of herb to solvent. The trick is to find the correct proportion of herb to solvent and the lowest alcohol-to-water ratio for the most efficient extraction. The labels of some commercially available tinctures give a ratio; for example, 1:2 means 1 part of solvent per 2 parts of herb. Dosage when using tinctures varies widely; for guidelines, consult the Resources listed on page 215.

INFUSED OILS

Olive and other vegetable oils are also used to extract the medicinal constituents of herbs and can be applied externally to bruises, strains, and various skin ailments. Infused oils are also the base for herbal salves. Store them in glass, preferably amber glass, to protect them from light.

Here is an easy method of infusing fresh herbs in oil. Gather the clean, fresh herb of choice and allow it to wilt for a couple of days to reduce its moisture content. Without washing it, chop the fresh herb in a food processor or mash it with a mortar and pestle, then warm it gently with enough oil to cover in a double boiler over barely simmering water for 3 hours. Stay close by and stir the herb-oil mixture occasionally, making sure that it does not boil. Squeeze the mixture through a jelly bag or fine-mesh cotton cloth into a glass jar. Allow it to stand undisturbed for a week while water and impurities settle to the bottom. Carefully decant the oil into oven-sterilized amber glass bottles and store them in the refrigerator.

SALVES AND BALMS

To make an herbal salve, or balm, warm an herbal oil with beeswax, cocoa butter, or other thickening agents, then pour it into containers and cool to harden. Many salves combine various herbal-infused oils with small amounts of essential oils added for therapeutic properties and fragrance, and sometimes a preservative such as vitamin E or benzoin powder is included, though salves and balms keep for a long time because they contain no moisture or air pockets. Small tins of salve are easy to carry in your purse or pocket.

Herbal Remedies

EASY-DOES-IT-TEA

Mellow out with a cup of this pleasant-tasting and gently relaxing tea before bedtime.

½ cup dried chamomile
½ cup dried lemon balm
¼ cup dried hibiscus flowers
¼ cup dried peppermint

Combine the herbs and store them in an amber glass jar or a tin with a tight-fitting lid. Steep 1 heaping teaspoon in 1 cup of boiling water for 5 minutes, strain, and enjoy.

COLDS AND FLU TEA

This is a time-honored remedy for colds, flu, sinusitis, and other respiratory tract infections. Dried herbs are recommended because they are available in the winter, when coughs and sniffles are most common, and are easy to measure in the correct proportions.

½ cup dried peppermint leaves
½ cup dried yarrow flowers
½ cup dried elderflowers

Combine the herbs and store them in an amber glass jar or a tin with a tight-fitting lid. At the first signs of illness, steep 1 tablespoon of the tea mixture in 1 cup of boiling water. Drink up to 5 cups a day, very hot. Drink the tea often until symptoms abate. The action of the tea is enhanced by a hot footbath, made with a strong decoction of thyme or the three herbs used in the tea.

ELDERBERRY HONEY

Elderberry honey can be taken as a cold preventative, as a medicine if you do catch a cold, and for coughs that linger at the tail end of a cold. The berries' decongestant and diaphoretic actions are enhanced by flavonoids that seem to prevent viruses from entering cells.

  3 cups fresh elderberries, cleaned

  1¾ to 2 cups honey

Warm the honey in a saucepan over very low heat, making sure that it does not boil. Then, rinse and drain the elderberries, remove stems, and pick off any shrunken or moldy berries. Measure the cleaned berries into a clean wide-mouth quart canning jar. Pour the warmed honey over the berries, filling the jar almost to the top. Stir gently to get rid of any air bubbles, then top up as necessary. Cover the jar with a canning lid and screw the ring on firmly. Place the jar in a bowl to catch any drips. Put the jar where you will see it and remember to shake it daily for 3 weeks. As the berries release their juice, the honey thins and turns ruby colored. At this point, strain out the berries and bottle the syrup. Store in the refrigerator. Take 1 to 2 tablespoons a day, straight or dissolved in a glass of hot water, as a good-tasting tonic during the winter months. If you catch a cold, increase the dose to 1 tablespoon four times a day.

ECHINACEA TINCTURE A LA JEAN

Dig the roots of 3- to 4-year-old echinacea roots in the fall, after the tops have died down. Carefully remove the offsets around the crown and replant them to start new plants. Wash the tangle of roots as best you can and chop them into ¼- to ½-inch pieces. Weigh them on a kitchen scale and put them in a clean glass canning jar. For each ounce of echinacea root, measure 2 ounces of 100 proof vodka (a weight-to-volume ratio of 1:2). Be sure that the vodka comes to within ¼ inch of the top of the jar. The jar should hold about 10 ounces of root and 20 ounces of vodka. Cap it tightly, store it in a dark cupboard, and shake the tincture daily for 3 to 4 weeks. Strain and bottle in amber glass—or, if you like, leave the roots to steep indefinitely and use the tincture directly from the canning jar.

CALENDULA–INFUSED OIL

Calendula is wonderfully healing and rejuvenating to the skin. Massage this oil directly into the skin, or use it as a base for salves and creams.

Pack freshly picked, unwashed calendula flowers into a clean, dry glass canning jar. For the highest quality, use only the petals and discard the calyx. Cover them completely with light olive or canola oil. Use a stainless steel knife to work any air bubbles out of the jar. Cover the jar loosely and set it on a plate in case any oil spills over. Steep the flowers in the oil for 3 weeks, stirring occasionally. For a primo, extra-strength oil, remove the flowers and repeat the process with the same oil, using fresh flowers. Then, strain the oil through a piece of old white sheet or other fine cloth. Allow the oil to settle, then pour into glass bottles, making sure that any drops of moisture are left behind.

JEAN'S ROSE PETAL ELIXIR

Jean Galbreath, my "right-hand woman" at Silver Bay for several years, recommends this beautiful liqueur for sipping and for sharing.

> 2 cups clean, organically grown red rose petals,
>   loosely packed
> 1/4 to 1/2 cup honey
> Light rum or brandy

Pack the rose petals into a clean pint glass jar. Add the honey, then top up with rum or brandy. Let it sit for 2 weeks, shaking daily, then strain. The finished liqueur will be a beautiful deep red color. As Jean says, "It's guaranteed to lighten the spirits."

ST. JOHN'S WORT–INFUSED OIL

Harvest St. John's wort tops as they first come into flower. For a truly primo oil with high concentrations of hypericin and related compounds, pick only the unopened yellow flower buds.

> 1/2 cup H. perforatum *buds*
> 1 cup olive or grapeseed oil
> 1/4 teaspoon lavender essential oil (optional)

Place the flower buds in a glass jar, cover them with the oil, and allow them to steep for at least 1 month. Exposing the jar to full sunlight will hasten the infusion of constituents into the oil. Shake the jar occasionally, making sure that the oil covers the buds. The oil will gradually turn deep red. Strain it through a piece of muslin or old sheet, squeezing to extract as much oil as possible. Add 1/4 teaspoon of lavender essential oil per 1 cup of strained infused oil if desired and use within a year or two.

BUMP AND BRUISE BALM

Reach for this golden balm when you hit your thumb with a hammer, walk into the corner of a table, or when similar mishaps occur. It's soothing when rubbed on strained or aching muscles.

> 1/3 cup infused St. John's wort oil
> 1/3 cup infused calendula oil
> 1 ounce pure beeswax, chopped
> 10 drops lavender essential oil

Warm the St. John's wort and calendula oils in a small glass or stainless steel pan placed inside a larger pan of simmering water (it's best to have a pan just for this purpose). If there is sediment or bubbles of moisture on the bottom, warm the oils for 30 minutes or so. The moisture bubbles will rise to the surface and break. Add the chopped beeswax and let it melt. To test the consistency of your salve, spoon a tablespoon of the mixture onto a piece of foil and let it cool. For a firmer salve add a little more beeswax; to make it softer, add more oil. When the consistency is just right, remove the pan from the heat and stir in the lavender essential oil. Strain through a muslin cloth if desired. Pour into small containers such as miniature jelly jars and allow the balm to set. Label it with ingredients and date.

To clean the pan, wipe it with a paper towel while the fats are warm, then rinse it with hot water and finish the job using dishwashing soap.

Herbal Crafts and Home Uses

"For use and for delight" is the motto of the American Herb Society. That word "delight" figures prominently in old herbals, too, suggesting that the authors in their wisdom described the value of herbs in medicine, cooking, and other practical uses, but also honored herbs' timeless appeal to the senses.

Since earliest times, peoples around the world have relied on herbs in weaving and dyeing fabrics, caring for animals, and countless other practical applications. They have also made use of their delightful qualities. The ancient Egyptians were famous for their herbal perfumes, anointing oils, and cosmetics. In olde England, herbs were strewn on the floors of castles and cottages to mask unpleasant odors, and bouquets of herbs were carried for a similar purpose. Later, the Victorians popularized herbal crafts including potpourri making, and transformed the herb bouquets into "tussie mussies," or herbal nosegays.

We can learn from the past and utilize both the practical and sensual properties of herbs. Herbs can decorate your home, scent your rooms and clothing, and pamper your body. Enjoy!

Home Decor

One of the simplest ways to enjoy herbs is to literally bring them into your home. Potted herbs, casually placed in a sunny window or trained formally as topiaries, contribute their living presence to your home environment. You can always reach out and crush a leaf and savor its aroma or tuck it inside a letter to a friend.

Herbs also give pleasure in fresh bouquets. Herbal bouquets may be as simple as a child's bunch of dandelions or a single old-fashioned rose in a vase. More elaborate herbal nosegays, are truly a delight to the nose. These were a specialty at Silver Bay Herb Farm, often made up of 20 or more scented herbs from the cutting garden. In more conventional bouquets, flowering herbs offer vivid or subtle color, fresh scents, and interesting foliage. Roses and lavender quickly come to mind, but also try monarda, anise hyssop, echinacea, basil, oregano, and almost any flowering herb. Rose geraniums, lemon verbena, rosemary, mint, sage, and many other herbs offer fragrance. Bay leaf, fennel, sweet cicely, lovage, parsley, and angelica are only a few of the herbs with varying leaf textures and shapes.

Herbs can help make special occasions memorable. Hop vines festooning arbors and gazebos are perfect for outdoor galas. Children, especially young girls, have fun making herbal hair garlands or other favors to take home from birthday parties. In wedding bouquets and flowers, herbs can deliver a romantic message via the language of flowers.

Fresh floral materials last only a few days, but arrangements of dried herbs can provide years of enjoyment. Garlic braids and herb bunches in the kitchen are close at hand for the cook and create a cozy, country feeling. Dried herb leaves, flowers, and seed pods can be transformed into gorgeous wreaths, topiaries, and garlands. For inspiration, attend demonstrations at herb farms, garden centers, the Northwest Flower and Garden Show, and similar expositions. Books and magazines are also full of ideas.

Herbal Fragrance Crafting

In *The Art of Simpling* (1657), William Coles declared that herbs do "comfort the wearied Braine with fragrant smells, which yeild a certaine kind of nourishment..." I've always found that working with herbal fragrances gives me a sense of well-being. There is no logical explanation, but perhaps because the sense of smell is connected in the brain with memory and emotion, it touches me on a deep level where logic has no place.

Traditional potpourri is a combination of flower petals, herbs, spices, and fixatives. To make moist potpourri, salt is added to partially dried botanicals; the colors turn drab brown, but the scent lingers for years. For dry potpourri, flower petals and herbs are completely dried before blending, so their colors are preserved. Sachet mixtures are basically the same ingredients, finely ground. Potpourri for simmering is made of harder materials such as rosemary and bay leaves, fennel seeds, and whole spices, which keep their shape when simmered. (See recipe below.) Potpourri and sachet mixtures may be sewn or tied into all sorts of pretty "sweet bagges," and "dream pillows" for scenting linens, promoting sleep, and other purposes, depending on the ingredients.

Beauty and the Bath

For centuries, herbs have been used to heal and rejuvenate the skin. One of the most pleasant ways to avail yourself of these benefits is by taking herbal baths. This can be a great way to unwind, whether as an evening ritual, romantic interlude, occasional treat after a stressful day, or playtime for your kids. In Europe, the therapeutic effects of herbal baths are widely accepted. Herbal bath salts, infusions, body rubs, soaps, washing waters, and spritzers can all be made at home with herbs from the garden. Calendula, elderflower, comfrey, chamomile, rose petals, and St.

John's wort are among the herbs mentioned in this book that are good for the skin.

Making herbal cosmetics is a fascinating and enjoyable hobby. Your own high-quality dried herbs, tinctures, and oils can go into making all-natural skin creams, lip balms, soaps, and masks that rival any commercially available products. Sometimes the line between medicinal and cosmetic skin products is blurred, since both can have therapeutic effects. Except for general hints, herbal cosmetics are beyond the scope of this book, but consult the references listed in Resources for more details.

The recipes and suggestions for the "herbal lifestyle" in this book are starting points, meant to be adjusted until they are expressions of your creative self, just right for you. I hope that by putting herbs to uses both practical and pleasant, you will experience the delights of herbs and derive that "certaine kind of nourishment" that has brought joy and satisfaction to generations of herb lovers.

Herbal Craft Recipes

KITCHEN POTPOURRI

Bay leaves give this aromatic blend a slightly exotic quality. The recipe makes one batch; for a gift-size quantity, use dried bay leaves and quadruple the recipe.

2 cups water

3 large bay leaves, preferably fresh

1 teaspoon whole allspice berries

1 teaspoon cloves

1 3-inch cinnamon stick, broken

Combine the ingredients. To use, simmer in 2 cups of water on very low heat for a few days, adding water to the pot as needed.

SCENTS OF SUMMER POTPOURRI

Inspired by the Victorians' rose jars, this potpourri captures the essence of summer. Keep it in a closed container and open it for special occasions, or fill bags and pillows so its aroma becomes part of the scent you call home.

> 6 cups dried petals from fragrant "old roses"
> 1 cup dried lavender flowers
> 1 cup dried rose geranium leaves
> ⅓ cup orris root chunks
> 6 drops rose geranium essential oil
> 6 drops lavender essential oil
> 1 cup dried bay leaves, thyme, sweet marjoram, mint, or other herbs
> 2 tablespoons coriander seeds
> 1 3-inch cinnamon stick

Collect and dry rose petals, lavender flowers, and rose geranium leaves during the summer. Store them in jars or tins until you are ready to assemble your potpourri. In a small jar with a tight lid, combine the orris root chunks with the essential oils. Cover and let stand overnight or for up to a week. Combine the dried rose petals, lavender flowers, and rose geranium leaves in a glass gallon jar with a tight-fitting lid. With a hammer, pound the bay leaves, thyme, coriander seeds, and cinnamon stick on a hard surface between layers of old denim. Add the crushed spices and the scented orris root mixture to the petals in the jar. Put the lid on tight and age for about 6 weeks, until all the aromas marry into one splendid perfume. Place the jar in the freezer for a few days to kill off any insect eggs, then package the potpourri in decorative tins, sachet bags, or other containers.

CARMELITE WATER

The original formula has been distilled by Carmelite nuns since 1611. It is said to relieve headaches, and also makes a refreshing after-bath spritzer. I just love the scent of this updated version.

> 1 cup lemon balm leaves
> 1 cup angelica leaves
> Peel of 1 lemon
> 1 teaspoon crushed coriander seed
> 2 whole nutmegs, crushed
> 2 teaspoons crushed cinnamon
> 2 cups witch hazel extract (Dickinson's is best)
> 1 cup orange flower water

Chop the lemon balm and angelica leaves and bruise with the lemon peel. Crush the spices with a mortar and pestle or with a hammer between layers of canvas or denim. Combine the herbs and spices with the witch hazel extract and keep in a sealed jar for 2 days. Then stir in the orange flower water and keep in a sealed jar, shaking daily, for 2 to 3 weeks before use. Strain into a decorative pump-style bottle.

ROSE GERANIUM–LEMON VERBENA SPRITZER

Simple to make and wonderfully fragrant, this spritzer is gently astringent, normalizing and renewing to the skin. The glycerine is naturally moisturizing. Put it in a pump spray bottle, and use it as a refreshing after-shower spritzer.

¾ cup fresh rose geranium leaves

¾ cup fresh lemon verbena leaves

1 cup witch hazel extract (Dickinson's is best)

1 cup distilled water

1 tablespoon vegetable glycerine (optional)

Wash the rose geranium and lemon verbena leaves and chop them together. Combine the witch hazel extract and distilled water in a clean stainless steel or glass pan and put it on the stove to heat. Add the chopped herbs and bring the mixture almost to a boil. Reduce the heat and simmer for 3 minutes. Remove from heat and cool. Strain the infusion through a coffee filter or finely woven cloth. Put it in a pump spray bottle and use within 2 months.

LAVENDER-OATMEAL FACIAL SCRUB OR MASK

Ordinary, kitchen-variety rolled oats are the basis for this excellent cleansing scrub that exfoliates and nourishes gently, leaving your skin feeling as fresh and soft as a baby's. Lavender adds antiseptic and antibacterial qualities as well as its fine scent. Distilled lavender or rose water is also beneficial to the skin; if neither is available, plain water may be substituted.

¾ cup rolled oats

1 tablespoon lavender flowers

Lavender or rose water

1 tablespoon white or green French clay,

  for facial mask

Combine oatmeal and lavender in a blender or coffee-type grinder. Grind to a fine powder and store in a glass jar with a tight-fitting lid. For cleansing, tie your hair back and place 1 tablespoon of the powder in

your palm. Moisten with a little lavender or rose water, or plain water. Rub the paste on your face, using a circular motion. Rinse with warm water and pat dry.

To make a facial mask that removes impurities and tightens pores, add the clay when blending the oats and lavender. White clay is very finely powdered and gentle on sensitive skin; for oily skin, green clay may be substituted. Moisten the mixture as directed above; allow the mask to remain on your skin for 5 to 30 minutes before rinsing. Mist with Carmelite Water or Rose Geranium–Lemon Verbena Spritzer.

ROSEMARY AND PEPPERMINT-OATMEAL FACIAL SCRUB OR MASK

Follow directions for Lavender-Oatmeal Facial Scrub or Mask, replacing the lavender flowers with 1 ½ teaspoons each dried rosemary and peppermint leaves. This makes a stimulating scrub or mask that helps keep your skin "youngly."

CALENDULA-ORANGE FLOWER FACIAL SCRUB OR MASK

Follow directions for Lavender-Oatmeal Facial Scrub or Mask, replacing the lavender flowers with 1 tablespoon dried calendula petals. Use orange flower water instead of lavender or rose water for a scrub or mask that is both healing to the skin and delightfully aromatic.

LAVENDER EYE PILLOW

Everyone can use one of these restful pillows, perfect for afternoon naps or for going to sleep with the light on at night. They exclude light and give off the relaxing scent of lavender.

Choose a tightly woven fabric, perhaps cotton with a sleep-associated pattern such as stars, planets, or clouds, or a satin or silk that feels cool on the skin. One quarter yard is enough for at least four pillows. Keep your pillow simple, or embellish it with ribbons, trim, tassels, piping, or buttons (avoid metal).

Cut two rectangles 4 inches wide by 9 inches long. Pin the right sides together and sew around all four sides, ½ inch from the edges, leaving a 2 ½-inch opening on one end (backstitch at both ends of stitching). Clip the corners, turn the fabric right side out, and iron carefully.

Combine ½ cup of dried, cleaned lavender flowers with 1½ cups of flax seeds or rice. Using a funnel over a bowl, loosely fill the pillow with the mixture. Pin the opening shut and overcast by hand with neat, closely spaced stitches.

Lie back, put your feet up, place the pillow over your eyes ... and relax. Alternatively, warm the pillow in the microwave for a few minutes, then use it to relax tight muscles in your shoulders or neck.

MAKING A GARLIC BRAID

Braiding garlic is easy once you get the hang of it. If you don't grow your own garlic, make arrangements with a farmer to sell you some with the tops still attached. You can soften dried tops by misting them or dipping them in water briefly, but be sure to dry the finished braids quickly to avoid mold. Remove any dirt clinging to the skins.

Select three large heads of partially dried soft-neck garlic. Lay them on a flat surface, stems toward you, so the heads form a triangle with the largest one at the top. Tie the necks together with raffia or fasten them with a rubber band. Hold the stems together and lay a fourth head in the center of the triangle. Grasp the stems tightly and bring one of the outside stems across the first and fourth stems to hold them in place. Repeat this with the other outside stem, then proceed French-braid style, adding new heads until the braid reaches the desired length. As you work, keep the braid in contact with the flat surface. To finish, braid the stems for a few inches, then tie them off with raffia, bend them back to form a loop, and tie again. After a few tries, you'll be able to make tightly woven braids with nicely spaced heads that lay flat when hung. Whether plain or dressed up with ribbons or dried flowers, the braids make great kitchen decorations and gifts.

GARLIC-HOT PEPPER SPRAY

Homemade garlic and hot pepper bug sprays have been popular for years, and—according to studies at the University of California Davis and the Henry Doubleday Research Institute in England—they work. Garlic was found to be effective against caterpillars, aphids, pea weevils, Japanese beetles, and other pests, as well as certain plant diseases, including downy mildew, bean rust, and bacterial blight on beans. Might be worth a try on your bee balm and mint. If you have some dried nettles or nettle tea on hand, add it to the mix for a super-duper spray.

½ cup or 2 medium bulbs (3 ounces) garlic, chopped

4 long cayenne peppers or other hot peppers,
   fresh or dried

2 teaspoons mineral oil

2 cups hot water

3 teaspoons non-detergent soap flakes, or liquid non-
detergent soap (such as Dr. Bronner's)

Chop the garlic coarsely (no need to peel it) and combine it with the other ingredients in the blender. Put a towel over the top to avoid splashes, turn the blender on low, then blend on high speed until pureed. For the most potent spray, allow the mixture to steep overnight. Then strain through a cheesecloth (wear gloves) and store in a glass jar. When ready to use, dilute ¼ cup of the mixture in 5 cups water and spray on plants.

fifty

herbs

V: Fifty Herbs

So many herbs,
so little space. From among
the hundreds of herbs that can
be grown in the Pacific
Northwest, I've chosen
just fifty for inclusion
in this book.

My goal was to present a balanced and complementary selection that highlights the versatility of herbs. Whether they are annuals or perennials, ground covers, shrubs, or trees, these herbs are relatively easy to grow in a variety of environments. Some are native plants, perfectly adapted to local conditions; others were introduced and went wild; and most need to be planted and tended. Each herb has at least one outstanding attribute, be it as seasoning, tea, landscaping, or medicine; many have multiple uses. For some herbs, several species and varieties are listed when they are notable for leaf or flower coloration and form, productivity, growth habit, scent, or other distinctive characteristics. Personal preference was also a factor in the selection process, and I admit to a penchant for certain herbs.

Together, these fifty herbs offer an array of flavors, colors, textures, and medicinal qualities that can enhance an herb lover's life in many ways. Other wonderful herbs I would have liked to include—hawthorn, ginkgo, lady's mantle, hyssop, yarrow, Oregon grape, orris root, poppy, horehound, motherwort, plantain, and red clover, to name a few—await future investigation. I hope that you will be inspired to go beyond this book and learn more about the remarkable plants we know as herbs.

Angelica

Common name: Garden angelica

Latin name: *Angelica archangelica*

Latin and common family names: Apiaceae/Umbelliferae (Carrot family)

Varieties and cultivars: Red angelica, *A. atropurpurea;* Dong quai, *A. sinesis;* Seacoast angelica, *A. lucida;* and others

Description: Towering above other plants, angelica

is one of the most impressive garden herbs. The plants are often 6 feet tall and about 4 feet across. Lower leaves are bright green, deeply lobed, notched at the edges, and arranged in triangular groups on stout 2- to 3-foot stems. Upper leaves flatten into sheaths that clasp the stems. Flower stalks are thick and hollow, branching near the tops with secondary seed heads. The globular heads of greenish flowers and ripe seeds measure up to 8 inches across. Thick, tapering taproots usually have two or three side roots, all with pale flesh. Ripe seeds are buff-colored, ridged ovals about ¼ inch long, with ruffled wings along the sides. The entire plant has a fresh aroma reminiscent of wild places. The related species *A. atropurpurea* has burgundy-colored stems; *A. lucida* or seacoast angelica is one of several species native to the Northwest. **Caution**: Angelica can be confused with other umbelliferous plants that are poisonous. Be sure that you have identified it correctly!

Planting information and cultural directions: A native of the far north, angelica is extremely cold-hardy. Usually described as biennials, angelica plants actually live until they bloom and produce seed, which can take up to four years. Gardeners who wish to prolong the life of their plants can cut off all emerging seed stalks, making the plants more or less perennial. Angelica grows to be huge where the soil is rich and moisture is plentiful. By growing it in poorer, drier soil or in a pot the height can be limited to 3 or 4 feet. It adapts well to full sun or partial shade, even growing under trees.

Propagation: Angelica's big seed heads produce copious amounts of seed. It remains viable for only about six months, so plant it fresh or keep it in the freezer for longer storage. If you don't grow your own seed, obtain the freshest available and sow it thickly and shallowly in March, either in flats or directly in the garden where plants are to grow. The first seedling leaves are long and narrow, followed by notched, trifoliate (three-part) leaves. Thin plants or transplant seedlings to 2 feet apart. Offsets develop on roots that are at least two years old; these can be separated in early spring or fall to produce new plants.

Year-round care: Although mature angelica plants compete successfully with weeds and grass, keep young plants weeded, especially early in the season. Small seedlings are easy to transplant, but larger plants resent being moved around because of their large taproots. Occasionally, plants need staking as the seed heads enlarge, but mostly you can just leave the plants alone and enjoy them. Cut the seed heads off unless you want a carpet of baby angelicas, and remove the spent seed stalks to keep your garden looking neat.

Pests and diseases: Aphids are one of the few pests attracted to angelica. Wash them off with a strong jet of water, or use an insecticidal soap to banish them from your plants.

Harvesting and preserving: Cut the stems for confectionery use while the plants are young and tender, before seed heads begin to form. Harvest leaves for teas in early summer before they become tough. Dry them on trays in a dehydrator. Dig the roots in autumn at the end of their first growing season. Wash and peel the roots, then make tinctures from them or slice and dry them in a dehydrator. To harvest seed

1 Angelica's globular seedheads provide a dramatic focal point in the midsummer garden.

2 Pick young leaves and flower buds of anise hyssop for a delectable addition to salads, or let the honeybees enjoy their abundant nectar.

3 | **4**
5

3 Sweet basil, one of the best loved of all herbs, can fill a room with its intense perfume.

4 The pied beauty of 'Dark Opal' basil seedlings has been bred out of more recently introduced purple cultivars.

5 'African Blue' basil's attractive foliage blends with colorful annuals in this mixed planter; its flowers come later.

6 The succulent stems and leaves of borage have a mild cucumber flavor; its sweet flowers earn borage the nickname "bee bread."

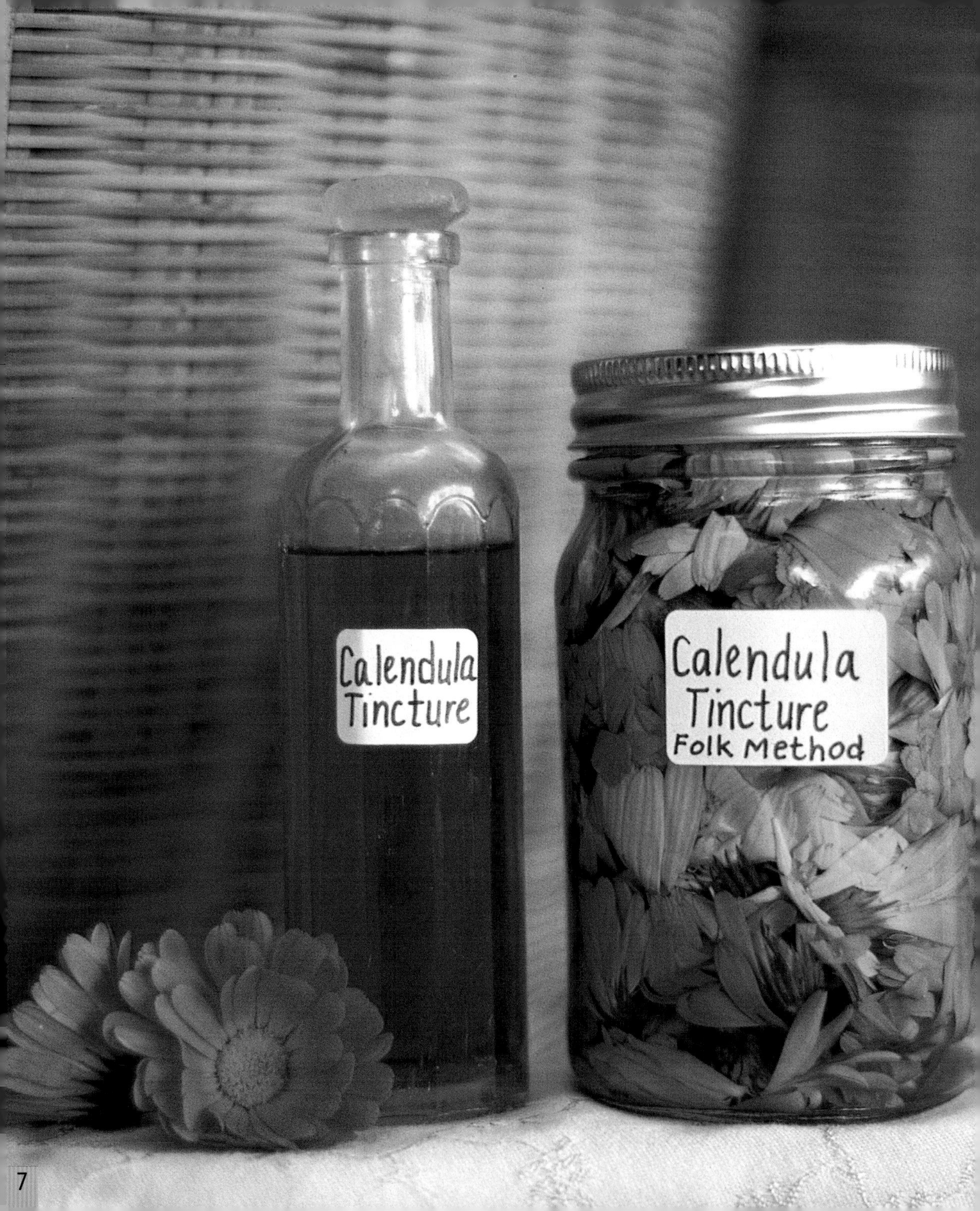
Calendula
Tincture
Calendula
Tincture
Folk Method

8 9
10

7 Calendula flowers in a tincture or alcohol extract can be used in compresses, creams, and lotions to heal and beautify the skin.

8 Brilliant calendula petals add pizazz to salads, soups, and quiches.

9 Musky-scented catnip leaves are calming to humans, in contrast to their wildly euphoric effect on many felines.

10 Chamomile flowers, valued chiefly for their gentle relaxing qualities, are ready to harvest when their centers begin to turn pale brown.

11 **12**
13

11 Garlic chives' flat leaves, buds, and starry white flowers are a favorite in Asian soups and stir-fries.

12 Airy cilantro blossoms have a soft, pinkish hue.

13 Bell-shaped flowers and double coils of buds distinguish comfrey from digitalis and other look-alike plants.

14 Dill in flower at the waterfront gardens of Silver Bay Herb Farm.

15 *Echinacea purpurea*, the purple coneflower, is a beautiful ornamental and a potent medicinal herb.

16 Echinacea's "cone" is made up of vibrant orange quills and tiny disk florets; the drooping mauve "petals" are ray florets.

14 15
16

18

17 Elder has been called "the medicine chest of the country people" in recognition of the many uses of its flowers and berries. Frothy elder flowers revitalize the skin, help chase away colds, and promote restful sleep.

18 Licorice-flavored fennel freshens the breath and improves digestion.

19 Feverfew's bitter leaves contain compounds that can prevent migraines; its daisy-like flowers brighten the garden.

20 Flexible hop vines twine up arbors and walls, and make excellent herbal decorations for festive occasions. The inconspicuous flowers shown here develop into cone-like stobiles used for beer-making and medicine.

21 Homegrown, freshly grated horseradish root added to dips, spreads, and sauces wakes up the taste buds.

22 Sweet-scented lavender is a perennial garden favorite; 'Hidcote' types, as the one shown here, have the darkest flowers.

23 Lemon balm lives up to its time-honored reputation for dispelling melancholy and uplifting the spirits

24 The clean scent of lemon verbena refreshes the body and the senses.

25 With its intriguing flavor, reminiscent of celery and allspice, lovage is one of the great undiscovered seasoning herbs.

26 Lovage seeds can be steeped in wine to make a digestive tonic.

27 Variegated pineapple mint will thrive in a moist, shady area.

28 Fragrant monarda or bee balm graces the garden, attracting butterflies and honeybees.

26

27 28

29 Nasturtium flowers come in a marvelous range of colors from pale yellow and cream to vivid pink, orange, scarlet, and burgundy.

30 Edible flowers, like the nasturtiums and violas shown here, brighten the garden and add panache to salads and desserts.

31 In late summer, nettle seeds hang in clusters until they ripen and drop.

32 In early times, the strong fibers within nettle stems were woven into canvas, rope, tablecloths, and clothing.

33 Young nettles are a delicious spring tonic, rich in chlorophyll and other blood-building nutrients.

31
33 32

34 Greek and common pink-flowered oreganos in bloom are usually surrounded by a busy contingent of bees. Both are shown here against a background of gray santolina.

35 Parsley has great flavor, good looks, nutritional benefits, and breath-freshening qualities.

36 In late summer, rugosa rose bushes may display ripe hips while their flowers are still blooming.

37 Multipetaled and intensely fragrant, 'Charles de Mills' is a quintessential old-fashioned rose.

38 'Rose of Bengal' scented geranium has outstanding flowers and a rose-patchouli aroma.

39 (Following page) Their many uses in aromatherapy, cooking, cosmetics, and medicine qualify roses as bona fide herbs.

36 37
38

40 41
42 43

44

45

40 Trailing rosemary spills over a cement wall like a living fountain. Above left, an upright variety of rosemary; above right, sedum 'Autumn Joy.'

41 'Berggarten' sage is a fine-flavored, big-leaved variety that quickly forms a large silvery mound.

42 Golden sage (left) and tricolor sage (right) are compact, ornamental forms of the popular culinary herb.

43 The elegant notched leaves of salad burnet have a mild cucumber flavor.

44 Macerate freshly picked St. John's wort buds and flowers in olive oil to make a soothing balm for sore muscles, bruises, and sprains.

45 Close examination of the brilliant yellow flowers of St. John's wort reveals irregular black dots along the margins.

46 Evergreen, cold-tolerant winter savory imparts a hearty flavor to casseroles and bean dishes.

47 Sorrel leaves have a refreshingly acidic tang.

48 Sweet woodruff is combined with white wine or fruit juice in the traditional "Mai Bowle" to celebrate the arrival of spring.

49 The anise-and-clove flavor of fresh French tarragon is so strong it can numb the tongue.

50 With careful selection of varieties, thymes can provide months of continuous bloom.

51 Thyme is an indispensable culinary herb; popular varieties include French, English, caraway, nutmeg, lime, and variegated lemon, shown here.

46

47

48 49
50 51

53 54
55

52 The sweet, cloying aroma of valerian flowers hardly gives a hint of the penetrating scent of its sedative roots.

53 Dainty violas, also known as Hearts Ease, are pictured here in their classic tricolor form.

54 Violas in yellow, white, and pastel shades expand the gardener's palette.

55 Watercress adds a peppery bite to sandwiches, soups, and salads.

56 Griffins, perhaps symbolic of the magic and mystery of herbs, once stood watch at the University of Washington's Medicinal Plants Garden.

57 Comfrey, fennel, and sweet cicely weave together into a foliar tapestry.

58 Red-flowered monarda attracts hummingbirds to this country garden.

59 A basket of herbs and edible flowers destined for the farmers' market.

56

57

PICKLING D...

ARUGULA
...Delicious nutty,
...lad, soo

SAG...
Poultry di...bread...
pasta, ve...rk...

Nasturtium
Peppery ...er-sala
vinegar

Stock
Edible flowe...
radish f...

BABY DILL
...ato salad, salmon,
...ess...aios

...INT
...eshi...in te...
...uli, fruit

ILANTRO
...as, bean dishes,
...cken soup, guacamole

SAVORY
Bean dishes, me...
dressings, ...ge...

60 Flats of seedlings, off to an early start in the greenhouse.

61 A culinary herb garden can be surprisingly compact

62 A simple bouquet of calendula, anise hyssop, fennel, and edible chrysanthemum blossoms is perfect for a picnic table centerpiece.

60

61

63

64

63 Garden-fresh herbs at bargain prices tempt farmers' market shoppers.

64 Nasturtiums and a happy frog sing a song of summer.

65 Potted lavender and other elements of this garden vignette can easily be moved to vary the scene.

66 A well-placed bench is an invitation to enjoy this lush gardenscape.

67 (Following page) A glorious array of edible flowers with 'Alaska' nasturtium leaves in the center. Clockwise from top right: calendula, nasturtium, lavender, and arugula. Blue borage flowers are scattered throughout.

for flavoring, clip off the heads when the seeds reach full size but are still green and moist. Strip them from the heads and use them promptly or freeze them until later. For garden seed or craft use, wait until the seeds turn from green to light tan. Cut the seed heads on long stems and hang them to dry for a week or two, or cut the stems short and dry them in a basket or other open container. Unless you are using the heads for decoration, rub the seeds from them, making sure they are insect free. For the best protection against insect damage, store seeds in glass jars in the freezer.

Garden uses: Small wonder that ancient cultures revered this plant: it commands admiration as it rises above the garden like a protective angel. It is outstanding in a foliage garden, offering rich textural effects that keep changing as the oversized leaves, stalks, flower heads, and seeds develop during the growing season. Its neutral green blends with any color combination, but particularly complements euphorbias, hellebores, lady's mantle, mullein, and other herbs in the yellow to chartreuse range, or grays like santolina, artemesias, and verbascums. Situate tall angelica in the back of the border, or in the center of the garden as a focal point.

Culinary uses: The leaves and stems of angelica have a fresh, complex aroma and a strong flavor. Candied angelica stems are recommended in many herbals for cake decoration. Always one to experiment, I have peeled the young stems as directed and simmered them in sugar syrup. The result was brownish, barely chewable stems in a singularly delicious syrup. This syrup is a treat over ice cream or as a base for a fruity punch. The candied stems I purchased for comparison at a Paris street market were bright green but flavorless. Angelica is grown commercially as an ingredient in various alcoholic beverages, notably vermouth, Chartreuse, and Bénédictine. To make a pleasant aperitif wine, steep angelica leaves in a Johannisberg Riesling; sip it before dinner or use it to poach fish.

Craft and home uses: Angelica produces a bountiful quantity of seeds, easily a gallon from just one plant. This is far in excess of a home gardener's needs for propagation. The extra seeds, with their unusual shape and texture, make an attractive addition to potpourri. The unusual, globular seed heads are also striking as room decor when dried and arranged in a vase. Freeze them first, to get rid of insects. Dried angelica root, peeled and sliced, is said to be an aromatic fixative for potpourri.

Medicinal uses: Angelica's Latin name suggests the reverence the ancients felt for this plant, which they regarded as the sovereign remedy for almost any ailment. Medieval monks prescribed angelica elixirs for digestive problems and lung ailments, and their formulas provide the basis of modern digestive spirits. A rich folk tradition persists in Northern Europe, where angelica has been used for centuries as an aromatic tonic and digestive stimulant. Scientific studies have corroborated these traditions. The herb has been found to stimulate gastric juices and liver function, improve the appetite, and ease flatulence and colic.

The *British Herbal Pharmacopoeia* lists angelica as a specific for bronchitis associated with vascular deficiency. It is regarded as an expectorant and used for chest coughs, colds, and flu. In China, ten species of angelica are used medicinally. Dong quai (*A. sinesis*), known as the "woman's ginseng," is esteemed as a blood-building tonic, liver stimulant, and menstrual cycle regulator.

Angelica may be taken in the form of infusions, tinctures, cough syrups, powdered root, bitters, and elixirs.

Anise Hyssop

Common names: Licorice mint

Latin name: *Agastache foeniculum*

Latin and common family names: Lamiaceae (Mint family)

Description: What's in a name? Neither anise (*Pimpinella anisum*) nor hyssop (*Hyssopus officinalis*), this handsome herb is actually a cousin to the mints, most closely resembling catnip in size and growth habit. It is a 2- to 3-foot bush with erect, branching, square stems that rise from a dense root clump. Its 3-inch leaves are opposite, notched, pointed, and soft to the touch. Rubbed between the fingers, they give off a pleasant fragrance that hints at their delicious flavor, a combination of sweet anise and root beer, perfect for garden sampling. The leaves are tinged with lavender, especially at the growing tips, and the color is echoed in 2- to 4-inch spikes of densely packed lavender blue florets. Each flower head produces copious amounts of tiny, rounded brown seeds. Seedlings germinate in May when the soil warms to about 60°F and can be recognized by their opposing pairs of crinkly, ruffled leaves with light lavender veining.

Planting information and cultural directions: Anise hyssop prefers full sun and humus-rich soil with abundant moisture, but also grows well in partial shade and drier soils. Adding compost, well-rotted manure, or organic fertilizer before planting helps to produce vigorous, healthy plants. They are hardy to about 15°F, but do not always survive the winter, either because of poor drainage or mysterious factors.

Propagation: Anise hyssop is easy to start from seed, sown in flats or in the ground in early spring. Cover the seeds with ¼ to ½ inch of soil and keep them evenly watered. Plants reseed in the garden but do not become weedy, perhaps because the ripe seed is a favorite of small birds.

Year-round care: Protect small and newly emerging plants from slugs, and keep them weeded until they are no longer vulnerable. Sidedress with fertilizer about once a month. These naturally shapely plants do not need pruning, but pinching back the tips encourages the production of tender growth. Allow the flowers to ripen into seed heads if you wish, but cut back the woody stems when you do your autumn garden cleanup. It may be helpful to label the plants so you will remember where they will be coming up when winter is over.

Pests and diseases: Many a gardener has blamed the demise of her anise hyssop plants on winter's cold when slugs were the real culprits. Vigilance is the key here, because these pests not only mow down the seedlings but return to feast again and again on newly emerging shoots. Look out especially for tiny gray slugs that seem innocent but wreak havoc, and thwart them by whatever method you prefer.

Harvesting and preserving: Gather the fresh tips of anise hyssop as needed, using your thumbnail or a clipper to pinch them from the stems above the second or third pair of leaves. To dry leaves for tea, cut the stems at the base of the plant and hang in bunches of about six stems, fastened with a rubber band. In two to three weeks, strip leaves from the stems and store them in glass jars with tight-fitting lids.

Garden uses: A mature anise hyssop in bloom, is a striking plant and one of the very best nectar producers for honeybees. It is a fine addition to the edible landscape with its lavender-tinged leaves, compact habit, and the strong vertical lines of its flower spikes. It is showy enough for the flower garden, under roses, paired with the long-blooming Siberian wallflower 'Bowles Mauve,' or true geraniums in rose and purple hues. In the herb garden, try growing it with lavender or echinacea. For a lovely effect in a large planter, let it rise above a cascade of peppermint-scented geraniums or beside the upright 'Mabel Grey,' with cherry- or apricot-colored nasturtiums hanging down in brilliant contrast.

Culinary uses: The tender tips of anise hyssop, picked with the young flower buds, are one of the best-tasting additions to a summer greens mixture. You can also make an excellent tea by pouring boiling water over a large handful of leaves; serve it iced, straight up, or combined with Earl Grey tea. Four Seasons chef James Walsh played up the anise flavor in an anise hyssop sorbet with a splash of Sambuca liqueur.

Arugula

Common names: Rocket, Rocket-salad, Roquette, Rucola

Latin name: *Eruca vesicaria* ssp. *sativa*

Latin and common family names: Cruciferae/ Brassicaceae (Mustard or Cress family)

Varieties and cultivars: Rustic arugula, *Eruca selvatica*

Related plants: Dame's rocket, *Hesperis matronalis*

Description: Arugula is a favorite Italian annual with dark green, rounded, deeply lobed leaves like those of a radish but smooth and shiny. Clusters of four-petaled white flowers are carried on 2- to 3-foot stems. Seedlings have two oval leaves similar to lettuce. The leaves and flowers have a nutty flavor, becoming hot and spicy as the plant grows older and the weather warms. Tiny brown seeds are formed in pods at the top of the stalks, completing the entire life cycle of the plant in three to four months. Arugula reseeds freely and is hardy enough to survive all but the coldest maritime Northwest winters. The related rustic arugula, *E. selvatica*, has stronger-flavored, narrower leaves and yellow flowers. Unwisely, I allowed it to reseed after one season in my garden and it promptly became a pest. Dame's rocket or *Hesperis*, the purple cottage-garden flower, is a more distant relative.

Planting information and cultural directions: Arugula flourishes in a rich, moist soil with partial shade or full sun. It is easy to grow, requiring only basic weeding and watering. Plants grown in the cool weather of spring and fall have the most delicate flavor. A crop sown under cover in early spring will produce a welcome supply of tasty leaves for early salads. Like all members of the cabbage family, it is a heavy feeder, so give it ample fertilizer and avoid planting it in the same place each season.

Propagation: Sow seeds directly where they are to grow. They germinate quickly. To maintain a continuous harvest, make your first sowing in mid-March and continue sowing every three weeks through September. If you space the plants 6 inches apart, they will grow to the size of a leaf lettuce in rich soil. For European-style mesclun salads, sow thickly in rows or bands; within a few weeks you can cut handfuls of tender 2- to 3-inch leaves.

Pests and diseases: Protect your arugula from flea beetles by placing spun-bonded polyester row cover over it. Light and moisture can get in, but pests are kept out.

Harvesting and preserving: For best flavor, harvest arugula leaves when they are 2 to 4 inches tall. You can harvest leaves of larger plants singly as needed, including the small ones growing up the flower stem. For mesclun, cut back baby plants to about 1 inch from the base, drench the bed with Regular Solution Fish Fertilizer, and more leaves will grow back quickly. Flowers are edible and taste good. Arugula does not dry or freeze well.

Saving your own arugula seed is easy, although it means giving up some garden space to lanky plants until they mature. Harvest seeds just when the pods start opening and the seeds inside are brown, not green. Be sure to label them, because they look just like the seeds of other mustard family members.

Garden uses: Arugula is a quick filler but doesn't hold its good looks for long. Its green rosette makes an attractive addition to a kitchen garden and effectively contrasts with the grays of lavender and sage. It soon bolts and loses its compact form, but the cream-colored flowers stay on the plant for a long time. Bolting plants look untidy, so you may want to pull them out and add them to the compost heap.

Culinary uses: My mom calls arugula "peanut butter plant," but to me it tastes more like toasted walnuts. Tender young arugula leaves make any salad or sandwich a gourmet treat. Try a bed of arugula leaves topped with sliced Bosc pears and goat cheese, thin slices of Walla Walla sweet onion, and walnut-raspberry vinaigrette, garnished with arugula blossoms. Or combine arugula with Gorgonzola, spiced pecans, and fruit such as dried cranberries, fresh orange, apple, or pomegranate with a basic vinaigrette dressing.

Older leaves, added toward the end of cooking, are a piquant addition to potato soups. At Silver Bay, chef Barbara Figueroa wowed picnic guests with a fabulous concoction of buckwheat pasta with a goat cheese sauce and lots of wilted arugula.

Medicinal uses: Once used to prevent scurvy and relieve coughs, arugula is generally regarded as a nutritious but nonmedicinal herb.

Basil

Common names: Sweet basil, Italian sweet basil

Latin name: *Ocimum basilicum*

Latin and common family names: Labiatae/Lamiaceae (Mint family)

Varieties and cultivars: 'Cinnamon,' 'Dark Opal,' Large Green, 'Citriodorum' (Lemon), 'Crispum' (Lettuce Leaf), 'Purple Ruffles,' 'Piccolo,' 'Spicy Globe,' 'Thai,' and many more

Description: Basil is one of the most beloved culinary herbs, and is sometimes called the "herb royale" or king of herbs. There are dozens of distinct varieties in popular use, originating in Italy, Greece, Thailand, India, Africa, South America, and the

United States. Some are very old, others are modern selections; all are highly aromatic. Their intense and complex flavors of sweetness and spice, citrus or camphor differ according to the balance of aroma components of their essential oils. The more unusual varieties are seldom available commercially, and very rewarding to grow.

Sweet basil (*Ocimum basilicum*), the most popular variety, is a bushy plant that grows 2 to 3 feet tall. Its shiny, deep green leaves are almond shaped, curve upward slightly, and grow in opposite pairs on short stems. They are about 2 inches wide and 2 to 3 inches long, with smooth or slightly toothed edges. Stems are square and branch out from a single trunk. Compact clusters of buds form atop the branches, then elongate into spikes encircled by whorls of six flowers. The two-lipped white blossoms attract bees to the garden. Sweet basil has a heady scent described by the English poet Drayton as "wondrous pleasing." Linalool and geraniol, also present in lavender and roses, contribute to its floral sweetness. Peruse seed catalogs and try to decide between named cultivars, such as 'Italian Sweet,' 'Italian Large Leaf,' 'Broad Leaf Sweet,' 'Genovese,' and 'Genova Profumatissima.' They are all wonderful for fresh culinary use and pesto, pesto, pesto.

'Mammoth' and 'Large Leaf' are milder-flavored varieties, with leaves up to 4 inches long. They are impressive to behold, and ideal for wrapping foods. The 'Lettuce Leaf' or 'Crispum' variety has large, ruffled leaves and a soft flavor. It is one of the oldest basil varieties, and handsome in the garden. 'Napoletano' also has crinkled leaves, and a mellow flavor.

Piccolo or small-leaved basils (*O. b. minimum*) are an interesting group characterized by masses of tiny leaves, just ⅛ inch to 1 inch long. They have been Mediterranean favorites for centuries. 'French Fine Leaf,' 'Fino Verde,' or 'Fine Green' plants can grow quite tall, and their small leaves have excellent flavor. 'Nano Compatto Vero' and 'Fino Verde Compatto' are smaller versions, at 12 to 15 inches. Bush basils, including 'Basilico Greco' or 'Greek Bush,' 'Green Bush,' and 'Compact Green Bush' form an attractive green mound 6 to 8 inches tall that may spread 12 to 15 inches across. 'Spicy Globe' is a miniature with tiny leaves that forms a compact mound about 8 inches tall.

Modern cultivars of ancient purple varieties (*O. b. 'Purpurascens'*) include 'Osmin Purple,' which has very dark leaves and stems and a sweet scent. Its leaves are smaller than 'Red Rubin,' a smooth, garnet-leaved beauty that reaches 18 to 24 inches. 'Dark Opal,' from which it was selected, is less uniform in color, with leaves that may be mottled and streaked with green. 'Purple Ruffles' is a gorgeous ornamental plant with uniformly deep purple, ruffled leaves. All these varieties are pleasantly aromatic and flavorful.

Some people find it surprising that basil may also be citrus flavored. *O. citriodorum* or lemon basil, described by Gerard in *The Herball* (1597), grows only to 12 inches and has small, sparse, light green leaves with a delicious lemony taste. 'Sweet Dani,' an award-winning 1998 introduction, is a robust 24- to 30-inch shrub with large, olive green leaves. Citral content up to 68 percent gives them a sweet and intense lemon scent and flavor. Johnny's Seeds of Albion, Maine, offers 'Mrs. Burns' Lemon,' an heirloom plant cultivated in New Mexico for sixty years, described as "the most lemony of all," and 'Lime' (*O. americanum*), a small plant with a "distinctly zesty aroma of lime."

The exotic spice-scented basils owe their captivating aromas to high levels of methyl cinnimate. One of my personal favorites is 'Cinnamon,' a vigorous 26- to 30-inch plant with purplish, voluptuous cinnamon-scented stems, leaves, and flowers. 'Anise' basil is similar but distinctly licorice-ish. 'Thai' and 'Siam Queen' are smaller plants, admirably suited to container growing. Nichols Garden Nursery of Albany, Oregon, lists the unusual 'Mexican Cinnamon Spice,' a "refined spicy sweet basil ideal for drying."

'African Blue Basil' or 'Kasar' (*Ocimum* x 'African Blue'), a relatively new introduction, is a sterile hybrid of 'Dark Opal' crossed with camphor basil. Propagated only from cuttings, it has rounded, downy, bluish leaves with purple veining, dark purple stems, and light purple blossoms. It is agreeably pungent though less sweet than some other varieties, and when in flower is very ornamental. It is more hardy than most basils, and can survive a month longer outdoors. It is also easier to grow as a perennial indoors.

Planting information and cultural directions: Give basil your sunniest spot. In tropical climates, this heat-loving plant is a tall, luxuriant perennial, but in the Northwest it takes all the sun it can get, and grows rapidly only in the heat of summer. Cover transplants with spun-bonded polyester row covers to encourage quick growth. Technically, basil is hardy to 32°F, but the leaves turn black at about 40°F, well before the first frost. Treat it as a very tender annual.

All basils do best in a moderate to rich soil with steady, ample moisture. Irrigate with drip or soaker hoses if possible to prevent dark spots on the leaves. Work compost and organic fertilizers into the beds at planting time, then feed the plants liquid fish fertilizer twice a month to sustain growth. Six plants provide a year-round supply of fresh leaves, dried leaves, and pesto for a basil-loving family, but plant a few extra to allow for the unexpected.

Propagation: Some growers sow basil seed directly into the garden when the soil warms in late May. Since basil takes about two months to mature, this makes for a short season. For an earlier start, sow basil seeds indoors at two-week intervals beginning in mid-March. Seed germinates in six to ten days at 60° to 70°F. A gel-like coating forms around the seeds once they are moistened; keep them evenly moist to prevent it from hardening around the emerging shoots.

Transplant the tiny seedlings to 2-inch pots and grow them until they have at least two sets of leaves. They are very vulnerable at this point, so be sure to harden them off gradually until they are well adapted to bright sunlight and night temperatures. Wait until soil temperatures are 60°F at night before setting basil out.

Try transplanting one batch of plants in mid-May, spaced 8 to 10 inches apart, and a second batch two weeks later with similar spacing. In mid-June, sow a row or two of seed directly into the garden for late summer harvesting. Space direct-sown rows of basil about 2 feet apart, thinning the plants gradually (savor those thinnings!) to about 9 inches apart.

Year-round care: To prolong your harvest, you can

pot up plants from the garden in September and bring them indoors where it's warm. With proper light and care, they can survive through the winter, and you can enjoy fresh basil during the coldest months.

Pests and diseases: Slugs love basil as much as humans do, and they can mow down rows of seedlings overnight. Protect your plants using any of the methods described in the section on Organic Pest and Disease Management in Chapter 1.

Flea beetles chew numerous tiny holes in the leaves. If the infestation is severe, dust the plants with rotenone on a still, dry morning. The tomato fruitworm, also known as the corn earworm, can do tremendous damage even to large plants. Spraying with Thuricide saved my basil from total devastation one year.

Fusarium wilt is a fungus disease, transmitted by infected seed, which has wreaked havoc with Hawaiian basil production. The University of Hawaii is working to develop resistant varieties, but meanwhile reputable seed suppliers test seed rigorously for this disease. Basil is also subject to various stem rots when overwatered.

Harvesting and preserving: Your first picking of basil will probably be in mid- to late June. When the plants are 6 to 8 inches high and have four sets of leaves, pinch off the stems just above the third set of leaves. Two new stems, each with its own leaf pairs, will grow from the leaf nodes. When picking pounds of basil at a time at Silver Bay, I set a paper bag inside a plastic bag and moved it alongside the plants as I harvested with both hands simultaneously. My thumbnails were stained, but I was enveloped in a divine aroma.

Religiously pinch back those leafy tips and flower buds. I have observed that if flowers are allowed to open, the plants shift into reproduction mode. They then develop fewer, poorer-flavored leaves and tough, woody stems, a process that seems impossible to reverse once begun. So keep picking that basil, and your plants will produce an abundance all season.

Many commercial growers wait to begin harvesting until the plants are larger, then clip branches that are long enough to bunch. If you buy bunched basil by the pound for making pesto, you'll be paying about a third of the cost for unusable stems.

Basil is a delicate herb that requires gentleness and proper handling. If bruised, crushed, or packed down, it turns black; left in the sun or standing in water, the stems and leaf veins turn brown. It will keep beautifully if you pick it in the morning while the leaves are moistened with dew, use my double-bag system, and refrigerate it promptly.

Hang small bunches of basil to dry in a warm, airy place. When they are brittle to the touch, store them in a glass jar away from heat and light. For maximum flavor, rub the leaves from the stems just before use.

The intensity of basil's flavor is best preserved by freezing. When frozen by themselves the leaves turn black, but combining them with oil seals out air and keeps them bright green. Many chefs purée whole leaves in olive oil and freeze the resulting paste in small containers (ice cube trays work well for home use). Or take out a pesto insurance policy against winter menu blahs by grinding basil with olive oil, garlic, Parmesan cheese, and pine nuts.

Garden uses: While all basils are handsome as ornamentals, certain cultivars are particularly striking in the landscape. Dwarf bush basils form bright green spheres about 9 inches tall that make a beautiful edging for formal beds or along curving pathways. Colorful 'Osmin' and 'Purple Ruffles' make dramatic statements when massed, or alternated with green basils, grayish sages, or lavenders. Long-lasting 'African Blue' is beautiful in bloom. Since the basils are annuals, they can quickly fill in spaces between slower-growing perennials.

As a container plant, basil has it all—good looks, compact habit, and plenty of variety in texture, color, and size. A luxuriant basil garden spilling out of an old wheelbarrow or wine barrel can be a garden centerpiece. Group individually potted basils on the front steps, define a path with them, or move them around for changing effects. Low-growing bush basils are perfect for window boxes and other containers.

Culinary uses: Sweet basil is practically indispensable in the kitchen, its sweetness a versatile accent to many flavors. Handle fresh basil leaves carefully to prevent bruising, and add them toward the end of cooking time for maximum flavor. Chef Monique Barbeau, formerly of Fullers in the Seattle Sheraton, stacks basil leaves in a bundle, then carefully slices them into chiffonade ribbons to sprinkle over fabulous entrées.

Basil is a classic complement to tomatoes, whether chopped and lavished on fresh slices, mixed with cottage cheese and chives as a stuffing, blended in gazpacho, or added to marinara sauce for pizza and pasta dishes. It is delicious in marinades and sauces for grilled or baked chicken, salmon, prawns, steaks, and other meats. It does wonderful things for soups such as Italian minestrone, French pistou, and hearty lentil. Fresh leaves are layered with sun-dried tomatoes in sensational summer tortas, and contribute spicy nuances to rich cheesecakes and other desserts.

'Lettuce Leaf' and other large varieties are great for wrapping foods like tabouli and other grain salads, grilled shrimp or chicken, and baked eggplant with feta cheese and garlic. 'Fino Verde' and other small-leaved varieties can go straight into the cooking pot without chopping, and they are very chic for garnishing.

Specialty basils can excite a creative cook's imagination. Lemon-flavored basils are memorable with fish and chicken, fruit desserts, or any dish that benefits from a twist of lemon. Purple basils are a visual delight in salads, especially when contrasted with yellow tomatoes, orange calendula petals, and dark green lettuce. They also make colorful pestos. 'Cinnamon' and 'Thai' basils, often combined with cilantro and mint, add an addictive flavor to Asian noodle dishes, soups, and chicken and beef dishes. Once you've tasted them in an authentic Thai spring roll or Vietnamese pho soup, nothing else can substitute.

To put up basil for the winter, try making some crystal-clear jellies, delicate or robust herbal vinegars, and dried herb blends. Pesto sauce stored in the freezer is like summer in a jar. Use it in the classic manner as a sauce for pasta, spread it on fish or chicken before grilling, or slather it on sandwiches and pizza dough. Add it to soups, omelets, deviled eggs, salad dressings, dips, and sauces. *Recipes from a*

Kitchen Garden, by Renee Shepherd and Fran Raboff, contains several intriguing recipes that utilize various basils.

Craft and home uses: In Mediterranean countries, pots of basil are often set on windowsills to repel flies and mosquitoes. Sprigs of fresh leaves are pretty in tussie mussies and other bouquets, while dried seed spikes are aromatic in everlasting bouquets. Dried sweet and lemon basils lend a fresh note to potpourri.

Medicinal uses: Basil is not an important medicinal herb, though it does have some therapeutic effects. Traditionally, an infusion of fresh basil leaves is regarded as relaxing to the nervous system. The leaves are also carminative, digestive, and antimicrobial.

Aromatherapy: Sweet basil oil is used in the cosmetic industry to scent soaps and toiletries, and in natural insect repellents. It is valued in perfumery for its aroma, reminiscent of mignonette. Diluted in a massage oil it relieves sore muscles and rheumatic pains.

Bay

Common names: Bay laurel, Sweet bay, Bay leaf tree, True bay, Grecian bay, Turkish bay

Latin name: *Laurus nobilis*

Latin and common family names: Lauraceae (Laurel family)

Varieties and cultivars: 'Turkish,' 'Aurea'

Unrelated plants: California laurel, *Umbellularia californica*; Mountain laurel, *Kalmia latifolia*; Myrtle, *Myrtus communis*; English or Cherry laurel, *Prunus laurocerasus*

Description: The word "classic" describes bay trees well, alluding to their lovely shape, time-honored use in cooking, and their importance to the ancient Greeks and Romans, who revered this tree, associating it with nobility, victory, and immortality. References to their custom of crowning emperors, victors, and poets with bay-leaf wreaths endure in expressions such as "earning one's laurels" and "poet laureate."

With their glossy, lance-shaped evergreen leaves and handsome form, bay trees are ornamental in any herb garden. The stiff, dark green leaves are 2 to 4 inches long, in opposing pairs on short stems, and so beautifully shaped and veined that their likeness adorns sculptures and buildings. The bark is reddish green to grayish, with the main stem developing an interesting stippled, wrinkled texture. Bay trees often produce multiple stems and suckers. In their native Mediterranean climate, they are hardy perennials that can reach 60 feet in height. In the Northwest, they are semihardy, growing about half that tall unless pruned back. After an especially mild winter, clusters of pale yellow fringed flowers may bloom at the base of the leaves in spring, but the decorative (and inedible) purple berries seldom ripen here.

Other plants sometimes confused with sweet bay are the California bay or California laurel (*Umbellularia californica*), which has narrower leaves only about 1 inch across; mountain laurel (*Kalmia latifolia*), a poisonous plant with odorless leaves and pink flowers; myrtle (*Myrtus communis*), a frost-tender evergreen shrub with aromatic leaves; and English or cherry laurel (*Prunus laurocerasus*), the large-leaved fast grower often planted as a screening hedge.

Planting information and cultural directions: Although bay trees are slow growing for the first few years, by the fourth year they reach a height of 4 feet and start bushing out rapidly. Each branch can grow about 3 feet a year. The trees' height and shape can be controlled by training, and their dense foliage makes them excellent subjects for topiary work (see below). Give them a rich, well-drained soil mix, and feed potted trees occasionally with a regular solution of fish emulsion or slow-release fertilizer.

Since bay trees are hardy only to about 25°F, they are often grown in pots set outside or sunk into the ground in summer and wintered indoors. If you wish to try growing yours outdoors, give it a very protected spot where it will be out of the wind. Cover the base of the plant with a heavy mulch of compost, leaf mold, or sawdust. You may have to wrap the tree with blankets to keep it from freezing in severe weather.

Propagation: Bay trees are notoriously difficult to propagate. Viable seeds are hard to find, and cuttings can take six months or longer to root, even under a misting system. I have read about taking suckers from established plants and layering branches growing low to the ground, but have no personal success with these methods. It's easiest to buy a young plant.

Year-round care: Bay trees go dormant in the winter and need minimal light and water. I've kept plants outdoors through light freezes, but during cold snaps when temperatures hover around 20°F they need protection. A humid garage, sheltered porch, or cool greenhouse is the best place to keep them. If you must bring them into the house, try to avoid dramatic temperature changes, and mist the leaves often. When buds begin to swell along the stem, move the plant into the light and work some All-Purpose Fertilizer Mix (see Chapter 1) mix into the soil

around it, about ¼ cup per gallon of soil in pot. Water plants and mist the leaves once a week. Set the tree outside in late March or April, fertilizing it once a month with half a cup of Regular Solution Fish Fertilizer. There is no need to prune your bay until it has become fairly large. Then trim back branches above leaf nodes during the growing season to achieve a compact, bushy plant.

Pests and diseases: Bay trees are generally healthy and pest free, but watch out for disk-shaped scale insects. These creatures begin life as six-legged nymphs, and in their final egg-laying stage attach themselves to the stems and undersides of leaves and suck nourishment from them. Scale insects produce a sticky honeydew attractive to ants, which carry the infestation to other branches. The honeydew also encourages the growth of black, sooty molds that can slow photosynthesis. Wash off molds with insecticidal soap. Scrape off scale by hand, or spray plants with Sunspray dormant oil (a highly refined petroleum product) before leaf buds open in spring. Follow directions on the label carefully to avoid leaf burn. The laurel psyllid is another sucking insect that may attack bay plants, causing cupping of terminal leaves. The problem is seldom severe, but can be controlled with pyrethrum spray if necessary.

Harvesting and preserving: Fresh bay leaves are an herbal luxury, and I love to pluck them straight from the tree year-round. They are fuller flavored than the more commonly available dried leaves, which are also fine—unless they are old. For convenience, decoration, or gifts, hang bunches of six or eight stems to dry in a warm location out of the sun.

When harvesting them, be sure that new leaves at the tips of branches are full grown and leathery or they will shrivel up. For flat leaves, allow them to partially air-dry, then press them in a book.

Garden uses: Bay trees have long been popular as the focal points of herb gardens, and are often planted in the center of a round garden or as twin pillars alongside a path. Even when small, their evergreen foliage gives them an elegant look that enhances formal and informal gardens alike.

By clipping and pinching branches during the growing season, bay trees can be kept reasonably sized, or shaped into globes, hedges, or topiaries with several pom-poms or other fanciful shapes. Multiple trunks can be braided while plants are young, a technique called "pleaching" that creates a striking effect when the trees mature. Bay tree topiaries in decorative pots are often set on the steps of European homes and shops, a custom Northwest city dwellers might well adopt.

Every few years it's necessary to repot bay trees to give them a fresh lease on life. When they are large, it's a project. During the dormant season, tip the pots sideways and ease out the plants. Use a hand pruner to clip roots that conform to the shape of the pot or are growing out the bottom. Move plants to larger pots with new, enriched potting soil, or, in the case of large plants, repot the reduced root ball in the same container with fresh soil.

Culinary uses: Versatile bay leaves belong in every well-stocked spice cabinet. They are indispensable in the cuisines of France, Italy, and other Mediterranean countries. Use them whole and add them to the pot early. One bay leaf is generally recommended to season six portions, but I often triple that amount, especially for short cooking periods. Cineol, eugenol, and pinene contribute to bay's cinnamon-clove-pine flavor, which the leaves release slowly. Long simmering or steeping brings out this flavor, so bay leaves are used in soups and stews, when cooking dried beans (especially pinto and flageolet) and spaghetti sauce, marinades, court bouillon, and herbal vinegars. Formerly, bay leaves often seasoned custards, rice puddings, and other bland dishes, uses that really highlight the herb. A good blending herb, bay is an ingredient in a classic bouquet garni or "broth posy," as well as spice mixtures for pickling and mulling. It's best to remove the leaves before serving, although in our household a "bay leaf watch" is sometimes in effect, and I've tried to convince my family that it's good luck to get the bay leaf.

Craft and home uses: Simmer a few bay leaves on your stove and your home will be filled with the warm, subtle aroma that perfumers prize for toiletries, especially for men. Bay leaf combines well with scents as diverse as rum, citrus, rosemary, pine, roses, lavender, and spices. It often appears in recipes for potpourri.

Medicinal uses: The Greeks and Romans used bay leaf both medicinally and ceremonially, believing that it enhanced memory and spiritual awareness. Since the Middle Ages it has been regarded as an antiseptic, digestive, and regenerative herb, and is used externally to alleviate rheumatic pain and sore muscles. An oil pressed from the ripe berries is applied to sprains and bruises.

Aromatherapy: The greenish yellow essential oil

distilled from bay leaves and twigs has a warm, powerful aroma. It is reputed to have antiseptic, antifungal, and bactericidal qualities, and to promote healing after serious illness. Experimentally, its supposed calming and blood-pressure-reducing properties are being investigated.

■ Borage

Common names: Bee bread, Burrage

Latin name: *Borago officinalis*

Latin and family names: Boraginaceae (Borage family)

Varieties and cultivars: Common borage, White-flowered borage

Description: Borage is a large, fast-growing annual, related to comfrey and forget-me-nots. It is loosely pyramidal in shape, with hollow, juicy stems and a single taproot. Its soft, oval leaves are rumpled and lightly scratchy due to tiny hairs on both sides. Plants are 2 to 4 feet tall and about 2 feet around, growing largest in rich soils. The herb is easily distinguished by its pretty blue or pinkish flowers that look as if they were cut with tiny star-shaped cookie cutters. A black cone of anthers rises from a white area at the center of each flower. A rare form of borage has pure white blossoms. The flowers are held tightly within a hairy calyx and form in drooping clusters (racemes) at the end of branches. There may be buds, blossoms, and ripe and unripe seeds in the same cluster. There are four seeds per calyx; when ripe they turn black, hard, and angular, and drop to the ground.

Planting information and cultural directions: Growing conditions in the Northwest are perfect for borage. Like most annuals, this herb matures quickly, requiring only eight weeks from seed to seed. It is very easy to grow and generally takes care of itself. It does well in a sunny or partially shaded spot with average to dry, well-drained soils. Plants grow bigger in moist, rich soils. Borage reseeds so generously that often a second generation of plants will spring up beneath the original plant. If this is not to your liking, it's easy to transplant or weed out the babies.

Propagation: Borage can be started indoors, but seeds sown directly into the garden germinate readily and will often overtake transplants. Sow them as soon as the ground can be worked, in February or March. Space the seeds 4 to 6 inches apart and cover them with about ½ inch of soil. As seedlings grow, thin them to about 12 inches apart. It takes just one plant to keep you in borage year after year. Seeds that drop in autumn lie dormant until temperatures reach about 60°F, then sprout in quantity. If you want to start with a plant rather than seeds, look for a healthy young seedling with large, rounded leaves. Older borage plants do not take kindly to transplanting.

Year-round care: Because of its short life span, borage is not a plant that requires year-round care. You will probably trim the plants back a little as you use the leaves over the course of the season. Pull them out when they start to turn yellow and shrivel as their end approaches. A sharp frost will turn the plants black. If you are too busy to fuss with them, just leave them alone and they will quietly disintegrate.

Pests and diseases: Destructive pests and diseases are seldom a problem with borage.

Harvesting and preserving: Despite its vigor and

size, borage is essentially a delicate herb that must be handled gently. It is primarily used fresh since its subtle flavor cannot really be preserved by drying or freezing. To harvest the flowers, grasp the calyx with one hand and pull gently on the black anthers with the other. Place flowers directly into a plastic bag on a tray lined with damp paper towels. If they must be held for more than one day, leave the prickly calyxes on till just before serving to keep the flowers fresher. Refrigerate flowers and leaves immediately after picking. When making punch, I cut back whole plants from the borage patch in my garden, then pluck off the flowers and refrigerate them separately for use as a garnish.

Borage seeds are hard to harvest because they ripen at different times and drop immediately. In the herbal research gardens of Purdue University, the ground beneath the plants was covered with black plastic, making it easy to suck up the fallen seeds in quantity with large shop vacs. Patient gardeners can simply bend down and pick up the ripe seeds under mature plants.

Garden uses: With its tendency to grow fast and loose, borage is good for filling in empty spaces between perennials, especially in young gardens or early in the season. It provides a soft, green effect and, in warmer parts of the region, can be covered with blossoms by early April. It is an undisciplined plant that tends to sprawl, so its good looks are temporary. But it is of value as a bee plant; its flowers produce such generous amounts of nectar that borage is nicknamed "bee bread." Perhaps the enhanced pollination that results is one reason it is said to be a good companion plant for tomatoes, cucumbers, and squash.

Culinary uses: Borage flowers are edible, and make an attractive and mildly sweet garnish for tea sandwiches, salads, and punch. Most chefs turn the anthers downward for the prettiest presentation. Candied, the flowers are used to decorate cakes. To make a festive ice ring for a punch bowl, place borage and other edible flowers in a ring mold, fill with water, and freeze. Young borage leaves can be chopped fine and added to salads, and older leaves are good in punch. In traditional use, the leaves and flowers were steeped in wine to gladden the mind. Although often likened to cucumber, the mild, refreshing flavor of borage eludes easy identification.

Medicinal uses: Over the centuries, borage has enjoyed a reputation for elevating and comforting the spirits after illness or hard study. "I Borage bring always courage," according to an ancient Greek saying; Pliny called the plant "euphrosinum" and believed that it "maketh a man joyful and merry, brings comfort, and drives away melancholy." Although consistent, these claims remain unproven. As a folk remedy, borage tea continues to be taken for depression, exhaustion, and menopausal symptoms.

Recent discoveries indicate that borage seed oil is nature's best source of gamma-linoleic acid (GLA). This substance, also found in evening primrose oil, is promising for treatment of PMS, eczema, migraines, and essential fatty acid imbalances. It is not feasible to extract the oil at home, but the seeds can be gathered, ground, and added to bread as a dietary supplement.

Fresh borage leaves (but not flowers) have been found to contain small amounts of pyrrolizidine alkaloids, the substances that have given comfrey a bad rap. Although the amounts contained in a glass of borage punch would be minute, ingesting large amounts of fresh borage leaves is not advised.

Calendula

Common names: Pot marigold, Garden marigold

Latin name: *Calendula officinalis*

Latin and common family names: Compositae/ Asteraceae (Aster family)

Varieties and cultivars: 'Fiesta Gitana,' 'Kablouna,' 'Pacific Brights,' 'Pink Surprise,' 'Pot Marigold,' 'Touch of Red,' and others

Unrelated plants: *Tagetes* species, such as African or French marigold

Description: Calendula, the old-fashioned marigold, is beloved for its sunny yellow or orange blossoms that have culinary, cosmetic, and medicinal qualities. They are compound flowers, with single or multiple rows of colorful, notched petals (ray florets) and same-colored to chocolate brown centers (disk florets). They bloom profusely throughout the summer, one flower atop each stem, tending to flag somewhat in hot weather. Plants grow 1 to 3 feet tall depending on variety, and have many-branched, fleshy stems with light green, centrally veined, 2- to 6-inch leaves and long, pale taproots. As a child I was fascinated by calendula's unusual and varied seeds, some curving and sharply ridged, others ringlike and smooth. Later I learned that this is a textbook example of heterocarpy (bearing different fruits). A half-hardy annual, calendula survives to about 25°F, making it through mild winters in sheltered locations or if protected from hard frost.

Planting information and cultural directions: For best results, give the plants moderately rich soil, ample moisture, and full sun to partial shade. Keep the flowers picked and remove every seed head to prolong blooming. If flower production dwindles, try cutting plants back by half and feeding them with Regular Solution Fish Fertilizer—before long they should look better than ever. Some commercial growers spray the plants with liquid kelp to increase production. Alternatively, make a second sowing one month after you sow or set plants out.

Propagation: Sow calendula seed indoors in February or March, or outdoors March through June. Overwintered seed from autumn sowing also does well, and calendula reseeds freely, often popping up as soon as very cold weather is gone. Seedlings have a pair of 2-inch narrow leaves, tapering toward the stem.

Pests and diseases: Insects sometimes chew the petals of calendula blossoms, but usually the damage is limited to a few flowers and not worth bothering about. Before using flowers for cooking, examine them carefully for tiny insects, which can be washed off easily.

Harvesting and preserving: Cut calendula for bouquets when the flowers have opened fully, preferably in late morning when they are free of dew. Carry a clean bucket filled with warm water, and immerse stems as soon as they are cut to keep them fresh longer.

For culinary or medicinal use, it is most practical to pick the flower heads with their green bracts but with no stem attached. Harvest in the heat of the day when resin content is highest. The bracts are sticky, so you'll want to wash your hands afterward.

To dry calendula, place whole heads in single layers on screens in a warm, airy place or in a dehydrator. Make sure the receptacles (flower centers) are completely dried out before storage, or the entire batch will mold. The outer petals are most desirable for medicinal purposes; you can use the entire dried heads or twist off the petals as needed.

Garden uses: Attractive new cultivars with special flower characteristics and colors as well as a bushy growth habit are now available. At this writing, the Thompson and Morgan catalog lists eleven varieties, including 'Pot Marigold,' the old single-petaled orange variety preferred by many herbalists, along with 'Pink Surprise,' 'Touch of Red,' and compact 'Fiesta Gitana.' Other seed companies offer a 'Pacific Giant Mix' of semidouble flowers in shades of cream, yellow, apricot, and orange, and 'Kablouna,' an elegant cut-flower variety with dense, crested flowers and short quills in yellow, gold, and apricot.

Culinary uses: Calendula has become a popular edible flower, reviving a tradition that dates back at least to the ancient Romans. Its easy cultivation and golden color made it an inexpensive substitute for saffron, and it was used to color and flavor buns, cakes, "drinkes, possets, and pottage." In *The Countrie Farme* (1573), Charles Stevens relates that a traveler to the Netherlands noted, "The yellow leaves of the flowers are dried and kept throughout Dutchland against winter to put into broths, physicall potions and for divers other purposes, in such quantity that in some Grocers or Spicesellers are to be found barels filled with them...."

Use the fresh flowers whole as a garnish, or sprinkle the colorful petals like confetti on salads, desserts, and entrées. Calendula has an affinity with eggs, whether scrambled, poached, or baked in custards. Fresh or dried, the petals are reminiscent of saffron in rice dishes, stews, and fondue.

Crafts and home uses: Calendula is a popular ingredient in cosmetic creams, lotions, skin washes, and soaps. It is gentle enough for babies and for people of any age with sensitive or problem skin. It can help clear up acne and eczema, while its estrogenic and astringent qualities rejuvenate mature skin.

Calendula flowers give fresh bouquets a simple charm. Dried whole, the flower heads brighten potpourris and are especially suitable with citrus mixtures. Chickens fed on calendula blossoms lay eggs with deep golden yolks.

Medicinal uses: Calendula has long been esteemed as a medicinal herb for both internal and external use. There are more than thirty constituents in the fresh flowers, including natural pigments, resins, bitter compounds, saponins (calenduloside), polyenes, alcohols, salicylic acid (aspirin's pain-killing ingredient), and essential oil. Numerous scientific studies confirm the healing properties of calendula flowers, which are gentle and nontoxic.

Calendula's value as a skin herb goes beyond cosmetics, because of its antiseptic, antifungal, astringent, and wound-healing qualities. In the form of a tincture, infusion, salve, cream, or homeopathic remedy, it is therapeutic for burns, scalds, sunburns, bruises, wounds, and slow-healing sores. An effective anti-inflammatory, it brings down swellings of sprains, insect bites, varicose veins, and contusions. It is also used in cases of athlete's foot, and to treat conjunctivitis.

Taken internally, calendula is regarded as a menstrual regulator, relieving cramps and easing menopausal symptoms. It is thought to stimulate the immune system in a subtle way, activating the body's healing mechanisms, and has a traditional reputation as an antitumor agent. These applications are being researched, and have shown some promise.

Catnip

Common names: Catnep, Nep

Latin name: *Nepeta cataria*

Latin and common family names: Labiatae/Lamiaceae (Mint family)

Varieties and cultivars: Lemon catnip, *Nepeta citriodora*; Dwarf catnip, Pink-flowered catnip

Description: Catnip is clearly related to the mints. Its leaves are grayish green, sometimes flecked with white, 2 to 4 inches long, pointed, with notched edges (margins). They are soft to the touch and give off a distinctive musky odor. They are attached in opposite pairs by short stems (petioles) to sturdy square stalks. White flowers shaped like tiny snapdragons form in tight clusters on spear-shaped heads at the tops of the stems. Catnip plants reseed freely, and the small brownish black seeds, each with a tiny white dot, remain viable for several years.

Of course the most intriguing characteristic of this plant is the attraction it holds for the feline species. There is something cat-ivating about its musky aroma, though this is not universally true—some cats ignore it. Some cats like it only fresh or only dried,

but some cats go truly bonkers over the stuff, exhibiting what is called "catnip response."

Planting information and cultural directions: A widely adaptable plant, catnip grows lush in rich soil that is continually moist, while in drier locations plants are smaller and leaves may take on a mauve tinge. In a single season, a catnip plant can grow from a seedling to a stocky plant 3 feet tall and just as big around. Plants prefer full sun or partial shade. The herb does well in pots, which can be moved away from cats as necessary. When sharp frosts hit, catnip plants die back to the ground. Unlike their more vigorous mint relatives, they don't always survive the winter.

Propagation: Sixteenth-century writer Thomas Tusser advised: "If you set it, the cats will eat it / If you sow it, the cats don't know it." In other words, direct seeding the herb is best, because cats may not notice plants grown from seed until their leaves are handled during weeding or harvesting. The seed germinates readily in soil temperatures around 60°F. Sow it thinly in rows 2 feet apart and keep seedlings weeded until they start getting big. You can also start plants indoors (away from cats) in tray packs or recycled tofu containers. It may be necessary to protect the bed with a mesh screen or other arrangement. Catnip self-sows liberally in good, moist soil, though flocks of small birds will harvest most of the seed if you don't gather it before they arrive in late summer.

Year-round care: Plants become straggly after flowering, so cut them back to keep a tidy appearance. Mulch the roots before winter sets in to help them survive cold weather, then remove the mulch in February or March when new leaves begin to appear.

Harvesting and preserving: A single healthy catnip plant will provide plenty of dried material if harvested two or three times during the season. When the flower heads are open, grasp a handful of stems and cut them back almost to the ground. Hang them in bundles of six to eight stems, not too large to interfere with good air circulation. When the leaves are brittle, strip them from the stems, rub them between your palms, and store in catproof glass jars.

Pests and diseases: While cats don't usually appear on lists of garden pests, some frustrated gardeners would certainly put them in this category. People have told me that wherever there is catnip, felines materialize to devour it, roll in it, and otherwise destroy it. I have heard of various methods of foiling felines. You can try sprinkling the perimeter of the plant with ground cayenne pepper, or buying large plants so that there is something left of them after cat orgies. The only surefire way to keep cats out is to put a fence around your catnip plants.

Garden uses: Although your cat or neighbor cats may thwart your intentions, keep in mind that catnip is nonetheless a plant to consider for the garden landscape. There is something restful about the soft gray of its foliage and its pale flowers. Placed toward the back of the border, it blends in well with more showy perennials of medium height. Light pruning enhances its pyramidal shape. Catnip is attractive to bees, but a strong infusion of the leaves sprayed on plants is said to repel flea beetles and ants.

Culinary uses: Before Chinese black tea was available in England, catnip tea was a popular beverage. The leaves are edible and though seldom eaten these days were once favored in salads.

Craft and home uses: Catnip-stuffed toys for kitty, whether simple sachets or more elaborate hand-sewn leather "mice" with tantalizing tails, are always popular items as gifts for cats or their owners.

Medicinal uses: Euphoric for cats, this herb is sedative to humans and promotes sleep. Nepetalactone, the major ingredient in catnip's essential oil, is similar to the valepotriates found in valerian, and has a sedative action on the nervous system. Catnip is also antispasmodic; it calms digestive upsets and dispels gas. Because of its diaphoretic (sweat producing) action, catnip is often recommended as a cold and flu remedy. It is mild and safe enough to use to help children through colds and fevers, insomnia, hyperactivity, diarrhea, and the restlessness of teething. The herb is taken as an infusion or a tincture.

Roman Chamomile

Common names: Chamomile, Camomile, English chamomile, Garden chamomile

Latin name: *Chamaemelum nobile*, formerly *Anthemis nobilis*

Latin and common family names: Compositae/Asteraceae (Daisy family/Aster family)

Varieties and cultivars: Lawn chamomile, *C. n.* var. 'Treneague,' *C. n.* var. 'Flora Pleno'

German Chamomile

Common names: Camomile, Hungarian Chamomile, Scented May weed

Latin names: *Matricaria chamomilla* (currently preferred), *Matricaria recutita*, *Chamomilla recutita*

Latin and common family names: Compositae/Asteraceae (Daisy/Aster family)

Varieties and cultivars: 'Bodegold,' 'Bona'

Related plants: Pineapple weed (Matricaria matricarioides), Scentless May weed (M. maritima)

Description: Roman chamomile is a hardy, low-growing perennial that forms a mat of bright green, feathery leaves. Its daisylike flowers are about 1 inch across, with domed yellow centers surrounded by single or double white petals (ray florets). The flowers are borne singly atop wiry stems 6 to 12 inches tall. Seeds are small and lightweight. The plants spread by creeping rootstocks and rootlets that develop from the lower stems. The entire plant has a distinctive aroma reminiscent of apples. 'Treneague' (also spelled Treanague) or Lawn chamomile is a selected nonblooming perennial variety; 'Flora Pleno' has double flowers.

Similar in appearance, German chamomile is classified as a different genus. Its more plentiful flowers have single, strongly recurved (drooping) petals, thicker leaves, and branching stems about 18 inches tall. Its scent and flavor are sweeter. The scientific names of these two kinds of chamomile have changed several times, resulting in confusion. The easiest way to tell them apart is to slice one of the domed centers (receptacles) in half. German chamomile has hollow receptacles; in Roman chamomile, they are solid. The cultivar 'Bona' has small, sweet blossoms particularly high in the medicinal compounds chamazulene and alpha-bisobolol; 'Bodegold' has the largest blossoms and yields, with a 6 percent average essential oil content.

Two weedy relatives sometimes mistakenly identified as chamomile are pineapple weed (M. matricarioides), a short plant with greenish receptacles and a pineapple scent that grows along or in gravel driveways and in lawns, and scentless May weed (M. maritima), a faintly aromatic plant that is most prolific when grown near the sea.

Planting information and cultural directions: Roman chamomile likes a sunny or partially shaded location and sandy, well-drained, slightly acidic soil. In richer soil, plants put out more lush foliage, but flowers may be fewer. You can prolong the harvest period by sowing seed or transplanting small seedlings as soon as the ground can be worked in spring, since plants go to seed in hot weather. To cover an area or fill in a garden feature, space plants 4 to 6 inches apart. Keep them well weeded, and cut back flowers during the first season to promote spreading. If you leave some of the flowers unharvested, plants will reseed in most soils.

German chamomile produces best in full sun and average soil. Sow or transplant in rows for ease of cultivation and harvesting. Weed by hand while plants are small. As with Roman chamomile, plants reseed freely.

Propagation: Vigorous chamomile plants of both kinds grow from seed sprinkled where it is to grow. Cover seeds lightly or press them into the ground, and keep them watered with a fine spray until they germinate, usually in one to two weeks. Alternatively, sow seed in flats in late February or March and transplant them to the garden when seedlings are about 2 inches tall. Volunteer seedlings can be transplanted from one spot to another while they are 1 to 2 inches tall, but larger plants do not transplant well. Sow Roman chamomile seed between stepping stones for a pretty effect.

After their first year, Roman chamomile plants can be divided with hand pruners or a sharp spade. This is the best way to propagate plants with desirable characteristics such as double petals or no flowers. Rooted pieces as small as 1½ inches will take hold if they receive water consistently. Press or tread them gently into the soil.

Year-round care: It is important to keep weeds from crowding out young chamomile plants. German chamomile plants die after one season.

Pests and diseases: Chamomile is relatively pest- and disease-proof in the garden, though small insects are attracted to the flowers. Take the steps indicated below to prevent damage to dried flowers when preserving them.

Harvesting and preserving: Commercial chamomile operations are mechanized, but for home gardeners patience or a specialized rake is required when hand-harvesting the small flowers in quantity. They are ripe when the centers begin to turn from bright yellow to light brown. Pluck or snip them without stems, and dry them on screens or newspapers at room temperature or in a dehydrator on low heat. Since the flowers do not all ripen at once, spend a few minutes harvesting them every few days, and you will soon have a good supply of primo organic chamomile. Put them in the freezer for a few days to protect them from insect damage. You may wish to let some of the seed heads ripen to ensure a crop of self-sown plants next year.

Garden uses: Roman chamomile forms a ground-hugging mat of bright green that spreads gradually to cover an area. It is lovely between stepping stones or along brick walkways. Mass planting emphasizes the beauty of this herb in flower; one of the finest displays I've seen is at the VanDusen Botanical Garden in Vancouver, British Columbia. German chamomile looks similar to Roman in bloom, but is less compact. Its stems tend to grow leggy and sprawl as the season progresses, so it is less useful as an ornamental plant.

Culinary uses: Chamomile is not generally regarded as a culinary herb. Its popularity as a beverage is due mostly to its calming properties, and it is often blended with peppermint or other herbs, spices, or fruit extracts to enliven its flavor.

Cosmetic uses: A simple infusion of chamomile is often recommended as a hair rinse, particularly for natural blondes. It is said to lighten the hair and bring out highlights. Chamomile is also popular as a skin herb, having soothing, emollient, and protective actions.

Medicinal uses: Centuries before Peter Rabbit drank chamomile tea to calm down after a tough day in the garden, this herb was esteemed for its relaxing, antispasmodic, antiseptic, and anti-inflammatory actions. Herbalists in ancient Egypt, Rome, and Europe were familiar with its beneficial effects, and their experience is validated by extensive modern research. Safe and reliable, chamomile is used today in dozens of products to treat various conditions.

Roman and German chamomile have somewhat similar constituents and actions, and there is long-standing disagreement on which is the "true" chamomile. In Europe, the annual German chamomile is considered medicinally superior, and it does contain more chamazulene, a constituent that is strongly ano-dyne (pain killing), antispasmodic, anti-inflamma-tory, and antiallergic. It is taken internally to relax all states of tension and to relieve dietary distur-bances such as stomachache, dyspepsia, cramps, gas, and bloating, especially when these are linked to emotional upsets. This is the chamomile generally favored in the United States for tea, made by steep-ing 2 teaspoons of the dried herb in 1 cup of boiling water for five to ten minutes.

Roman or English (perennial) chamomile is regarded as "true" chamomile in the British Isles. It possesses many of the same virtues and shares most of the actions as its relative, though to a lesser extent. It is often used externally in lotions, creams, and oint-ments for skin irritations, puffiness and swelling, sprains, wounds, diaper rash, and arthritis.

Aromatherapy: When distilled, German chamomile produces a dark blue oil, high in chamazulene and very expensive. The oil of Roman chamomile is light blue, changing to golden with age. Both oils are val-ued in aromatherapy for their calming, pain-reliev-ing, antiseptic, and digestive properties.

Caution: There is a small incidence of allergy to chamomile. To be on the safe side, do not ingest or use chamomile if you have a ragweed allergy.

Chervil

Common names: French parsley, Gourmet parsley

Latin name: *Anthriscus cerefolium*

Latin and common family names: Umbelliferae/ Apiaceae (Carrot family)

Varieties and cultivars: Flat-leaf chervil, Curled chervil

Description: Chervil is a dainty herb with finely textured, fernlike leaves and a subtle anise flavor, sometimes called French parsley or gourmet parsley. The herbalist Parkinson described it well in 1629: it is "of a pale yellowish greene colour, but when the stalke is growne up to seede, both stalkes and leaves become of a dark red colour: the flowers are white, standing upon scattered or thin spread tufts, which turne into small, long, round, and sharpe pointed seedes of a brownish blacke colour." Like parsley, chervil is an umbelliferous plant with a rounded shape and a single taproot, and may have flat or curly leaves; however, chervil is smaller and more delicate than its relative. Plants grow about 12 to 18 inches tall and 9 to 12 inches across. They are annuals, but their cold toler-ance often allows late-sown plants to overwinter, mimicking the growth cycle of biennials. Chervil closely resembles the wild poison hemlock, so it's important be certain of your plant identification.

Planting information and cultural directions: Fresh chervil is hardly ever available in markets, so if you want to enjoy its delicate flavor reserve space for a few plants in your garden or on your deck. It is easy to grow from seed, tolerates shade, thrives in cool weather, and holds up to cold—in short, it's an excel-lent plant for the Northwest climate. Give it moist yet well-drained soil with abundant humus. Since the plants bolt to seed quickly in hot weather, a place under deciduous trees is ideal for them, providing full sun in winter and partial shade in summer. Chervil is fast growing and has a short life span. For a steady supply of leaves, repeat sowings every few weeks through May, then resume sowing again in September when the weather cools down. If you allow some spring-sown plants to reseed, you'll soon have a second generation of plants that can overwinter and produce a generous harvest the following spring.

Chervil is a fine herb for containers, and is excellent in window boxes, hanging baskets, and containers on a deck. Some commercial cut-herb growers have found that plants grown in pots provide the greatest yield of leaves. Plus, it's easy to move potted chervil plants to full shade to delay bolting in the heat of summer, or to a sheltered spot for winter protection.

Propagation: Chervil seeds should be used when they are as fresh as possible. They are quite cold-hardy and can survive outdoors over the winter, but they require light to germinate. For earliest harvest, start plants indoors in late January or February. Sow the seeds on top of individual pots of moistened potting soil, sift a little peat moss over them, water lightly, and cover with plastic wrap. Remove the wrap as soon as germination takes place, usually seven to ten days. When transplanting, disturb the roots as little as possible.

Outdoors, sow seeds directly in the soil where they are to grow, as early as the ground can be worked. Press them into the soil and make sure they are kept moist. This is easiest to accomplish in early spring, when frequent rains will probably take care of watering. Weed seedlings carefully until they are big enough to compete with weeds—an application of high-nitrogen fertilizer, such as Regular Strength Fish Fertilizer (see Chapter 1) or dried blood meal, will

give them a boost. Some gardeners like to sow chervil thickly and cut the plants back to the ground when they are just 3 to 4 inches tall to stimulate regrowth. Otherwise, gradually thin plants in a row to about 6 inches apart, using the thinnings in the kitchen. If you allow plants to reseed, they can perpetuate themselves for years.

Year-round care: Once a patch of chervil has been established, it will almost take care of itself. Application of a 2-inch layer of compost or composted manure in spring, regular light weeding, and harvesting are about all that really needs doing. Moss may become a problem, particularly in shady spots. This indicates lack of soil fertility and poor aeration; improve the soil by digging in rotted straw or compost. To be sure you have chervil handy in the wintertime, keep a few potted plants in a cool greenhouse, sunroom, or sheltered porch. If you lift them from the garden, try to keep as much soil around the taproots as possible, and expect plants to die back temporarily, even when you are very careful in transplanting. Usually, they will regrow from the roots.

Pests and diseases: Watch out for aphids on your chervil, especially if you are growing plants indoors. Timely spraying with insecticidal soap will usually remedy the problem. In the garden, check the chervil when you are on slug patrol. Tiny white wireworms, the bane of carrot growers, are also said to like chervil, though I have not seen evidence of them in my garden.

Harvesting and preserving: Chervil is ready to harvest within six to eight weeks after sowing, depending on the weather. Snip or pinch stems at the base of the plant, generously while plants are growing quickly and more judiciously when growth slows during cool weather. The herb's delicate flavor diminishes greatly when it is dried, although it is still included in many fines herbes mixtures. Freezing will preserve the flavor best. Gather stems and blanch them in boiling water for one minute, then chill in ice water, pat dry, chop, and freeze according to directions in Chapter 3. Or, purée fresh chervil with a little water in the blender, and freeze in ice cube trays. Transfer the cubes to a glass jar and use within about six months.

Chervil seeds are ready to harvest when their color changes from light to dark brown. Gather them by hand before they start to drop, air-dry them at room temperature for a week or two, and store them away from heat and moisture.

Garden uses: Chervil is very pretty in a window box, planted densely by itself or interplanted with other herbs and flowers. During the winter months, it can be just the thing to fill in those empty spaces in your planters.

Culinary uses: In French cuisine, chervil (*cerefeuil*) holds a place of honor, both for its sweet anise flavor and the beauty of its leaves. Along with chives, parsley, and tarragon, it is one of the four traditional fines herbes, which are used liberally to flavor fish, meats, and vegetables, and are greatly favored for omelets, soufflés, and other egg dishes. It adds something special to carrot soup, leek and potato soup, spinach soup, and potato salad. It is a key ingredient in béarnaise and ravigote sauces, and delicious in a cream sauce served over carrots, potatoes, and other vegetables. Minced or separated into leaflets called *plushes de*

cerefeuil, it makes a lovely garnish for puréed soups, vegetables, and meat platters. It is also an elegant addition to salads, and has the advantage of being available during cooler weather when salad choices tend to be limited. Add chervil during the last few minutes of cooking, or use it uncooked, to preserve its bright green color.

Medicinal uses: Chervil is out of fashion as a medicinal herb, but this was not always so. Pliny declared that it will "comfort the cold stomach of the aged," and Evelyn called it "exceedingly wholesome" and "chearing the spirits." Its Latin name, *cerefolium*, reflects that it was once regarded as a mental stimulant and was thought to have rejuvenating powers. In folk medicine it has been used internally as a digestive and diuretic, and externally as a poultice for rheumatic pains and bruises.

Chives

Common name: Chives

Latin name: *Allium schoenoprasum*

Latin and common family names: Liliaceae (Lily family)

Varieties and cultivars: Common, 'Forsgate,' 'Grolau'

Garlic Chives

Common name: Garlic chives, Oriental chives

Latin name: *Allium tuberosum*

Latin and common family names: Liliaceae (Lily family)

Description: Chives' versatile onion flavor, easy care, neat appearance, and compact growth habit have placed them among herb gardeners' top favorites.

They grow in a clump like miniature green onions, with deep green, tubular leaves a foot high, crowned with globular pink edible flowers in the spring. There are a few named varieties, notably 'Forsgate,' a vigorous grower with showy flowers, and 'Grolau,' which is particularly suitable for forcing indoors in winter. Ripe seed heads are light brown and papery. Left alone, they will drop generous quantities of pure black, sharply angled seeds to reproduce in the garden.

Less well known is their close relative, garlic chives, which have flat, solid leaves and a sweet flavor that hints of garlic. Their star-shaped white blossoms are tinged with green, and bloom in an airy ball on stems that rise about 8 inches above the leaves. The unopened buds are edible, as are the interesting green knobs that hold unripe seed. When ripe, these casings split open to reveal angular black seeds. Garlic chives also reseed freely. Both varieties are frost-hardy perennials.

Planting information and cultural directions: Chives will grow in almost any garden soil, but do best in full sun to partial shade and in a moist soil rich in organic matter. For bumper crops, amend the soil with rotted manure or compost before planting. Weed the plants well as they become established, taking care to keep grasses out. The roots of some grasses look just like chive roots and are difficult to remove, and if even a small piece remains the grass will grow back.

Propagation: Dividing plants is the preferred method of increasing stock. It is as easy as pulling clumps apart and replanting them, and produces good-sized plants in a single season. Alternatively, sow seeds of either kind of chives thickly in a seed tray or flat in March (indoors) or April (outdoors). Once the grasslike seedlings are about 3 inches high and have developed sturdy roots, take a sharp knife and cut 2-inch squares, as you would a cake. Each of these squares will become a clump. Tuck them in the ground, and within a few months they can be harvested. When the plants are three years old, dig them up in spring or fall and divide each one into four plants. It doesn't take long to grow a big chive patch.

Year-round care: Once the plants bloom, the leaves begin to shrivel and turn yellow, so harvest them steadily to forestall flowering. In late fall, the entire plant dies back. This is a fine time to mulch your plants generously with compost or manure to get them off to a flying start in spring.

To extend the harvest season, allow the plants a period of rest after they die back, then dig them up during a mild spell in January or February and bring them into the house or greenhouse. You'll soon have a fresh crop of chives for cutting.

Harvesting and preserving: Cut chives from the bottom, about 2 inches from the ground, to stimulate new growth. If you take just a handful at a time rather than chopping off all the leaves, plants have enough greenery to regenerate quickly.

Fresh chives really are best. You can dry chives in the microwave or in the dehydrator at low heat, but freezing preserves the flavor and texture better. Remove tough flower stems, then chop and spread chives on cookie sheets according to directions in the section on Freezing in Chapter 3.

Pests and diseases: Insect problems with chives

are minimal. Although uncommon, the most serious problem is rust, a fungus that appears as orange spots on the leaves. Dig and burn affected plants, and start over with healthy plants in a different location.

Garden uses: Chives make charming edging plants along paths. Try planting them with lower-growing herbs such as thyme or compact bush basil, with a background screen of taller calendulas, mature sages and lavenders, or scented geraniums behind them. The reedlike form of chives is an interesting counterpoint to the textures of Italian parsley, nasturtium, or rosemary. Although they die back in winter, they also provide early color in the garden when their pink flowers bloom.

Chives and garlic chives are excellent choices for container plantings. One big plant in a gallon pot on the deck might be sufficient; chives are also good companion plants in mixed planter boxes and strawberry pots.

Culinary uses: Chopped chives have myriad uses in the kitchen, since their mild, agreeable flavor goes well with almost anything. They have lots of vitamins A and C, plus iron, calcium, phosphorous, and some of the antibiotic sulfur compounds found in garlic. For best flavor and aroma, use them raw or cook them just enough to heat them through and turn them bright green.

Chives and garlic chives are great in dips and dressings, cream cheese spreads, and herb butters. To avoid a stringy texture, use a knife to chop the chives rather than putting them in the blender or processor. For elegant appetizers, roll a cheese ball or small rounds of fresh goat cheese in freshly minced chives.

Chives also have a special affinity with potatoes, whether new potatoes, potato salad, vichyssoise and other potato soups, or baked or scalloped potatoes. Garlic chives, cut in inch-long pieces, are delicious in stir-fries, pad thai noodles, and spring rolls, and can give salads a refreshing Asian twist.

The mauve flowers of chives and white blossoms of garlic chives are among the best edible flowers. Twist individual florets from their stems and scatter them liberally over salads, soups, and entrées. They also make delicately flavored herbal vinegars.

Craft and home uses: Chive flowers hold their shape and color when dried for everlasting wreaths and bouquets. Harvest them while their color is bright and uniform, to prevent ripe seeds from dropping as they dry. Reach down to the bottom of the stem and snip or break them off, then bunch and hang them upside down.

Cilantro and Coriander

Common names:

Cilantro (leaves and roots): Green coriander, Chinese parsley, Mexican parsley

Coriander (seeds): Dizzycorn

Latin name: *Coriandrum sativum*

Latin and common family names: Umbelliferae/ Apiaceae (Carrot family)

Varieties and cultivars: 'Common,' 'Slowbolt' or 'Slo Bolt,' 'Festival,' 'Jantar,' 'Santo'

Description: A penetrating odor and equally strong flavor characterize cilantro, while its alter ego, coriander, has a subtle pungency. Both an herb and a spice, this is one of the world's earliest flavorings, and it remains an international favorite. Young cilantro leaves are deep green, flat, and rounded with serrated edges, rather like Italian parsley. Seed stalks form quickly, topped by feathery leaves and airy umbels of edible pinkish white flowers with enlarged outer petals. Flowering plants are 1 to 4 feet tall, depending on growing conditions, with a single taproot.

The seeds of cilantro, which form in dense clusters, are technically fruits, and contain two seeds within a thin husk. They are $1/8$ inch in size, round, and ribbed. Green seeds have an intense flavor; they are buff colored when ripe and known as coriander seed.

Cilantro is a fast-growing annual, completing its life cycle within just three months. For years, it was bred to bolt and produce coriander seed quickly. Since the leaves are now appreciated as well, slow-bolting strains such as 'Jantar,' 'Santo,' and 'Slow Bolt' have become available. 'Festival' is an especially early cultivar.

Planting information and cultural directions: Cilantro flourishes throughout the Northwest. Ideal growing conditions are a sunny location, well-fertilized soil with good drainage, and steady watering. Keep the plants weeded, especially when they are small. Mature plants going to seed may need staking to prevent them from falling over.

Cilantro is a good choice for potting up, although its life cycle is short. It can also be grown indoors under plant lights. In pots or planter boxes, sow clusters of seeds. Use the leaves when they are young and prolific.

Thickly sown bands of cilantro, about 4 inches wide, are productive and easily harvested. Single rows waste garden space, and broadcasting seed results in beds that are exasperating to weed. Cilantro will tolerate light frost, and protection with spun-bonded polyester row covers extends the harvest of fresh leaves by at least two weeks.

Propagation: For best results, sow coriander seed about $1/2$ inch deep, directly where it is to grow. Keep the soil moist until germination occurs, usually in two to three weeks. Seedling leaves are narrow and elongated. If you transplant young cilantro plants, be very gentle with the taproots.

Begin sowing in March or early April and continue at three-week intervals for a continuous supply of fresh leaves. Cilantro reseeds freely.

Harvesting and preserving: Harvest cilantro when the plants are 3 to 6 inches tall. Pull them out by the roots, snip the large outer leaves, or use the "cut and come again" method: grasp a handful of plants and cut them back to the ground. Drench them with a Light Fish Fertilizer Solution (see Chapter 1), keep them well watered, and the plants will come back. You can repeat this process four or five times a season as the plants reach harvestable size.

Though assertive, the flavor of fresh cilantro is not easily preserved. When there's no fresh cilantro in my garden, I buy it at the grocery store. I do freeze the leaves as pesto or in salsa. Dried cilantro is not worth using.

Coriander seeds are ready to harvest when they begin to turn the color of toast. Left on the plants too long, they darken and begin to drop. With your fingertips, roll them from the stems into a paper bag or bread pan. Spread them out on screens in a warm place to dry, then shake them in an $1/8$-inch mesh sieve to clean. Use them in cooking or sow them next year.

Pests and diseases: Slugs and insects steer clear of cilantro, and though a roving caterpillar may occasionally take a bite, it's nothing serious. Powdery mildew and fusarium wilt can cause problems if air circulation is inadequate, but generally the plants are disease free.

Culinary uses: The assertive flavor of cilantro (or green coriander) is appreciated worldwide, yet for some people it's an acquired taste. It is *muy necesario* in salsa, albóndigas and cilantro soups, ceviche, and other Mexican specialties. The leaves are a staple flavoring in Southeast Asian dishes such as dipping sauces, Thai mushroom soup, and Vietnamese chicken soup, and the roots are eaten too. In India, the leaves are pounded with spices into fresh chutneys that serve as condiments. Its use is so prevalent in China that it's called Chinese parsley. Fresh cilantro is good with steamed clams, black bean soup, in stir-fries, and in chicken or crab salads.

Coriander seed has a complex flavor that is warm and sweet with a citrus twist. Like other spices, it is best when freshly ground, but be forewarned by the old nickname, Dizzycorn—supposedly, inhaling its aroma can make you dizzy (move over, nitrous oxide). Often roasted before blending, coriander seed adds a mellow sweetness or tempers the fire of chiles in many spice blends with exotic names, including garam masala and the curries of India, tabil and harissa of North Africa, zhug of Yemen, and Ethiopian berbere. For recipes, see *The Complete Book of Spices*, by Jill Norman.

Western cooks traditionally use ground coriander seed in baking and to flavor lamb, pork, and other meats. Try adding ½ teaspoon or more to your favorite recipe for spice cakes, gingerbread, or pineapple upside-down cake. Whole seed is used for pickling cucumbers and meats, or distilled for an oil that flavors gin and vermouth.

Garden uses: The scalloped, deep green leaves of compact young plants add texture to container plantings, and the delicate laciness of the pinkish flowers fills in gaps in the garden, but the effect in both cases is short-lived. Because of its fast life cycle, cilantro is probably best grown in annual beds and replaced by other plants later in the season.

Craft and home uses: Coriander seeds are used in dry and simmer-type potpourri.

Medicinal uses: Coriander seed has long been regarded as an aromatic stimulant. It was an ingredient in a famous cordial, which also included lemon peel, nutmeg, cloves, cinnamon, angelica root, and spirits of wine. Currently, coriander is considered to stimulate digestive juices, reduce spasms, and dispel gas. It is often combined with strong-tasting herbal laxatives to improve the flavor and ease cramps.

Aromatherapy: Colorless coriander seed oil has a woodsy, spicy fragrance. It contains 55 to 75 percent coriandrol, carvone, anethol, geraniol, and other components. The essential oil lends a warm note to perfumes including Chanel No. 5, Le Jardin d'Amour, and Coriandre. Medicinally, it is used in pharmaceutical digestive preparations, and it shows promise as an antiviral, antifungal, and larvicidal agent.

Comfrey

Common names: Knit-bone, Bruisewort, Healing herb

Latin names: *Symphytum officinale, S.* x *uplandicum* var. *'variegatum,' S. caucasicum*

Latin and common family names: Boraginacae (Borage family)

Varieties: Common comfrey, Russian comfrey, Variegated comfrey

Description: In established comfrey plants, a neat cluster of sharply pointed leaves emerges in early spring and grows rapidly to a clump about 3 feet in height and circumference. The long, pointed leaves often reach 1½ feet in length, and are covered with short, scratchy hairs. Hollow, branching flower stems develop with leaves that grow progressively smaller toward the top. The stems end in curled spirals of double buds that open into diminutive bell-shaped blossoms, usually lavender, which hang downward on twin stalks. Clusters of four seeds develop in tiny cups, as with comfrey's relative, borage. The entire plant smells like fresh cucumbers. The plant soon loses its compact appearance and sprawls inelegantly unless cut back to the ground, stimulating the growth process to begin anew. Comfrey roots are thick, fleshy, and many-branching. They are chocolate brown on the outside and creamy white on the inside, with a brittle texture and fresh aroma.

Planting information and cultural direction: For those who do not believe they can succeed in growing herbs, comfrey is the ultimate confidence builder. It adapts to sun or shade, soils that are rich or poor, acid or alkaline, and any temperature the Northwest delivers; it is insect resistant and truly awesome in its persistence. It reaches its maximum size in rich, well-drained soils and partial shade, and only in drought conditions or extremely poor soil will it fail to thrive. Choose its location carefully, because once in place comfrey is almost always there to stay. To control this prolific plant, grow it in a contained area. For a comfrey row or patch, space plants about 3 feet apart. P.S.: *Never* rototill a comfrey plant!

Propagation: Comfrey is extremely easy to propagate by root cuttings or division of the crowns. A piece of root the size of a peanut will take hold and flourish—in fact, attempts to move or eradicate comfrey usually result in frustration because you end up with more plants instead of fewer. For the greatest number of plants from a limited supply of roots, dig the roots at any time of year and cut them into pieces 1 inch in diameter or larger. Plant them horizontally 3 to 6 inches deep, keep them watered, and within a month or so small plants will develop. Larger plants are produced by using a sharp spade to slice the crown of an established plant into smaller clumps about 5 inches in diameter. Don't worry if you cut some of the roots. Keep the clumps watered and stand back. It is possible to start comfrey from seed, but more difficult and therefore seldom attempted.

Year-round care: Little care is required for comfrey plants. To keep them compact, cut back the entire plant to the ground two to five times each season as necessary.

Pests and diseases: I can't think of a thing that bothers comfrey.

Harvesting and preserving: For fresh use, pick

comfrey leaves or dig the roots as needed. To dry the leaves, harvest while they are young and bright green, not yellowing. Cut out the thick midrib and slice the leaves crosswise, then arrange on trays and dry at 110°F until brittle. Alternatively, dry in the microwave. Dig the roots in early spring or late autumn when the leaves have died back and the plants' medicinal constituents are concentrated. Scrub, slice ¼-inch thick, and dry at 110°F. Make sure the roots are completely dehydrated before storing them in glass jars, and keep them away from heat and light.

Garden uses: Unusual varieties of comfrey that feature red or blue flowers or variegated leaves are said to be smaller and more manageable than common comfrey, which is seldom considered ornamental. Comfrey's long, pointed leaves can add interesting texture or simply blend in with other plants, but since it can become invasive, is so difficult to remove, and dies back in winter, it is best to plant it in an out-of-the way place rather than in a flower or vegetable garden.

Comfrey can play an important role in compost making. The considerable leaf mass of a mature comfrey plant, cut several times in a season, can add plenty of high-nitrogen green material to the pile. In addition, the leaves contain calcium, phosphorous, potassium, and trace minerals drawn deep from the subsoil. Just be very sure that there are no ripe seeds, and that no pieces of root are attached to the base of any comfrey leaves that go into the compost pile.

Comfrey leaves are an ingredient in some compost-starter kits. Submerged in water for about two weeks, they dissolve into a high-potassium "tea" or liquid fertilizer that gives plants a quickly absorbed boost.

Culinary uses: Comfrey is not recommended as a culinary herb. In the folk tradition, the leaves were boiled as greens and used to make a tea with demulcent and restorative properties, but controversy in the 1970s centering around the presence of pyrrolizidine alkaloids in comfrey has made most people cautious about ingesting comfrey in any form. Also, young digitalis leaves, which are toxic, can be mistaken for young comfrey leaves with disastrous results.

Medicinal uses: As knit-bone, comfrey has been valued for centuries as a folk remedy to speed the healing of broken bones, sprains, bruises, wounds, and skin problems. Studies show that this is due to the presence of allantoin, a cell proliferant that speeds healing by promoting cell division, and rosmarinic acid, an anti-inflammatory. Allantoin is present in all parts of the plant, but is most concentrated in the roots. Roots and leaves also contain tannins, which have an astringent effect, and soothing mucilage.

Enthusiasm for comfrey as a medicinal and fodder plant peaked in the late 1970s, before Japanese researchers found that rats placed on a diet high in comfrey developed liver cancer. The controversy that erupted continues to this day. Comfrey came under closer scientific scrutiny, and it was found that the problem centers around the liver-toxic pyrrolizidine alkaloids (PAs) present in comfrey roots (and to a lesser extent the leaves). The possibilities of problems developing after long-term ingestion are now better understood. However, it is good to know that fresh roots have about ten times more PAs than fresh leaves, and that leaves picked early in the season contain much higher concentrations than mature leaves in autumn. Also, according to one study, water extracts of comfrey leaves actually decreased tumor growth and increased survival time in cancer patients.

Currently, many herbalists feel that thousands of years of use are enough to establish the safety of this herb when taken internally in moderation. Others believe that internal use should be avoided completely. It is generally agreed that there are no problems with comfrey for external use. Because allantoin is very effective in healing skin problems, from minor cuts and scrapes to sore nipples and slow-healing sores, it is an ingredient in many salves and ointments. It is not recommended for deep wounds, lest the surface heal over quickly when infection remains at a deeper level. In my own experience, comfrey-leaf poultices and baths were very soothing after childbirth, and my torn skin healed very quickly. For more information, consult *Comfrey: Fodder, Food and Remedy* by Lawrence D. Hills, and S. Foster, "Comfrey: a Fading Romance."

▌Dandelion

Common names: Lion's tooth, Piss-in-bed, Devil's milk bucket

Latin name: *Taraxacum officinale* (formerly *Leontodon taraxacum*)

Latin and common family names: Compositae/ Asteracae (Daisy/Aster family)

Varieties and cultivars: 'Ameliore'

Description: Dandelions are so ubiquitous in lawns, waysides, and gardens that almost anyone can recognize them. Surprisingly, there are hundreds of natural variations of this common plant. Moreover, dandelions are sometimes confused with look-alike false dandelions, which are unrelated and have dissimilar constituents.

Dandelion's brilliant yellow flowers, actually made up of tiny tubular florets, appear on leafless hollow stems. After blooming, the flowers close up, then reopen as a "round downy blowbal" (to quote the sixteenth-century herbalist Gerard) with parasols that carry the seeds skyward. Deeply notched, pointed leaves give this herb its name, *dent de leon* (tooth of the lion), although leaves vary in shape, some being quite smooth at the edges. They are 6 to 12 inches long, shiny, and completely hairless (even the back of the midrib) and radiate outward from the root. In the 1885 classic *The Vegetable Garden*, Mme. Vilmorin-Andrieux describes selected cultivars including Moss Leaved, Cabbaging, and Very Early dandelions. A modern French variety, 'Ameliore,' has been selected for improved quality. There are also red, frilly, or slow-bolting "dandelions" from Italy, where bitter plants are highly regarded, although many of these are variations of chicory (*Cichorium intybus*).

Dandelion roots are long, cylindrical, and brittle. They are dark on the outside and whitish inside, and, as any gardener knows, difficult to remove once established. All parts of the plant exude a bitter, milky latex when cut. Dandelions draw minerals from many soil layers into their deep roots, which also loosen and aerate the soil. Dandelion haters sometimes take extreme measures to kill this tenacious plant.

Planting information and cultural directions: Throughout the Northwest, dandelions grow wild for the picking, making it unnecessary to expend any effort cultivating them. They like full sun, but exist in the most inhospitable soils and situations, including cracks in the sidewalk. Plants with leaves up to 12 inches long and plump, juicy roots are produced in the richer, moister soils of vacant lots and meadows. Keep an eye out for a good patch of large dandelions in an unpolluted environment, where you can harvest all you like when the time is right.

Growing dandelions on purpose makes sense if you really like them or plan to market them. By cultivating them in optimal conditions, you are assured of an abundant crop of leaves and large, straight roots. When planted at the same time, they mature together, which facilitates harvesting in quantity. Just don't let them go to seed, and be sure to dig out the entire root or you will definitely be growing dandelions again! Choose a sunny spot with fertile soil and enrich it with potassium by working in greensand or wood ash. Sow the seeds in March or April about an inch apart and 1/2 inch deep. Thin plants to 6 inches apart and keep them weeded (why does this sound like a contradiction in terms?). Leaves will be ready to harvest by late summer, roots in spring or fall of their second year.

Propagation: As evidenced by its wide distribution, dandelion is a remarkably successful plant. Not only can the airborne seeds travel up to 5 miles, but any piece of the root left in the ground will also grow into a new plant. Even plants dug out of the ground and left to die can draw enough energy from their roots to bloom and produce ripe seed. To grow large plants, buy improved seed through a mail-order catalog or larger nursery and follow the directions above.

Year-round care: Blanched dandelion leaves are a gourmet item that can replace costly Belgian endive as a winter salad ingredient. The simplest way to blanch the leaves is to gather them together and cover them with a bucket or large coffee can when winter approaches. Weigh it down with a rock or brick and wait. Deprived of light, the leaves lack chlorophyll and become creamy white, tender, and relatively mild in flavor. You can also dig up the roots, bring them into a shed or cellar, and keep them dark, as you would when forcing endive. Harvest the tender leaves as they sprout.

Pests and diseases: Known as an all-season bee plant, dandelion is a boon to honeybees and a host of other harmless insects that feed on the sweet nectar of its flowers. Fresh dandelion seems to be invulnerable to pests and diseases, but the dried, unroasted root is attractive to various insects in storage.

Harvesting and preserving: Unblanched dandelion leaves are mildest when eaten while young and tender, before the flower buds develop. Cut the whole plant at the base, or hand pick the tenderest inner leaves. Wash well. You can dry the leaves or blanch and freeze them, but they are better fresh and are available most of the year. Or make an alcohol or vinegar extract of the leaves to preserve their healthful qualities in a convenient form.

Because of dandelion roots' brittleness and proclivity to resprout from root fragments, they must be dug with care to avoid breakage. This is easiest when the soil is damp. Using a trowel or spade, dig downward slowly and patiently until you can lift out the entire root. The medicinal properties of the roots vary depending on the season, so the correct time for harvesting is determined by their intended use. The best months to harvest them for use as a liver and digestive tonic are October or November, when the tops are dwindling and the roots are plump with a rich store of inulin (a carbohydrate that breaks down into fructose without requiring insulin) and other nutrients. By spring, the roots are slimmer and contain little inulin but high concentrations of taraxacin and other water-soluble bitter principles that promote healthy function of the urinary system. Harvest them before plants begin flowering.

To dry dandelion roots, harvest them as directed, wash them gently, and lay them on screens in a warm place. Remove top growth if you wish, keeping in mind that it is important not to break or cut the roots, which would allow the sap to leak out. After about two weeks, the dried roots should be brittle enough to snap when bent. Store them in tins or glass jars, but check them regularly for insect damage and use them within about six months.

For many herbalists, an alcohol extract of fresh dandelion-root tincture is the preferred method of preserving the active principles of the root. This is because the inulin contained in fresh roots is soluble in alcohol, while in dried roots it has solidified and is soluble only in hot water. Dig the roots as directed, wash them gently, and pack them with or without their tops in a clean glass jar. Cover them with 100 proof vodka, label clearly, and allow to steep for six weeks before using.

Dandelion "coffee" is a dark, pleasantly bitter brew rich in minerals and inulin. To prepare it, scrub fall-harvested dandelion roots, cut the tops off just above the crowns, and air-dry the roots for a few days. Chop them in ½-inch pieces, spread them on a baking sheet, and roast at 250°F until dark and brittle. Stored in dark glass, they will keep for years. Grind them in a coffee mill and simmer for 10 to 15 minutes before drinking.

Culinary uses: In a salad of early spring greens, tender dandelion leaves are as chic as they are healthful. I can testify that a person can come to appreciate the bitter flavor, but for the unconvinced, chop the leaves fine and they won't even be noticed. Books on herbs, wild edibles, salad greens, and even general cookbooks offer many recipes for cooking with dandelions, which aid digestion of fatty foods. Dr. Peter Gail's fascinating booklet, *On the Trail of the Yellow Flowered Earth Nail—A Dandelion Sampler,* features more than seventy recipes, including Dandelions in Buttermilk Gravy, Pâté of Leafy Greens, Ciccoria Fagioli, Blanched Dandelion Crowns au Gratin, Dandelion Flower Fritters, and even Dandelion Meringue Pie! Traditional beverages include Dandelion Stout, Dandelion Fizz, Dandelion Cordial, and delicate Dandelion Wine.

Medicinal uses: The respect dandelion has earned from herbalists outweighs the contempt in which this plant is generally held. More than one herb company has chosen this plant as its emblem, the gold flowers perhaps symbolic of the riches it offers. Its Latin name is probably derived from *taraxos* (disorder) and *akos* (remedy)—that is, the Official Remedy for

Disorders. The plant is high in vitamins A, B, C, and D; potassium; iron; calcium; magnesium; and phosphorous. It also contains protein, fiber, pectin, bitter principles that stimulate the liver, and inulin. It is the plant's combination of high nutritive values with powerful medicinal constituents that makes it such a revered herb.

By the 1600s, European herbalists were using dandelion as a liver restorative and diuretic. Similarly, country wisdom has long prescribed dandelion leaves and roots as a spring tonic to cleanse the body of toxins accumulated over the sedentary winter months. Modern research shows that the bitter principles activate the taste buds, which in turn stimulate the liver, a crucial organ that filters toxins and purifies the blood; the herb also stimulates bile production and helps to keep the entire digestive system in good working order. Studies indicate that dandelion is helpful even in serious liver conditions, supporting its use around the world as one of the best herbs for repairing liver damage. It is also thought to have a beneficial effect on acne, eczemalike skin problems, and rheumatic conditions because it breaks down acids and impurities stored in the muscles and blood. It is nontoxic, safe even in large doses, and can be taken over a long period.

Dandelion greens are among the top four leafy vegetables in overall nutritional value according to the United States Department of Agriculture. They are also known for their strongly diuretic effect, and are excellent for treating urinary problems and fluid retention of all sorts while restoring potassium lost through increased urination. Their French nickname,

Pissenlit (piss-in-bed), is a cautionary description of the effects of eating dandelions before bedtime.

Dill

Common names: Dill

Latin name: *Anethum graveolens*

Latin and common family names: Umbelliferae/ Apiaceae (Carrot family)

Varieties and cultivars: 'Bouquet,' 'Long Island Mammoth,' 'Vierling,' 'Dukat' or 'Tetra,' 'Fernleaf,' and others

Description: Dill is an attractive annual herb with feathery, bluish green leaves, and umbels of tiny yellow flowers. The bases of the leaves clasp the hollow stems. Dill grows from a single taproot to a height of about 18 inches, and in fertile soil can reach 4 feet. Bunches of stalks topped with plump, bright green, unripe seeds are often seen in grocery stores in late summer when cucumbers are ripe. As dill seed ripens it turns brown, ridged, and flat. It is ready to harvest about three months after germination.

'Bouquet,' 'Long Island Mammoth,' and 'Vierling' are tall varieties that produce large umbels of green seed for pickling. 'Dukat' (also called 'Tetra') and 'Fernleaf' are extra-leafy dwarf types for fresh-cut dill weed or baby dill leaves. They are good choices for growing in containers.

Planting information and cultural directions: Choose a sunny location out of the wind with a fairly rich, moist soil. Keep the young plants weeded and watered, and that's about all it takes for success.

Propagation: Sow dill seed directly where it is to grow (or transplant carefully). I scatter the seed thickly in bands 4 inches wide, which results in nice stands of baby dill that are much easier to weed and harvest than broadcasted seed. Seed germinates in seven to twenty-one days. Two long, narrow seedling leaves are followed by feathery true leaves.

If pickling dill is your object, timing your planting to have it when cucumbers are ripe can be a gamble. The best insurance is to keep sowing every three weeks from late March or early April through June. Seed germinates poorly during hot weather. Keep harvesting baby dill, leaving some plants to mature, and you will get it right. Or, sow dill in rows 10 inches apart and thin to allow 4- to 6-inch spacing between plants.

For extended harvests of baby dill, make sowings through late August and blanket them with spun-bonded polyester row covers as the weather cools. Late plantings can survive light frosts. Dill reseeds abundantly in the garden.

Pests and diseases: In my experience, aphids are the only insects to attack dill. Insecticidal soap is a good organic control, or, if the problem is not severe, simply wash the cut dill well before using it.

Harvesting and preserving: To harvest baby dill, cut the entire plant to the ground using scissors or hand pruners. If your plants were sown in bands, you can cut a handful with one snip. Drench the cut row with Regular Fish Solution Fertilizer, keep it watered, and within weeks a second cutting will be ready. Or, allow a few plants, spaced 4 to 6 inches apart, to remain until mature. You can pick large individual leaves from the stalks as needed. For pickling dill, cut the seed heads when they are large, green, and

plump. Harvest ripe seed heads when they flatten and turn brown and the stems are drying out.

My favorite way to preserve dill is to lay the green seed heads on a baking sheet, freeze them, then rub the seeds off and transfer them to glass jars. They are very pungent and are easy to use in any recipe that calls for fresh dill. Alternatively, dry chopped dill leaves in a dehydrator at 90°F for bright green dill weed, or freeze chopped leaves.

Garden uses: As an annual, dill's place in the garden is temporary, yet its lively color, strong vertical lines, and shapely seed heads make it quite ornamental. Consider it as a backdrop for other plants in a border, for adding height to groupings in planters, or as a quick-growing foliage plant that has an excellent filling or softening effect.

Craft and home uses: Dried dill seed heads are attractive woven into herbal wreaths, garlic braids, and other decorations for the home. The dried leaves and essential oil are included in relaxing blends for herbal sleep pillows.

Culinary uses: Dill is one of the most widely used culinary herbs. Most people are familiar with its flavor—dill pickles have been an American standby since the days of the pickle barrel at the old general store. Yet baby dill (fresh young dill leaves), dill weed (dried young leaves), pickling dill (green seed), and dill seed (ripe seed) each have a distinct flavor.

Baby dill is most delicate, and it is delicious with many vegetables, including fresh cucumbers, beets, green beans, carrots, cauliflower, potatoes, and peas. It's also good in vinaigrette or creamy dill dressings for coleslaw and potato salads. Dill is often paired with salmon or other fish, in a cucumber-dill sauce, yogurt sauce, or dill aïoli. It is a great favorite in Eastern European and Scandinavian countries. My cousin Cilla served a beautiful appetizer at her New Year's Day feast in Norway: a slice of gravlax on buttered white bread, topped with a sprig of perfectly fresh dill. Baby dill should be used fresh or added toward the end of cooking time, since its flavorful essential oil is very volatile. For this reason, dried dill weed has less flavor than fresh baby dill, although it makes an adequate substitute.

Crisp cucumber pickles, Dilly Beans (see recipe in Chapter 4), and pickled asparagus are enhanced by two or three heads of pickling dill packed in each jar. Fresh or frozen green dill seeds have a concentrated fresh-dill flavor. Green seeds, along with fresh leaves, are great in herbal vinegars and butters. I freeze the seeds, then chop them coarsely for use in winter potato salads, tomato soup and borscht, and cooked vegetable dishes.

The high carvone content in dill seed gives it a strong flavor similar to caraway. It is used in pickling spice mixtures, sauerkraut, mustards, and breads.

Medicinal uses: The word *dill* is thought to derive from the Norse word *dilla*, meaning to lull. The use of dill seeds as a mild sedative, digestive, and carminative herb was recorded by ancient writers and is still prevalent in folk herbalism. According to Galen, the second-century Greek physician, "Dill procureth sleep." Insomniacs may find relief from a cup of tea made by steeping 1 to 2 teaspoons of dill seed in a cup of water taken at bedtime. The *Physicians' Desk Reference for Herbal Medicine* recommends dill seed to prevent and treat disorders of the gastrointestinal tract, kidney and urinary tract, spasms, and sleep disorders. Chewing the seeds is said to cure stomachaches, dispel gas, and sweeten the breath. Currently, there is scientific interest in dill as a cancer preventive, since plants high in essential oils may help to eliminate carcinogens from the system.

Aromatherapy: The essential oil distilled from dill seed contains carvone, limonene, phellandrene, eugenol, pinene, coumarins, and other substances. Oil from the leaves is of similar composition, but with a lower carvone content. The oil is considered to be bactericidal, as well as being responsible for the various medicinal effects of the plant. "Gripe water," made by adding 2 to 4 drops of dill essential oil to $\frac{1}{4}$ cup of water, is a standard remedy for colic in babies.

Echinacea

Common names: Coneflower, Purple coneflower, American coneflower

Latin name: *Echinacea purpurea* (formerly *Brauneria purpurea* and *Rudbeckia purpurea*)

Latin and common family names: Compositae (Daisy family)

Varieties and cultivars: 'White Swan,' 'Bright Star,' and others

Related species: *E. angustifolia, E. pallida, E. paradoxa* var. *paradoxa*, and others

Description: *Echinacea purpurea*, the purple coneflower, is both a highly decorative perennial and one of the most popular medicinal herbs. Seldom is such beauty combined with such powerful healing properties. Its showy flowers have a central raised disk or "cone" composed of vibrant orange quills and tiny florets arranged in a spiral pattern, which is encircled by drooping mauve petals. Stems are dark, stiff, branching, and rise 2 to 4 feet above a mound of leaves. The leaves are long, oval at the base and narrowly pointed at the tips, lightly hairy with notched edges, and decrease in size up the stem. The roots are white inside and dark outside, fleshy, and somewhat tangled. A native of the midwestern prairies, this rugged plant tolerates drought and temperature extremes and will grow in all parts of the Northwest. The tops die down each winter, but plants can live for many years.

E. angustifolia, sometimes called "narrow leaved purple coneflower," is the smallest of the other echinacea species at 6 to 20 inches tall. Its disk florets are purplish brown; stems are purple-green. *E. pallida*, the "pale purple coneflower," has long, narrow leaves with smooth edges; the flowers have sharply drooping petals in pink, purple, or white. It grows 16 to 36 inches tall. *E. paradoxa* var. *paradoxa* is a rare species that has yellow petals and smooth stems and leaves.

In the wild, *Echinacea purpurea* and *E. angustifolia* often cross, producing a variety of plant forms. Plant breeders have produced beautiful varieties with white petals, 6-inch flowers, and other ornamental characteristics.

Planting information and cultural directions: In its native habitat, purple coneflower grows in rocky, dry soils and open meadows or woodlands. It adapts to a variety of soils and conditions, generally preferring full sun and good drainage. Plants do fine in average to dry soil but grow big and lush with ample water and rich soil. This herb is a great choice for large planters. For best results, plant in a mixture of sand, humus, and peat. Water deeply and infrequently, preferably before leaves begin to droop.

Propagation: The easiest way to start echinacea is from small plants, increasingly available at herb farms and garden shops. After about three years, you can divide the roots of established plants in spring or fall. Be gentle as you separate young plants from the crowns, and wait a couple of years before taking more divisions. Starting echinacea from seed is a little tricky, but for the uncommon species, it is sometimes the only option. In nature, echinacea seeds lie frozen during the winter and germinate in spring while the ground is moist and cold. You can simulate the conditions that signal the seed to break dormancy by stratifying (chilling) them.

Try this tip from Mark Wheeler of Pacific Botanicals in Grants Pass, Oregon, one of the region's premier growers of medicinal herbs. In late autumn, sow rows of seed in flats of sterilized potting soil. Press seeds into the soil and sift a little peat moss over them. Water well, then leave the flats outdoors where they will be exposed to the elements but safe from animals. A cold frame is ideal for this. Check on them periodically, and in early spring you will see the seedlings with their pointed tips and two rounded leaves poking out of the soil.

An alternative is to sow seeds in moist sand (in a handy recycled tofu container, perhaps) as directed above. Put a plastic bag around the container, seal it up, and refrigerate it. If your refrigerator looks like mine, a bag or two of sand toward the back of one of the lower shelves will hardly be noticed. Check occasionally to see whether any seeds have sprouted. After one to three months, place the container in a warm, well-lighted place and keep it watered. Germination should occur in about three weeks.

Year-round care: Echinacea plants are low maintenance. Top dress in April and May for the best flower displays. Keep plants weeded and water them on a regular basis or whenever they begin to look dry. Cut back spent flower stalks unless you want to harvest your own echinacea seeds or leave them for the birds.

Pests and diseases: Slugs are the greatest threat to echinacea plants. They devour seedlings and chew down tender shoots that emerge from the crowns in spring. If not controlled, they can exhaust the plants beyond recovery. Inspect the plants in cool mornings, evenings, or wet weather, and get rid of any slugs you find.

Harvesting and preserving: Harvest the aerial parts of the plant—stems, leaves, and flowers—for teas and tinctures when the plants are in full bloom. Dig roots in late autumn, after the seeds have ripened, for maximum levels of medicinal constituents. Scrub roots well, chop or split them lengthwise, and air-dry them. Harvest seeds when they look black and dry. Rub them out of the cone, dry on newspapers for a week or two, and store in a dry place out of direct sunlight.

Garden uses: One of the loveliest ornamentals in the herbal world, purple coneflower merits inclusion in large and small gardens alike. Its foliage has a neat,

fountainlike habit, and the tall flowers with their orange centers, pink petals, and green foliage provide contrasts that command attention. City gardeners can grow echinacea successfully in planters, ornamental borders, and planting strips. It is seen increasingly in park plantings, attesting to its beauty and durability. The plants combine well with cosmos, lilies, late-blooming lavenders, and ornamental grasses. Where more room is available, echinacea is striking massed in drifts. Approaching Trout Lake Herb Farm in southern Washington, you cross a charming covered bridge and proceed along a driveway lined with echinacea, then encounter fields of it, which in full bloom is truly a spectacular sight.

Medicinal uses: Echinacea is one of the most popular medicinal herbs worldwide, and among the most intensively researched. In clinical trials it has been shown to stimulate the immune system and help the body to resist disease, fight infection, and heal wounds. It is nonspecific and nontoxic, making it safe and effective for treating many illnesses and conditions. Echinacea appears to work in several ways to boost the body's resistance to bacterial activity. Primarily, the herb stimulates production of white blood cells (leucocytes, lymphocytes, and phagocytes), which destroy bacteria, viruses, and possibly tumor cells as well. Clinical studies in Europe and the United States have proven echinacea's benefits, but researchers have yet to pinpoint exactly how and why the herb is so effective.

In the United States, echinacea has become well known as an herb to take at the first symptoms of a cold or flu. Its ability to prevent the illness entirely or mitigate its effects and speed recovery is generally recognized, though controversy over its effectiveness erupts periodically. The herb's immunity-enhancing properties have also gained attention as a subject of research for AIDS, rheumatoid arthritis, and other diseases of the immune system. These uses sometimes overshadow echinacea's other healing properties. It is a powerful remedy for all kinds of bacterial and viral infections, including staph, strep, and the herpes virus, and is effective as a "blood purifier" in cases of acne, boils, abscesses, and the like. In Europe it is available in creams, ointments, and lotions that are applied to cold sores, swellings and inflammations, septic sores, and wounds that are slow to heal. The tincture or decoction (tea) is used as a mouthwash for gum diseases.

All species of echinacea have generally similar actions and effects. *Echinacea purpurea* is the only species grown on a commercial scale; wild stands of other species may be endangered. In the United States, echinacea is most commonly available in tincture or tablet form. Good-quality tincture makes your mouth tingle.

▌Elder

Common names: Elder, Elderberry

Latin name:

Coast red elderberry: *S. callicarpa* (or *S. racemosa callicarpa*), and others

Blue elderberry: *Sambucus caerulea*

American elderberry or North American sweet elder: *S. canadensis*

Black elderberry: *S. melanocarpa*

Related species: European elder, *S. nigra*

Varieties: 'Madonna,' 'Yellow Variegated,' 'Guincho Purple', 'Johns,' 'York'

Latin and common family names: Caprifoliaceae (Honeysuckle family)

Description: Elder has a long, long history as a culinary, medicinal, and cosmetic herb and a reputation as a powerful, even magical plant. Although the folklore surrounding it usually refers to the European elder (*S. nigra*), many of the species native to the Northwest have similar attributes and uses.

The blue elderberry, *S. caerulea*, grows wild throughout the region in all except the coldest climatic zones. It is a deciduous perennial shrub, usually 10 to 20 feet tall but sometimes growing up to 40 feet, depending on conditions. Leaves are large, graceful, and similar in shape to walnut leaves. They are opposite, 6 to 9 inches long, each having five to nine pointed leaflets with serrated edges; the stems are hollow. In June or July, the plant is covered with a froth of tiny, star-shaped blossoms in flat-topped clusters (cymes) which the sixteenth-century herbalist Gerard described as "spoky rundles." These ripen in September or October into hanging bunches of round, purple, juicy berrylike fruits dusted with a waxy white substance that gives them a powder blue appearance. The three to five stones inside the berries each contain one seed. The black elderberry (*S. melanocarpa*) is the variety most common east of the Cascades; it is generally shrubby to 6 feet, with shiny black berries. The coast red elderberry, *S. callicarpa*, has small, pyramidal flower clusters that appear in late spring. Its bright red berries ripen in midsummer.

Named fruiting hybrids of American elderberry (*S. canadensis*) include 'York' and 'Johns,' which have sweet, large, tasty berries and form compact ornamental shrubs 6 to 10 feet tall. Two *canadensis* varieties are required for pollination.

Planting information and cultural directions: Elder trees are often seen growing wild by the roadside, especially at the outer edge of the woods, along ravines, or near streams and other moist places. They adapt well to any situation with partial shade and a moderately rich, well-drained soil. Starts dug from the wild or cultivars from a nursery are best planted in early spring or late fall.

Propagation: Patience is required for starting elder from seed, and germination can be erratic. Collect ripe fruit in autumn and mash it in a bowl. Fill the bowl with water and separate the seeds, which float, from the pulp. Rinse the seeds and drain them in a sieve. Make a special nursery bed and mark out rows about 1 inch deep and 6 inches apart. Sow seeds about 2 inches apart and fill in the furrow with compost. Mark the location carefully, since germination may take more than a year. Elder is more often propagated by taking 12-inch-long hardwood cuttings in late autumn (see Chapter 1), which can be planted out about one year later. It may also be possible to dig suckers that sprout from the tree's roots.

Year-round care: Since elder thrives in the wild, it obviously requires little care. If you have plenty of room, just let it grow. To maintain an elder as a reasonably sized shrub rather than a tree, grow it in a drier location or prune it back in March each year. Keep in mind that severe pruning will limit the shrub's flowering and fruiting.

Harvesting and preserving: Pick elderflower clusters when most of the blossoms are newly opened and spread them on trays or hang them in a warm location to dry quickly. Many of the flowers will fall off in the process; rub the rest off the stems when thoroughly dried and store the flowers in glass containers. Dried elder blossoms are very tiny and light cream to tan colored.

Harvest blue or black elderberries when they are dark blue with a white coating; coast elderberries should be bright red. Wash them gently and drain them on old towels. As with the flowers, dry the berries on the stems and separate them later, or pick them off the stems and preserve them in one of the preparations suggested below.

Garden uses: With their shapely leaves and plentiful berries, elder trees have a lush, almost tropical look. They are suitable for separating garden "rooms," for planting on large islands, as a screen or windbreak, or for the back of the garden. In Britain, elder is often planted in hedges, though superstitious gardeners are reluctant to cut or burn the tree lest it bring bad luck. There are ornamental varieties of *S. nigra*, including 'Madonna' with lime green and yellow variegated leaves, 'Yellow Variegated' with cream variegation on a dark background, and 'Guincho Purple,' which has leaves that turn reddish purple in the summer and red in the fall. All of these are about 8 feet tall and produce fruit if two varieties are planted for pollination. See Resources for sources of elder varieties.

Culinary uses: When people relied heavily on the

produce of their locale rather than imported foods, the culinary possibilities of elderflowers and elderberries were greatly appreciated. Maude Grieve, author of *A Modern Herbal*, says, "Elder Flowers, with their subtle sweet scent, entered into much delicate cookery, in olden days. Formerly the creamy blossoms were beaten up in the batter of flannel cakes and muffins, to which they gave a more delicate texture. They were also boiled in gruel as a fever-drink, and were added to the posset of the Christening feast." Elderflowers add a light muscat flavor to tea, sorbet, vinegar, and wine. They are charming sprinkled on fresh strawberries, applesauce, and other desserts. For sweet elder-blossom fritters, the entire heads are dipped in a light batter and deep fried. Elder Presse is a pleasant, lightly carbonated beverage flavored with elderflowers, produced in Canada, and available in specialty grocery stores.

With the berries of elder even more than the flowers, there is an overlap between culinary and medicinal uses. Delicious elderberry jams, jellies, and conserves are not so different from the robs (sweetened syrups) and unsweetened syrups used medicinally; all taste great on toast or pancakes, a fine example of phytocuisine. The berries are also used in pies, chutney, cordials, and wine. Elderberry juice is increasingly available in grocery stores.

Caution: Red elderberries should never be eaten uncooked; eating too many blue or black elderberries raw can cause allergic reactions or diarrhea.

Craft and home uses: When general use of elder was more prevalent, various parts of the plant were used. A light blue to lavender dye can be made from elderberries with an alum mordant, while a chrome mordant with the berries yields a purple dye. With the soft pith removed, elder wood was used to fashion popguns, flutes, and a stringed instrument called a *sambuca*, which gave the plant its Latin name.

Elder is regarded as an excellent skin herb. Elderflower water, made by infusing fresh or dried flowers in pure water or witch hazel extract, is mildly astringent and emollient, and traditionally used to tone the skin and clear up problems from acne to sunburn. Elderflower skin creams soothe chapped or mature skin, and may also help to heal psoriasis and eczema.

Medicinal uses: *The Anatomie of the Elder*, written by Dr. Martin Blockwich in 1644, testifies to elder's former stature as a medicinal plant. Every part of the plant was used, including the bark and leaves—both of which are violent purgatives. Elder's current popularity is largely the result of work by Dr. Madeleine Mumcuoglu of Jerusalem, Israel. Elderflowers contain an essential oil, vitamin C, and flavonoids including rutin, quercetin, and kaempherol. They have a diaphoretic action, promoting sweating and elimination of toxins through the pores, and they are decongestant, helping to break up and disperse mucus. Their relaxing qualities promote restful sleep, and are especially helpful with fussy children who are starting to get sick.

Besides tasting good, elderberries contain the same flavonoids as the flowers, and have the same diaphoretic and decongestant properties, plus diuretic and laxative actions. They equal rose hips and black currants as excellent sources of vitamin C, and also contain vitamins A and B. Dr. Mumcuoglu's scientific research, cited by Steven Foster in *Herbal Renaissance*, corroborates the traditional use of elderberries for symptoms of cold and flu, suggesting that flavonoids in the herb prevent the viruses from entering cells. Elderberry juice, syrups, and robs can be taken to prevent colds and flu; if you get sick, try 1 teaspoon of the dried fruit simmered in a cup of water, three to five times a day. Elder tinctures and extracts are widely available under the brand name Sambucus. Follow package directions for use. (Note: Anise-flavored Sambuca liqueur is not related.)

There is some evidence that the anthrocyanic pigments, which give the berries their color, improve eyesight and eye health, and also stabilize collagen, thus helping to prevent osteoporosis.

Fennel

Common names: Common fennel

Latin name: *Foeniculum vulgare*

Latin and common family names: Umbelliferae/Apiaceae (Carrot family)

Varieties and cultivars: Copper or bronze fennel, *F.* var. *rubrum*; Florence fennel, *F.* var. *Azoricum*

Description: With its feathery green leaves and branched seed heads, common fennel looks like oversize dill. Although they are related, fennel is a hardy perennial that is easily distinguished from dill by the sweet anise flavor present in all parts of the plant. Its finely cut leaves can reach 2 feet in length. They unfold gradually from sheaths that clasp the stalks. Glossy and bright in spring, the leaves lose their shine, growing dark over the season. Stems are succulent when young and become hollow with age. A seed stalk gradually rises up to 8 feet from the middle of the plant and produces umbels of small yellow flowers attractive to bees. Ripe seeds are about ⅛ inch long, greenish gray, ribbed, and oval. In the coldest areas of the Northwest or in deep shade, seeds ripen poorly. Fennel's large white taproots grow into sizable clumps by producing offsets. Plants die back to the ground in winter but reappear in early spring and can live for many years. Copper or bronze fennel is slightly more frost tolerant than common fennel and has dark reddish leaves with glints of copper. Florence fennel or finocchio, an annual relative grown for the tasty bulbous base of its stems, requires a long, warm growing season.

Planting information and cultural directions: A tough survivor, fennel is often found growing along roadsides or in vacant lots. Given enough sun, the herb will grow almost anywhere, but it does best in a fertile, fairly moist yet well-drained soil. Since the plants are hardy to −10°F, winter protection is seldom necessary, but be sure the roots are not in standing water. Fertilizer is seldom needed. To keep plants producing tender leaves, cut them back to the ground when they begin going to seed and water them well once or twice a week.

Propagation: Start fennel from seed sown in spring or fall, from small plants, or from root divisions. Large plants do not transplant well, especially in dry weather. This herb reseeds freely. The tiny seedlings have two long narrow leaves at first, then develop more characteristic feathery leaves and quickly grow to sizable plants.

Year-round care: To prevent an overabundance of

fennel plants in your garden, harvest *all* the seeds. Then cut back woody stems to the ground for a neat winter appearance. Divide the roots every three years in early spring or fall. Don't wait until they are really big, or it will be a really big task.

Pests and diseases: Aphids are fond of fennel, especially copper fennel. Usually, thorough washing before using the leaves is enough to remove bugs, but if not, insecticidal soap spray is an efficient control. If you find a horned green monstrosity munching on your fennel, it's probably the caterpillar of a beautiful swallowtail butterfly, so just let it be.

Harvesting and preserving: Young fennel leaves just emerging from their sheaths are tender and delicious—pick them fresh throughout the season. Seeds ripen unevenly, a few heads at a time. Cut heads of green seeds and dry them upside down in bunches for ornamental uses. Harvest ripe seeds when they turn light brown, before they start dropping. Spread seed heads on screens or hang them in bunches over a cloth or inside a paper bag for about two weeks, then rub off the seeds and store them in an airtight container.

Garden uses: Although it grows large, fennel makes a handsome backdrop in a perennial border or herb garden, and is also effective as a screen. Children love its licorice-stick flavor, so plant it near their play areas or in their own gardens. Ornamentally, copper fennel, with its burnished leaves, makes a dramatic contrast to gray plants such as dusty miller, 'Silver King' artemisia, cardoon, globe thistle, and artichoke, or white flowers such as Florentine iris (orris root plant). Copper fennel is also luscious with pale pink, apricot, or white roses, and it blends beautifully with other burgundy-colored plants including purple basils, shiso or beefsteak herb *(Perilla frutescens)*, bearded iris, and Japanese maples.

Culinary uses: Fennel has been a culinary herb for more than 2,000 years, and an element in Italian cuisine since the ancient Romans served young fennel shoots as a vegetable. It is used to flavor pork and other fatty meats, and adds interest to salads. In France, fennel leaves are traditionally wrapped around or stuffed inside oily fish before baking or grilling. The chopped leaves also flavor sauces for fish.

The seeds are more strongly flavored than the leaves, and have a sweet aftertaste. Nibble them straight from the garden while they are green and at their best. They perk up Italian sausage, spaghetti sauce, and fruit salads, and are combined with savory, thyme, and other herbs in French herbes de Provence. Fennel seeds are among the spices in chai, the steaming, milky tea of India. Sugared or toasted, they are served after meals as an aromatic breath freshener and aid to digestion.

Craft and home uses: Grayish green fennel seed heads are attractive and sturdy additions to herb wreaths, garlic braids, and everlasting bouquets. Due to their high oil content, they make aromatic firestarters that burn as hot and fast as pitch.

Medicinal uses: Fennel has a long tradition of medicinal use. Interestingly, the herb has enjoyed a long-standing reputation as a weight-loss aid with the ability to allay hunger pains. Historical references to this date back to the ancient Greeks. In *Nature's Paradise* (1650), William Coles wrote, "both the seeds, leaves, and root of our Garden Fennel are much used in drinks and broths for those that are grown fat, to abate their unwieldiness and cause them to grow more gaunt and lank." The herb's diuretic and fat-digestion-enhancing qualities have been established, but there is no modern research to back up the weight-loss claims. Still, a fennel tea diet might be worth a try! As noted in The *Physicians' Desk Reference for Herbal Medicine*, diabetics must check the sugar content before ingesting fennel.

Like dill, coriander, and other aromatic seeds, fennel is a carminative, digestive, and antispasmodic, and is often made into a mild tea to soothe colicky babies. It is also diuretic and taken for liver and gall-bladder problems. As Nicholas Culpeper wrote in 1666: "Fennel expels wind, provokes urine, and eases the pains of the stone, and helps to break it."

Fennel is often added to cough drops and syrups for its soothing, mildly expectorant effect. It is also thought to be beneficial to the eyes and eyesight.

Aromatherapy: The oil distilled from fennel herb and seed has similar constituents, chiefly anethole, which also characterizes anise seed. Known as "codex" fennel oil, it is used in cough preparations, carminative waters, and laxatives. It imparts a sweet, pleasant scent to room sprays and cosmetic products.

Feverfew

Common names: Featherfew, Featherfoil

Latin name: *Tanacetum parthenium*, also *Chrysanthemum parthenium* (formerly *Pyrethrum parthenium*, *Matricaria parthenoides*)

Latin and common family names: Compositae/Asteraceae (Daisy/Aster family)

Varieties and cultivars: 'Aureum,' Golden feverfew, Double feverfew

Description: Feverfew is unique in appearance and medicinal qualities, yet it has been classified botanically with chrysanthemum, chamomile, pyrethrum, and (currently) tansy. A hardy perennial that grows 1 to 4 feet tall depending on conditions, it has traits in common with all these plants. It is similar in growth habit to tansy, with straight, stiff, alternately branched stems that end in clusters of composite flowers that look like chamomile or button chrysanthemums. The yellow disk florets in the center have almost flat receptacles, unlike chamomile, and are surrounded by a ruff of short white petals. Bright green, sharply divided leaves emerge in early spring, and have a spicy aroma reminiscent of chrysanthemums. The wiry roots often put out rootlets. Seed is tiny, light colored, and plentiful. Variations include an all-yellow variety, a double variety that looks almost completely white, and 'Aureum,' a variety with single white flowers and yellow-gold leaves.

Planting information and cultural directions: Feverfew is a hardy, widely adaptable herb. Its drought tolerance earns it a place in a xeroscape garden, where it grows short and stocky. Given more moisture it is tall and luxuriant. Plants prefer full sun but also grow well in partial shade. Almost any well-drained soil is suitable for feverfew. The herb can also be grown indoors year-round in a cool, well-lit location.

Propagation: Although I never planted feverfew it popped up in my gardens at Silver Bay, compliments of a low-flying bird, I suppose. It also took care of its own propagation, self-sowing everywhere. In spring, a green carpet of seedlings emerged around feverfew mother plants.

If birds and mother plants do not oblige, sprinkle tiny feverfew seeds onto moistened sterile mix, press them in lightly, cover with plastic wrap, and water from the bottom. At 70°F, they will germinate in about two weeks. Feverfew can also be propagated from softwood heel cuttings. Mature plants can be divided in early spring or fall: cut apart sections of root, bury them shallowly, and keep them moist until they become established.

Year-round care: Feverfew plants are definitely easy care—in fact my maintenance regime for this herb consists mainly of tearing out plants growing where I don't want them. Beyond that, you may wish to thin volunteer seedlings to about 1 foot apart or transplant them to a location of choice while they are still small. The disintegrating seed heads are not very attractive, so cut flower stems back at the end of the season unless you want to encourage self-sowing.

Pests and diseases: Pungent feverfew deters insects and pests of every kind, probably because it contains pyrethrins. These substances are also found in pyrethrum (*Tanacetum cinerriifolium*), the herbal insecticide that kills many insects by paralysis but is nontoxic to mammals. Feverfew plants also seem to be untroubled by disease.

Harvesting and preserving: To dry feverfew flowers for everlasting arrangements, cut entire plants near the base when they are in full bloom, preferably on a sunny day. Fasten bunches of five or six stems with rubber bands and hang them in a warm, dark, airy place for about two weeks. Store them away from light and moisture.

Harvest the leaves for medicinal use any time. They are most potent just before the plants come into bloom. Follow the procedure described above for drying. Alternatively, strip the leaves from the stems and lay them in a dehydrator set at about 110°F. To freeze feverfew leaves, blanch them in boiling water for 1 minute, pat them dry, strip them from the stems, and follow general directions for freezing herbs in Chapter 3. Feverfew can also be preserved as a tincture.

Garden uses: Feverfew is especially suited to informal cottage gardens where serendipitous self-seeding does not upset a color scheme or strict design plan. In my rose garden, a sea of feverfew appeared unbidden as the understory layer, giving a very pretty effect. In an herbal or perennial border, highlights of white feverfew blossoms provide a unifying element.

Culinary uses: Feverfew is too bitter for culinary use.

Craft and home uses: Feverfew's abundant blossoms begin as early as May in warm areas, and continue for months. It makes a fine cut flower, nicely filling in holes and brightening up bouquets. With red bee balm and blue delphiniums, it's perfect in Fourth of July arrangements. The strong-smelling dried leaves are sometimes included in moth repellent mixtures.

Medicinal uses: In the late 1980s, feverfew became a high-profile herb after the publication of scientific studies showing that it can reduce the frequency and severity of migraine headaches more consistently than the leading prescription medicines. Until then it was a fairly obscure folk remedy despite a history as a medicine for allaying fevers, menstrual irregularities, stomach problems, and headaches that dates back 2,000 years to the first-century Greek physician Dioscorides. John Hill asserted in *The Family Herbal* of 1772, "In the worst headache this herb exceeds whatever else is known." Old-time herbalists usually recommended external application of this strongly bitter herb, binding it on the head or wrists.

In *The Illustrated Encyclopedia of Herbs*, Kathi Keville reports that E. S. Johnson and others at the City of London Migraine Clinic investigated its popular use as a migraine remedy. They found that for 70 percent of migraine sufferers who took feverfew, the herb consistently reduced migraine frequency and/or pain and nausea. Taken for at least four months, feverfew seems to work in several ways to prevent inflammation and constriction of the blood vessels of the brain. It is thought to inhibit the formation of inflammatory substances at the cellular level and is also a relaxant, easing smooth muscle spasms that may trigger migraines. Whatever the exact mechanisms, subsequent controlled studies at the London Migraine Clinic and at Nottingham University documented a clear association between feverfew and migraine relief. Feverfew's 70 percent success rate compares with 50 percent for conventional migraine drugs. So what's changed since 1772?

Feverfew is made up of at least thirty-nine constituents, including sesquiterpene lactones, volatile oils, tannins, bitter resins, and pyrethrin. Parthenolide, possibly with other sesquiterpenes, is regarded as the most active migraine-preventing constituent. Frozen, freeze-dried, and air-dried leaves are equally effective. The various botanical forms of feverfew, whether single, double, or yellow, seem to have equal effect, although the amounts of particular constituents vary among plants. Commercially available medications contain standardized amounts, which vary among manufacturers.

Feverfew's name derives from *febrifuge*, meaning fever-reducing. The herb's effectiveness in bringing down fevers, alleviating menstrual and premenstrual headaches, and reducing chronic inflammation is now being studied, with important implications for arthritis. Comparisons with aspirin, which is often taken for these symptoms, suggest that feverfew may actually work better for reducing fevers and controlling inflammation, and it does not interfere with blood clotting. The herb's other traditionally valued properties as a bitter digestive stimulant, antihistamine, uterine and menstrual regulator, relaxant, and insect repellent have not yet been extensively researched. Perhaps someday feverfew's potential as a botanical medicine will be fully realized.

Cautions: Some people develop sores or swelling in the mouth after eating feverfew for extended periods. This can be prevented by putting the leaves between slices of bread, or in gelatin capsules, before ingestion. Pregnant women should avoid feverfew because it acts as a uterine stimulant.

▌Garlic

Common names: Garlic, Stinking lily
Latin names: *Allium sativum, A. s.* var. *ophioscorodon*
Latin and common family names: Liliaceae (Lily family)

Varieties and cultivars:

A. sativum: 'California Early,' 'Silverskin,' 'Artichoke,' 'Italian Purple'

A. sativum var. *ophioscorodon:* 'Rocambole,' 'Spanish Roja,' 'Korean Red,' many more

Related plant: Elephant garlic, *A. ampeloprasum*

Description: Garlic is grown for its compound bulb or head of four to twenty-four cloves (technically, these are swollen leaves or fleshy scales), which develop at the base of the leaves, enclosed in a thin white or reddish sheath or skin. A short, thick cluster of roots is attached. Four or more flat, ribbed, lance-shaped leaves up to 12 inches long rise from the base of an upright, unbranched stalk (spathe). Rows of garlic in my gardens have been mistaken for daffodils or corn. Depending on variety and conditions, the stalk may wither away or produce a globe of small clove-like bulbils, or a globe of white or greenish flowers and angular black seeds. It may also be straight, curved, or coiled. Garlic is a perennial that requires a period of rest while the new cloves begin to form.

Essentially there are two types of garlic—hard neck and soft neck—and within these categories there are many varieties with various flavors, sizes, keeping qualities, and other characteristics. Soft-neck (*sativum*) varieties can be braided; hard-neck types (*ophioscorodon*, or ophio) form tough, unwieldy stems. Popular soft-neck varieties include 'California Early,' 'Silverskin,' and 'Italian Purple.' Hard-neck varieties include 'Rocambole,' 'Spanish Roja,' 'Korean Red,' and others. Elephant garlic, a different species, is gigantic, mild flavored, and a superlative keeper.

Planting information and cultural directions:

Garlic needs full sun and well-drained soil with plenty of nutrients. Although it takes several months to mature it doesn't require much space, so you can tuck it in among your flowers and vegetables or plant it densely in beds. Prepare the area by digging in compost, aged manure, or other organic material, plus All-Purpose Fertilizer Mix (see Chapter 1). Plant the cloves plump side down, about 1 inch deep and 4 inches apart. Mulch the entire planting with a 4- to 6-inch layer of straw or alfalfa hay to keep weeds down. For container gardening, follow the same general directions, omitting the mulch. It's a good idea to rotate garlic in the garden, growing it in a different place each year.

Propagation: Garlic can be propagated from seeds, bulbils that form at the base of the plant, or, most commonly, from cloves. Cloves grow biggest when planted in October through December, though they can be planted as late as March. Garlic will not freeze out in the Northwest, but it can rot with poor drainage. Young plants are often available in the spring at nurseries and farmers' markets.

Year-round care: Beginning in May, water your garlic to keep it from drying out. Pull or hoe weeds and keep applying mulch. For highest yields, break off the stalks before flower heads form. Quit watering as soon as the leaves begin to wither and turn yellow, usually in mid-July or August, to keep the sheaths from splitting. Plants are ready to harvest when they are about half yellowed, before they die down completely.

Pests and diseases: Garlic is so repellent to aphids, cabbage moths, slugs, and other pests that preparations made from it have long been used as insecticides (see Garlic Pepper Spray recipe, page 79). However, it is vulnerable to mold and fungus diseases. Gray or botrytis mold appears at harvest time after too much water late in the season. It can also be caused by cutting the garlic tops before proper curing. Infection begins with a leaf blight, moves into the neck of the bulb (which looks water soaked), then gray mold develops, turns the neck black, and destroys the entire bulb. Very ugly. To prevent gray mold, avoid overwatering late in the season and cure the bulbs well (see Harvesting and preserving, below).

Another serious disease, called white rot, has ravaged garlic plantings in recent years. The leaves of diseased plants decay at the base, turn yellow, and topple over. Gray or blackish filaments of rot appear in the neck and bulb, roots rot, and the plant can be pulled up easily. Destroy all affected cloves, clean up garlic plant litter from the garden, and avoid planting garlic or any other alliums in affected areas for up to ten years. To prevent this disease from getting your garlic, grow only certified stock. Your local County Extension Office can help you find sources and identify garlic diseases.

Harvesting and preserving: Dig garlic with a garden fork or spade on a dry day, taking care not to injure the bulbs. Remove dirt from around the bulb by stripping off the outer leaves down to the base. Clip off the roots if you wish. Lay the plants out or hang them in bunches of six to ten in a dry garage, shed, or basement, away from hot sun, rain, and dew. Turn them every few days and check to make sure no mold forms. After two to four weeks of curing, the cloves should feel hard and their skins papery. Bunch or braid them while the leaves are still pliant but damp, or simply remove the tops and store the heads in a mesh bag in a warm, dry area with good air circulation. If the cloves begin to sprout in spring, you can peel and freeze them in glass jars with tight lids.

Craft and home uses: Garlic braids are decorative as well as useful. Some people never eat the garlic but just hang the braids up for show. Outwardly they look great for years because the skins hold their shape perfectly, hiding the shrivelled cloves inside. See page 79 for garlic braid-making instructions.

Culinary uses: Volumes have been written on the gustatory pleasures of garlic, and festivals are dedicated to enjoying them. Its uses in the kitchen are endless. Raw, it is almost mandatory in green salads, whether a clove is used to discreetly rub the bowl or more is added flagrantly to herb vinegars and salad dressings. Because its taste mellows when cooked, garlic enhances the flavors of almost any savory dish. (Heat destroys the sulfur compounds that make garlic hot and odiferous.) It is sumptuous baked and spread on crusty French bread. Greek skordalia, Spanish sopa de ajo (garlic soup), French aïoli (garlic sauce), and the famous Thai Chicken with Fifty Cloves of Garlic are delicious garlicky offerings from the world's cuisines. Finish off a garlic-rich repast by chewing a few sprigs of parsley or mint, both high-chlorophyll breath fresheners.

Medicinal uses: Consider yourself lucky if you love garlic, because this versatile bulb is a bona fide medicinal herb as well as a kitchen staple. Its ability to promote health and kill disease organisms has been the focus of literally thousands of scientific studies during the past century. Its benefits have been recognized far longer. It has been part of the Chinese materia medica since 2000 B.C.; in ancient Greece it was called *theriac* or "heal all," and the first-century herbalist Charaka of India declared that it would be worth its weight in gold if it weren't for the smell.

That smell, by the way, is caused by the interaction of sulfur compounds in garlic's straw-colored essential oil, and does not exist until a garlic clove is cut or bruised. The garlic enzyme allinase reacts with the amino acid alliin to form allicin, and there's that smell again. Garlic breath is a result of allicin, converted into diallyl disulfide (an antibacterial compound), being excreted via the lungs. Many researchers believe that allicin is the most active healing component in garlic, but ajoene or other sulfur compounds vie for the credit. There may well be other therapeutic agents among this herb's 200 other constituents. Certainly it is nutritious, supplying vitamins A, B complex, and C; calcium; zinc; magnesium; potassium; phosphorous; iron; folic acid; and several amino acids.

Garlic ranks high on the list of important medicinal herbs because of its remarkable range of healing attributes. Eaten regularly as a basic part of the diet, it acts to build up the system, enhance immunity, and maintain general health. It also helps protect against some of the major diseases of our time.

▦ Promotes Heart Health

Garlic can prevent or slow the onset of heart disease, still the Western nations' number-one killer (33 percent), in several ways. Studies consistently show that it lowers artery-clogging LDL cholesterol and triglyc-

erides in the blood while increasing plaque-reducing HDL cholesterol. Thanks to its ajoene content, it is as effective as aspirin in preventing atherosclerosis by preventing platelets from building up inside blood vessel walls. This blood-thinning activity also reduces blood clots, protecting against stroke. Garlic also lowers blood pressure, an important factor in hypertension and heart disease.

▦ Natural Antibiotic

Garlic is one of nature's most potent broad-based antibiotics. The *Physicians' Desk Reference for Herbal Medicine* says flat out that garlic's antibacterial, antifungal, and lipid-lowering effects are proven. What's more, the herb destroys organisms that have become resistant to more narrowly focused pharmaceuticals, having the ability to kill or inhibit the growth of at least eight types of antibiotic-resistant bacteria, including several strains of staphylococcus. It is more effective against *Candida albicans* (the organisms causing yeast infections and thrush) than gentian violet and six other reputed antifungal drugs. And, unlike many prescription antibiotics, garlic actually enhances friendly intestinal flora while destroying pathogens.

▦ Benefits the Liver and Digestive System

Eating small amounts of garlic regularly protects the liver and aids the digestive system in general. Increased dosage successfully treats severe digestive disorders, such as gastroenteritis, intestinal bacterial infections, amoebic dysentery, and internal parasites.

▦ Enhances Immune System

Garlic's traditional use in treating respiratory infections and other lung ailments is also validated by scientific evidence. Its immune-system-enhancing effects help prevent colds and flu. Many people swear that chewing two or three garlic cloves at the first signs of a cold will stop it—well, cold. Researchers have noted success in treating established colds, coughs, bronchitis, and flu.

■ Cancer

In case that's not enough to convince you to eat garlic, this wonder herb has also been linked to cancer prevention and antitumor activity. At least nine epidemiological studies show that garlic decreases the incidence of cancer among those who consume it regularly. Its ability to dramatically activate natural killer (NK) cells seems to be a factor in this.

■ Other Claims

In folk medicine, garlic is also used to treat sinus congestion, fevers, asthma, whooping cough, diarrhea, hepatitis, earache, and many other ailments. The juice is put on warts, plantar warts, acne, and slow-healing sores. More research is needed to confirm these and other common uses of garlic.

■ Dosage

Traditionally garlic is taken as whole or mashed cloves eaten raw, mixed with honey, or added to cooked foods just before serving. It is also made into tea, syrup, oil, tincture, juice, and poultices. As a preventive medicine, the German government-sponsored Commission E recommends 4 grams a day, the equivalent of one large clove. For acute conditions, the dose is three to six crushed cloves. However, the social side effects of this regime do give one pause.

There are various commercial preparations that eliminate garlic breath, including garlic-oil capsules and deodorized garlic. Some preparations have allicin as the primary ingredient; some are based on other sulfur compounds. In addition to the lively controversy over which of garlic's constituents are most active, there is disagreement about which form is the most therapeutic. Some say the deodorized products are less effective; others claim that only enteric-coated capsules can shield allicin from destruction by stomach acids so it will pass into the system through the small intestine. If you opt to take commercial garlic products, you will probably want something standardized to 6 percent allicin per 100 mg, which should deliver a little more than the Commission E recommendation.

It will probably be years before all the controversy about garlic is resolved, and fresh discoveries may raise new questions. Meanwhile, I'll just keep things simple and take my garlic as people have done for the past 5,000 years: raw or cooked as part of my diet. Before trying it for serious conditions, I'll seek the guidance of a health-care provider, and that's my advice to you, too.

■ Hops

Latin name: *Humulus lupulis*

Latin and common family name: Cannabaceae (Hemp family)

Varieties and cultivars: 'Cascade,' 'Willamette,' 'Tettnanger,' 'Nugget,' 'Saaz,' 'Aureus' or 'Golden,' others

Description: Like Jack's fantastic beanstalk, hops grow quickly, with vigorous twining vines. They can easily reach 25 feet in height during a season. The stalks are slender but resilient and prickly, covered along their length with leaves and ending in curling tendrils. Leaves are dark green and deeply lobed and notched, resembling grape leaves. In female plants, small yellow starburst flowers are gradually transformed into clusters of *strobiles*, which have a papery texture and are shaped much like Douglas-fir cones. Their bracts and the tiny, bright yellow glands at their base contain the essential oil and bitter resins that give hops their flavor, aroma, and medicinal qualities. Small male flowers appear on separate plants that are not required for pollination. The tough, cold-hardy roots grow in a thick mass. Hundreds of tons of hops are produced annually in the Northwest; for a fascinating historical excursion, visit the murals and Hop Museum in Toppenish, Washington.

Planting information and cultural directions: Hops are adaptable enough to flourish in the hot eastern counties of the Northwest as well as the coastal region, and have been grown commercially on both sides of the mountains. They do best in a rich soil with ample moisture, in full sun or partial shade. Adequate support is a must, be it a trellis, pole, wall, or building. Commercially, hops are trained up tall poles and along huge cages with "ceilings" of wire mesh. Once established, a hop vine will outcompete almost any weed, growing larger as the years go by. Without support, hops grow along the ground in a big sprawling mound.

Propagation: Divide hop roots in early spring when new shoots are first emerging. Using a sharp spade, dig at the edge of the clump to expose the rhizomes. Look for pieces of root that have shoots less than 6 inches high and adequate rootlets, and separate these from the parent plant with sharp hand pruners. Plant where desired or in pots to recover from transplanting shock. Hops are also propagated by cuttings taken in midsummer or, rarely, from seed.

Year-round care: Ordinarily, home gardeners do not need to fuss over hops. Remove old stems from the base of your plants in late winter, and scratch a cup of fish meal or 2 inches of compost or rotted manure into the crowns if the soil is poor. As plants grow, tie or clip back errant vines that may threaten to carry off your lawn furniture. After heavy frosts kill back the vines, pull them down and compost them.

Pests and diseases: Aphids can be a problem with hops; if they arrive in droves, spray the plants every three days with insecticidal soap until the infestation is under control. Be sure to spray the underside of the leaves. One year my hops had such severe and recurring attacks of aphids that I had to tear down the plants, but that was after an exceptionally mild winter.

Hops are also susceptible to downy mildew, a fungus disease that diminishes yields and is devastating the Washington hop industry at present. Spray affected plants with a solution of ¾ teaspoon baking soda per quart of water.

Harvesting and preserving: Hop strobiles are ripe when their color changes from bright green to golden green. To preserve the maximum medicinal constituents and the best flavor for beer making, harvest the strobiles by hand and freeze them in glass jars. Pack them down well, since they are bulky yet lightweight. For pillows and the like, spread the strobiles out on racks to air-dry in a warm place indoors, or dry them carefully in the oven at the very lowest setting with the door slightly ajar. Store in airtight glass jars. When grown commercially, vines laden with ripe strobiles are cut and hauled by the truckload to separating plants. A drive through the back roads of the Yakima Valley in September is fun and a memorable experience.

Garden uses: Hops are an excellent plant for covering an arbor or gazebo, creating a shady bower, or camouflaging an unsightly feature with a wall of green. They do grow huge and may require clipping. The strobiles hang down prettily and are a natural topic of conversation, as well as a great backdrop for photos. A vine of Golden hops (*H. l. 'Aureus'*) is highly ornamental, with pale foliage and a less vigorous habit.

Culinary uses: The resinous flavor, intense bitterness, and preservative properties of hops have made this the preferred herb in beer making for centuries. Microbrew aficionados and home-brewing equipment suppliers can describe in detail the nuances of flavor imparted to beer by particular varieties. There is a tremendous commercial demand for hops; tour any good-sized brewery and you will be impressed by the quantities involved.

Young and tender hop stems (called bines), cut when they first emerge, can be steamed and eaten as a vegetable like asparagus. The strobiles are too bitter to be enjoyed as a seasoning on their own, but once made into beer they are used in recipes for anything from breads to baked beans to batter for fish and chips.

Craft and home uses: Fresh hop vines are delightful as decorations for garden parties, weddings, and other festive occasions. Their flexible stems can be tied with twine or ribbons to festoon doorways, arbors, and gazebos. Their graceful draping curves look like herbal bunting and provide a big effect with little effort. Lay smaller vines along the center of a long table, then tuck in statice and other fresh flowers for a simple yet elegant centerpiece.

Medicinal uses: The medicinal constituents of hops are contained in the strobiles and concentrated in the sticky golden powder called lupulin found at the base of the bracts. Other constituents include a volatile oil that contains more than a hundred substances, including antiseptic bitter resins, estrogenlike components, and gamma-linoleic acid (GLA). The volatile oil in hops has sedative and muscle-relaxing qualities, while the bitter principles have a salutary effect on the liver and digestive system. Because of these attributes, hops are listed in the *British Herbal Pharmacopoeia* as a specific remedy for restlessness with nervous headaches and digestive problems. A neighbor friend of mine, however, tried drinking hop tea and decided that he preferred his chronic insomnia! It is possible to mitigate the bitterness of hops by taking them in tincture or capsule form.

The estrogenic compounds and GLA in hops are believed to regulate menstrual cycles, ease cramps, and alleviate various problems associated with menopause. These compounds may also contribute to the long-standing reputation of hop baths and cosmetic creams that are said to rejuvenate and smooth the skin.

Horseradish

Common name: Horseradish

Latin name: *Armoracia rusticana* (formerly *A. lapathifolia, Cochlearia armoracia*)

Latin and common family names: Cruciferae (Mustard family)

Related plant: Wasabi, or Japanese horseradish, Japanese hot mustard (*Wasabia japonica*)

Description: Horseradish is a big perennial with long, penetrating roots that have been used for centuries as a medicine and condiment. The roots are yellowish outside and white inside, tapering downward to 2 feet with side shoots. They have a pungent aroma and a hot flavor when cut or bruised. The large, shiny leaves grow about 2 feet tall and 5 inches across on long stems from a basal cluster. They are deep green and coarse, wavy, and irregular at the margins. After the first year, clusters of small flowers with four white petals bloom in midsummer on stems that rise above the leaves. Seed is usually barren. The leafy tops die down in the winter, but early in spring the pointed, maroon-tinged leaves emerge from the crown and gradually unfurl. Plants are at their best for two to three years; after that the roots become increasingly tough and bitter.

Planting information and cultural directions: The object in growing horseradish is to produce thick, straight roots, and for this you need a deep, moist soil free of rocks and hardpan, in a sunny or partially shaded site. Horseradish plants are invasive, so keep them out of your main garden or contain them within it. For primo roots, excavate a hole 3 feet deep and 3 feet wide, loosen the soil, remove large rocks, and add compost, rotted manure, or other materials rich in humus, along with some wood ash or greensand for phosphorous. Avoid fresh manure, as this will cause the roots to fork. In February or March, set out cuttings, crown divisions, or a start from your favorite herb farm, spacing plants 10 inches apart.

Gardeners have devised special ways to grow straight horseradish roots in a contained space. One method is to drill drainage holes in the bottom of a 5-gallon plastic bucket, sink it into the ground and fill it with amended soil, then set horseradish cuttings into it. Another is to place an old-fashioned round drain tile 4 inches into the ground, fill it with good soil, then set root starts 2 inches deep within the tile.

Warning: Horseradish plants are difficult to remove, since as with comfrey a new plant will grow from any small piece left in the ground. I have a vivid memory of digging out a 20-foot row of horseradish plants. The roots went down 2 feet and the side roots seemed even longer. It took a while!

Propagation: Horseradish roots are remarkable in their will to grow, making it easy to propagate plants by making root divisions or cuttings from established plants in fall or early spring. Rub all side growth from a root and cut roots or rootlets into pieces 6 to 9 inches long and about the diameter of your little finger. Customarily, the tops of cuttings are sliced off straight across and the bottoms cut at an angle, so it's easy to tell which end goes up. Lay them at a 45-degree angle with the straight or wider end up, cover with about 4 inches of soil, and keep watered. Roots sold in the produce section of the grocery store provide material for crown division. Cut them into chunks or strips, allowing one eye on each, then plant these in prepared soil.

Year-round care: Once established, horseradish requires little attention beyond occasional watering and minimal weeding. Many gardeners don't even bother with that, since horseradish plants survive amid weeds and grass and will grow back on their own after they are dug out. However, the roots will be larger and of better quality if you take care of them. Renew at least part of your horseradish bed by digging in compost with a little wood ash or greensand around the plants in autumn or when you harvest roots.

Pests and diseases: "Healthy as a horse" is an expression that could apply to this plant, which is generally untroubled by insects or diseases. Leaves may be chewed a bit, turn yellow, or become spotted at times, but this seldom affects the roots.

Harvesting and preserving: You can harvest the roots in early fall of their first year, though their flavor is stronger after they have been touched by frost, and the yield is greater if you wait a second year. Pack the ground root firmly into straight-sided half-pint jars, top up with white wine vinegar, cover with a plastic lid, and keep in the refrigerator for use within three months, or freeze for up to a year. Alternatively, just keep a good-sized piece of scrubbed, peeled root in a glass jar in the freezer, and grate unthawed root as needed.

In areas where winters are mild, it is possible to leave horseradish in the ground and dig the roots anytime. Where the ground freezes hard for extended periods, lift the roots in late fall and store them in a shed, root cellar, or other sheltered location, covered with sand or earth to protect them from freezing.

Garden uses: While the long, wavy leaves of horseradish have an interesting form and texture, I do not recommend this plant as an ornamental because of its invasive tendencies.

Culinary uses: As a condiment, freshly grated horseradish packs a wallop of flavor, though the root has no odor until it is cut or bruised. Two constituents, synigrin and myrosin, exist in separate cells, but react together in the presence of water when the root is bruised, releasing a powerful mustardlike gas. The gas and the flavoring compounds associated with it are very volatile and begin to dissipate at once. The root also discolors quickly, so grate it into lemon juice or vinegar if it must be held before serving. Horseradish becomes bland in the presence of heat, so it is always used raw.

Horseradish is widely available in various forms—grated in vinegar, cream-style, in prepared mustards, and in tomato-based cocktail sauces. It is traditionally served with roast beef, fatty meats, oily or smoked fish, and oysters. Scrub the roots well, then peel and grate them. Add a little grated root to whipped cream, mix it with mayonnaise and Dijon mustard, or try a lighter sauce by combining it with yogurt, garlic, and lemon juice. Stuff pitted green olives with grated horseradish for an appetizer that will wake up the taste buds for sure, or add fresh horseradish to deviled eggs or mashed potatoes. Chicken soup flavored with chopped horseradish leaves is thought to be extra-good for those suffering from colds and flu.

Wasabi, that clear-your-sinuses green paste that comes with sushi, is a different plant species but has many similarities. Mixed with soy sauce, it becomes an addictive pleasure for dipping tempura as well as sushi, sashimi, and tofu. Like horseradish, wasabi has a hot flavor that dissipates quickly and is best used fresh. The paste, and occasionally the root, is available in Asian and gourmet-style supermarkets. Fresh wasabi root is expensive, but offers you a chance to try growing the herb by planting the root in moist soil as you would horseradish.

Medicinal uses: Historically, horseradish was valued as a medicinal herb long before it gained acceptance as a condiment. Hold some freshly grated root near your face with your cupped palms, inhale deeply, and you will experience a time-honored remedy for congested sinuses. Syrup of horseradish is still sipped for colds, bronchitis, and hoarseness. Years ago, in an NPR program about horseradish, I learned that no one in a horseradish processing plant ever catches a cold. Horseradish also stimulates the digestive organs, promoting a healthy appetite and complete digestion. It is diuretic and a proven antibiotic, helpful with urinary infections. Including the fresh root in your diet or eating small amounts at intervals during the day as a medicine is probably just as effective as taking it in syrup or tincture form.

Lavender

Latin name: *Lavandula* species:

L. angustifolia (vera or English lavender, previously *L. officinalis*): 'Vera,' 'True,' English,' 'Hidcote,' 'Royal Velvet,' 'Sharon Roberts,' 'Irene Doyle,' 'Silver Frost' ('Kathleen Elizabeth'), 'Rosea,' 'Jean Davis,' 'Alba,' Munstead,' 'Lady'

L. dentata (French)

L. latifolia (spike)

L. x intermedia (lavandin species): 'Grosso,' 'Fred Boutin,' 'Provence,' 'Seal'

L. stoechas (Spanish): 'Otto Quast,' 'Wings of Night'

Latin and common family names: Labiatae/Apiaceae (Mint family)

Varieties and cultivars: See Latin names above

Description: Lavender is an herb that has it all. It is a perennial evergreen shrub with narrow, opposite gray-green leaves, crowned in summer with spikes of fragrant purple blossoms. The corolla of the flower has two flat, lobed lips fused at the base, and attaches to the tubular calyx or pip, which is harvested for its concentration of fragrant oil. Plants grow from 1 to 3 feet high, depending on the variety, to which the flower spikes add another foot or two. Seeds are glossy brown nutlets.

There are about twenty species of lavender, and many named varieties of each, which sometimes leads to hair tearing. *Angustifolia* cultivars are the basic lavenders: familiar, hardy, fragrant, and easy to grow. They produce the highest-quality essential oil, and there are many beautiful cultivars. 'Vera,' 'True,' or 'English' are very hardy and reach 3 feet, with lavender blossoms on 2-foot stems. 'Hidcote' is a handsome 2-foot-high lavender with deep purple flowers; 'Royal Velvet' is also deep purple, but its stems are longer. 'Sharon Roberts' and 'Irene Doyle' bloom twice each season, in May and September. 'Silver Frost,' also known as 'Kathleen Elizabeth,' is characterized by almost white leaves and dark violet flowers. 'Rosea' and 'Jean Davis' are about 2½ feet tall and have pale pink flowers. 'Alba' is a 2½-foot plant with pure white blossoms. 'Munstead' grows smallest, at only about 1½ feet high, and has medium to deep purple blossoms on short stems. There are several named cultivars that resemble these standard *angustifolia* types, each a little different from the others. 'Lady,' a non-hardy and unexceptional performer, caused a sensation upon its release because it blooms in its first year when grown from seed.

Lavandula dentata (French) and *L. stoechas* (Spanish) are distinctive lavender species, with toothed leaves and plump flowers. Fast-growing and lovely in the garden but intolerant of frost, they also have less fragrance than other varieties. 'Otto Quast,' a *stoechas* cultivar, is sometimes sold as 'Rabbit Ear' lavender; 'Wings of Night' is a gorgeous compact variety. *L. latifolia* (spike lavender) is grown in the Mediterranean region for its relatively inexpensive essential oil. The *L. x intermedia* or lavandin varieties created by crossing *L. angustifolia* with *L. latifolia* are large, beautiful, fragrant, and hardy plants that bloom continuously through the summer. 'Grosso,' 'Seal,' 'Fred Boutin,' and 'Provence' are lavandins, all grown commercially for oil production.

Planting information and cultural directions: Lavender farms are springing up throughout the Northwest as more and more people discover the charms of this fragrant plant and the fact that conditions here are well-suited to growing it.

As you select a location for your plants, keep in mind that lavender is a Mediterranean native, well adapted to sun-drenched locations with chalky, rocky soils that drain quickly. The plants are extremely heat and drought tolerant, and they like sun, all day long. It's worth growing them in partial shade if you have no other choice, but they can't attain their best appearance or production, often growing spindly and lopsided as they stretch toward the light.

Average to poor soils are no problem for lavender, as long as they drain well and are not too acidic. If you have the type of Northwest soil that is perfect for rhododendrons, work 2 tablespoons of agricultural lime into the soil around each small plant at planting time. Don't bother planting lavender in a wet spot under fir trees.

Propagation: Except for lavandin hybrids, lavender can be started from seed, but germination can be difficult and the plants will not all be uniform. For best results, sow fresh seed indoors in the fall, keeping the soil temperature between 75° and 80°F. Seedlings are often grayish in color, with stiff leaves that smell like lavender.

One of my customers told me that her lavender self-sows. Every year, baby plants appear in quantity along her gravel walk. I was intrigued, since this never happens in my garden although the lavenders grow in dry soil and their seeds ripen well. Later, I observed a colony of French lavenders growing between the cracks of a city sidewalk and got the clue: the heat trapped by the gravel and cement was the key factor in germination.

Cuttings of all species taken in spring and fall root easily, though they grow slowly the first year. My favorite method is the "Dutchman's cutting." In February or March, before plants start putting on new growth, take heel cuttings (see Chapter 1) from your lavenders. Using a dibble, insert them in a seedbed outdoors. Mother Nature will probably take care of the watering, but you'll have to do the weeding. When new growth appears at the tips of the plants, they are rooted and ready to transplant.

Year-round care: Lavender plants require minimal maintenance. Fertilizing is optional, but a little lime scratched into the soil around the roots each spring makes for better blooms. Cut back all the spent bloom stalks in autumn, or spring at the latest. Dig tender varieties as frost approaches and pot them up to winter in a sheltered place. Cut them back at least by half in January or February, and set them out in the garden only after all danger of frost has passed.

After about five years, the stems of English lavenders become tough and woody. I've never had the courage to cut my precious lavenders back to the ground to rejuvenate them as I've done with sages. I *have* laboriously replanted them, however, digging deep holes and burying the stems. The results were not worth the effort. It's better to start fresh with two-year-old plants.

Pests and diseases: Lavender usually remains clear of insect pests and is not usually susceptible to disease. A few brown, withered leaves at the base of the stems is normal and does not indicate a problem. There is one disease, called shab, caused by the fungus *Phoma lavendulae* and spread via any cut or injury. Described in *Lavender, Sweet Lavender* by Judyth McLeod, shab causes individual branches to wither and die, while other parts of the plant seem normal. Growers may be tempted to leave plants for another season, in hopes that they will recover, but because they seldom do it is best to destroy them and start fresh in a new location.

Harvesting and preserving: For decorative bundles of lavender to hang up or give as gifts, harvest lavender while the buds are closed; opened flowers shatter when dried. Lavender destined for culinary uses and potpourri can be harvested in midbloom. Fasten bunches with rubber bands and hang them to dry in a warm, airy room out of the sun. For cooking or craft purposes, rub the pips off the stems over an old sheet and store in tins or glass jars.

Garden uses: A massed planting of lavenders of varying colors and heights is truly a beautiful sight. The herb's soft grayish foliage looks good year-round, providing a sense of repose in a garden of silver and gray shades, or offering a handsome backdrop for brighter colors. Lavender's neat, rounded shapes create undulating curves that can carry the viewer's gaze with quiet motion or direct it to a focal point. Dwarf lavenders are often planted with roses to create a fragrant and romantic atmosphere. Lavenders also make beautiful edging plants, releasing their scent as passersby brush against the leaves. Shorter varieties can define a path yet allow views of plants farther back in the garden, and taller varieties can serve a dual purpose as edging and screen or garden room divider.

Culinary uses: Lavender's unique, aromatic flavor earns it a place in the kitchen, especially in France, where lavender reigns as the queen of flowers. It is part of the versatile herbes de Provence seasoning, which is sprinkled on lamb, cottage cheese, and cooked vegetables such as carrots and zucchini. Lavender by itself is rubbed on lamb and other meats before roasting to give them a subtle distinction that is very French.

Queen Victoria loved lavender so much that she ordered "lavender conserve," a sweet condiment for seasoning meats and savory dishes, to be placed on the royal table every day. A few flower pips add a piquant flavor to Greek salads. Lavender is also good in tea cakes, shortbread cookies, and jelly. Lavender cooler makes a refreshing summer treat (see page 57).

Craft and home uses: The marvelous clean fragrance of lavender has been associated with cleanliness and personal care since antiquity. *Lavare,* the Latin root of its name, means "to wash." The Romans perfumed their banquet halls and baths with lavender. England's Victorians put it in potpourris, fainting cushions, and peace pillows.

Today it is a favorite fragrance in cosmetics, soaps, and perfumes, including Blue Grass, Paco Rabanne, and the famous Yardley Lavender. An easy way to scent your clothes and linens is to tie dried lavender into a handkerchief and toss it into your clothes dryer with a laundry load. In full bloom, the flowers are charming in nosegays, and their heads and stalks can be woven with ribbons into old-fashioned wands and fans for use as sachets. Dried lavender is popular in herbal wreaths and dried flower arrangements.

Medicinal uses: Traditionally, herbalists recommend an infusion of lavender to calm the nerves and revive the spirits. It is mildly sedative, useful in cases of tension headaches, insomnia, depression, PMS blues, and stomach upsets caused by stress. Antiseptic and antibacterial qualities make it an effective gargle for throat infections and bad breath. A strong infusion added to the bathwater soothes away irritations and relaxes the muscles of crabby children or anyone who has had a bad day. A lavender footbath revives tired feet.

Aromatherapy: Asked to name just one essential oil that is indispensable, many experts would choose *Lavandula angustifolia.* It is exceptionally versatile, very safe, and it has an almost ethereal perfume. This steam-distilled oil has more than a hundred constituents, principally linalyl acetate (to 40 percent), linalool (25 percent), cineole (to 33 percent), geraniol, lavandulol, lavandulyl acetate, turpineol, limonene, ocimene, and the antioxidant rosmarinic acid, among others. Most medicinal applications of lavender refer to this essential oil.

L. angustifolia oil, sometimes called "fine lavender oil," is considered superior to the oils of other *Lavandula* species and has markedly different effects. Spike lavender *(L. spica)* and lavandin oils contain higher concentrations of cineol and camphor. There is some mixing and mislabeling of lavender essential oils, so be sure that your source is reliable.

L. angustifolia oil is antibacterial, antifungal, antispasmodic, analgesic (pain relieving), and cicatrisant (prevents scarring). This oil is safe to use neat (undiluted) on the skin for insect bites, acne, boils, dandruff, and other skin problems, but more commonly it is an ingredient in many creams, ointments, and salves. These are applied externally to burns, eczema, strained muscles, sprains, bruises, and similar injuries.

Whether inhaled, rubbed on the skin, or added to the bath, *L. angustifolia* oil is thought to elevate the mood, promoting feelings of tranquillity and well-being. Consequently it is used to allay depression and nervous conditions. In compresses and vapor rubs it is placed on the chest to ease asthma and bronchitis, especially when stress or anxiety is a factor. The oil is also an ingredient in the smelling salts used to revive after fainting and shock.

Lemon Balm

Common names: Balm, Lemon balm, Heart's delight, Lemon mint, Melissa

Latin name: *Melissa officinalis*

Latin and common family names: Labiatae/ Laminaceae (Mint family)

Varieties and cultivars: 'Aurea,' 'All Gold'

Related plant: Lime balm

Description: Lemon balm is a herbaceous perennial with square, downy stems and soft, rounded or heart-shaped, crinkly leaves 2 to 3 inches long that are notched at the edges and have a musky lemon flavor and aroma. Leaves of the common variety are light green, 'Aurea,' balm has splashes of gold, while leaves of 'All Gold' are golden. Lime balm, a near relative, has a similar appearance but a less musky citrus scent.

Inconspicuous white flowers bloom in clusters at the leaf axils, producing $1/16$-inch, tear-shaped, light brown seeds. Plants increase in size gradually, but do not spread by runners like mints. They grow from a fibrous root system to a height of about $2^1/2$ feet. They die down in winter but are up again in very early spring. Lemon balm is hardy to at least 0°F, but its roots rot in standing water.

Planting information and cultural directions: Once established, lemon balm is one of the very easiest herbs to grow. It is a great confidence builder for children and beginning gardeners. Although it does best in rich, moist soil and partial shade, it will also grow in dry soils and full sun. The leaves tend to turn yellow and even brown at the margins if the plant is not watered regularly. Lemon balm grows well in a sunny bed, under benches in heavy shade, and even from cracks in the sidewalk. Still, it is not a pernicious weed, just a nice plant to have around.

Propagation: Seeds germinate readily under glass in spring, or can be broadcast in the garden in spring or fall. Plants can easily be divided in any season, but they reseed so freely that it is seldom necessary to assist in increasing their numbers.

Year-round care: I first discovered this herb growing vigorously alongside an old barn, the last evidence of a long-abandoned garden. It manages very nicely on its own, thank you. Other than weeding, maintenance is optional. To keep plants looking neat and healthy you might whack off their growth once or twice in summer. Weed out self-sown plants unless you like them where they are. Clip off dead stems in late fall or during early spring cleanup.

Pests and diseases: At times, garden webworms may shred the leaves or cause them to curl. They can be controlled with Thuricide (Bt.), which must be applied during the caterpillars' feeding stage. Other than that, plants are pretty much pest and disease free.

Harvesting and preserving: A vigorous lemon balm plant will yield up to three harvests each season. The delicate flavor is best when the herb is fresh, but the dried herb is handy during the winter. Careful handling is necessary to preserve lemon balm's color, fragrance, and flavor. Cut the stems off near the base before blossoms form, handling them gently to prevent bruising. Their quality deteriorates quickly if they are left lying around for long, so tie them into small bunches promptly. Hang them to dry them in a very warm, airy place until brittle, or dry in a dehydrator. Their green color is best preserved at about 105°F. Strip the leaves and store them in airtight containers.

Garden uses: Lemon balm will grow almost anywhere, and its gentle green harmonizes with most informal planting schemes. 'Variegata' or 'Aureus' ('Golden') varieties are especially nice in quiet places where the crinkled texture and unusual coloration of their leaves draws the attention of the observant. Take advantage of lemon balm's shade tolerance by combining it with nasturtiums, angelica, or lady's mantle. Lemon balm is also a pleasant addition to a tea garden or tussie-mussie garden, where it represents sympathy.

Melissa, the herb's scientific name, comes from words meaning "bee plant" in Latin and Greek. Honeybees love the nectar-bearing flowers, and in olden times beekeepers rubbed empty hives with lemon balm to invite a new swarm to move in. Small birds come to the garden in late summer to feed on ripe lemon balm seeds.

Craft and home uses: There are many ways to bring lemon balm's pleasant citrus aroma into your home. Traditionally, the herb was strewn on floors as an antiseptic and deodorizer. Simmer a handful of lemon balm in a pan of water to achieve the same effect. The herb is also popular in potpourri, particularly citrus blends.

Relaxing and uplifting, lemon balm is also among the best herbs to include in herbal sleep and bath mixtures, combining well with lavender, chamomile, rose petals, and hops. Or simply pour a quart of boiling water over a large bunch of fresh leaves and stems, steep for ten minutes, strain into your bath, and let *Melissa* work its gentle magic on you.

Culinary uses: Lemon balm adds a mild hint of citrus to green salads, fruit cups, and sorbets. Try it in stuffings for lamb, pork, or chicken, or in homemade mayonnaise with fish. It is also excellent in teas, or combined with fresh-squeezed lemons and frozen lemonade for a refreshing punch. The old custom of steeping lemon balm in wine as a tonic survives in the herb's use in liqueurs such as Bénédictine and Chartreuse.

Medicinal uses: Lemon balm's traditional use for calming the nerves, strengthening the vital spirits, and dispelling melancholy traces back to early Arabian herbalists. The noted physician Avicenna (A.D. 980–1037) recommended its cheering effects, and it was specified as a remedy for anxiety or depression. During the Middle Ages it was believed to have revivifying powers and was the main ingredient in various elixirs of youth. Carmelite Water, distilled since 1611 from lemon balm, lemon peel, nutmeg, angelica root, and other ingredients, was famous as a restorative. This legacy survives to the present in the herb's use as a tonic tea, mild sedative, and antidepressant.

Despite its mild flavor and gentle action, lemon balm is a potent medicinal herb. Its low concentration of essential oil (0.3 percent maximum), combined with its other constituents, produces positive effects that are not improved by upping the dosage. It is recognized by the German Commission E as a safe and effective tranquilizer and carminative. These benefits make the herb ideal for people who have digestive upsets related to nervous tension. It is current in the *British Herbal Pharmacopoeia* for flatulent dyspepsia, depressive illness, and nervous breakdown.

Lemon balm was once called Heart's Delight, a name that relates to the herb's uplifting effect on the spirits as well as its tonic effect on the heart and circulatory system. Lemon balm dilates the peripheral blood vessels, lowering blood pressure. The *Physicians' Desk Reference For Herbal Medicine* recommends that, since its essential oil is very volatile, it is best for calming purposes when used fresh, or, if dried, within six months.

This herb is highly regarded in Europe. According to Varro Tyler, author of *Herbs of Choice*, in addition to its use as a relaxant and antispasmodic, lemon balm shows promise in treating cold sores and genital lesions caused by the *Herpes simplex* virus. A standardized melissa cream that shortens healing time of lesions and decreases recurrence rate is available in Europe. Dr. Tyler cautiously suggests that a strong lemon balm infusion (2 to 3 teaspoons of finely cut leaves steeped in ½ cup water) is at least as effective as any commercial remedy available. Soak cotton pads in the fresh infusion and apply them to lesions several times daily.

Despite all its health-enhancing properties, lemon balm is generally deemed as unexciting as the boy next door. It is interesting to speculate that one day it may become the latest "hot" herb, elevated to the position of respect it deserves as an important medicinal plant.

Aromatherapy: Citronellol, geraniol (citral a), and narol (citral b) comprise 40 to 70 percent of the essential oil contained in lemon balm leaves and flowers. Other constituents include tannins, rosmarinic acid, and a bitter principle.

Not all that much has changed since John Gerard wrote in 1597 that lemon balm "maketh the heart merrie and joyfull and strengtheneth the vitall spirits." Modern-day aromatherapists esteem essential oil of melissa as a tonic and relaxant for the nervous system. Writer Julia Lawless described the oil as a remedy for the "distressed spirit."

Lemon Verbena

Common names: Lemon-scented verbena, Herb Louisa, Verbena, *Verveine citronelle* (France)

Latin name: *Aloysia triphylla* (formerly *Aloysia citriodora, Lippia citriodora, L. triphylla, Verbena triphylla*)

Latin and common family names: Verbenaceae (Verbena family)

Unrelated plants: Spanish verbena (*Thymus biamalis*), vervain (*Verbena officinalis*), garden verbena (*V. hybrida, V. hortensis*)

Description: Rub a leaf of lemon verbena between your fingertips and inhale, and you will understand why gardeners love this plant. The scent, strong and clean, is unmistakably lemon. Yet this herb is not in the citrus family and not a verbena—another example of the confusion of common names. Lemon verbena is a tall, rangy shrub that reaches 4 to 5 feet within one or two seasons. In warm climates like its native Chile and Argentina, it is more exuberant, reaching a height that amazes Northwestern gardeners. Glossy, pointed leaves about 3 inches long appear in whorls of three or four along twiggy stems, which are topped in late summer by triangular heads of tiny white to pale-lavender flowers. Plants rarely set seed.

Planting information and cultural directions: Growing lemon verbena is a bit more work than some other herbs, but it's worth the trouble. It loves sunshine and does best in a rich, evenly moist soil with good drainage. It tolerates dry soil but grows more slowly. Try to give your lemon verbena a protected spot, beside a wall, perhaps, or near the house out of the wind. Pinch back the stems regularly to keep the plants bushy.

This herb is unusual in that it is truly a deciduous perennial. At the first sharp frost its leaves turn dark, shrivel, and fall off, leaving bare woody stems above the ground. Plants are semi-hardy, surviving temperatures down to about 20°F in this dormant state. When the weather warms to about 60°F, the plants leaf out again.

Lemon verbena makes a good container plant indoors or out. Enrich your potting soil with compost, worm castings, or other organic material, and add some sand and perlite for drainage. Even indoors the leaves usually drop, although the plant's requisite dormancy period may be shortened.

Propagation: Lemon verbena is best propagated by cuttings taken in midsummer, when stems are firm but not woody. Cut 4-inch lengths that include a growing tip, remove the bottom leaves, and place the cuttings in sterile potting mix or sand with at least one leaf joint below the surface. Keep them at about 65°F, providing bottom heat with a heating cable or propagating mat if possible. Keep plants evenly moist, misting the leaves regularly until rooting occurs.

If you manage to obtain viable seeds, sow them thickly in potting mix, water them gently, cover with plastic wrap, and provide a high temperature—around 90°F. Watch them carefully and remove the

plastic wrap as soon as seeds germinate. Grow them in individual pots until soil temperatures are warm enough for planting outside.

Year-round care: Lemon verbena needs help to survive a typical Northwest winter. The safest bet for outdoor plants is to dig them from the garden in early autumn, pot them in sterile potting soil or peat moss, and bring them into a cool garage, sheltered porch, or greenhouse. Leave potted plants in their containers and carry or drag them to a protected place. Without their leaves, the plants look completely moribund. Don't despair: they are only dormant. Check them every three weeks or so, and give them just enough water to keep them from drying out completely. In early April, start looking for tiny dots of green along the stems. When those buds appear, it's time to rejoice!

If you don't mind a gamble, leave mature plants in the garden over winter. In late October, heap a blanket of straw or leaves around the base of the stems as insulation. Leave the twiggy skeleton unpruned to mark the place, and as a framework for next year's growth. Pull off the mulch when all danger of frost has passed, usually late April to early May. Be patient in the spring; before deciding that your cherished plant is history, wait and watch for signs of life. Sometimes plants don't leaf out until June. If frost has indeed killed the tops, don't give up. Prune back the old woody stems to encourage bushy growth from the base of the plant.

Pests and diseases: Lemon verbena is generally a healthy plant, but in the greenhouse or outdoors in dry conditions there may be problems with aphids, spider mites, and whitefly. Inspect plants regularly, and at the first sign of infestation spray with a jet of cold water. Make sure you get the underside of the leaves. If that is not effective, try insecticidal soap or a garlic potion. As a last resort, dust the plants with rotenone powder.

Harvesting and preserving: Judicious harvesting will help keep your lemon verbena handsome and compact. You can pluck a few leaves for soup or tea anytime, but if you need a greater quantity or your plant is beginning to sprawl, clip stems back by a third, preferably just before flowering when the scent and flavor are strongest. It's not being greedy and it won't harm the plant at all—the leaves will soon drop anyway and you might as well enjoy them. To dry, hang bunches of stems, place the leaves on trays at room temperature, or use a dehydrator. They will hold their fragrance and curl and twist into interesting shapes.

Garden uses: The most spectacular lemon verbena I've seen was in the gardens at the University of California at Davis. Two gigantic specimens covered an arbor, creating a bower of heavenly scent. While we can't expect such herbal magic in Northwest gardens, a well-tended lemon verbena is a lovely addition to the garden. Grow it near a path or bench so you can easily reach out and pick a leaf or do some casual pruning.

Lemon verbena lends itself well to topiary work. Pruned into a standard with straight stems and a ball of leaves at the top, plants can be quite ornamental and live for many years. They make fine centerpieces for potpourri or fragrance theme gardens, and lend a note of formality to a home or garden entry.

Culinary uses: Lemon verbena is worth growing for its luscious scent alone, but it has many other uses too. In cooking, substitute the leaves for lemongrass in Thai dishes, or use them to flavor sorbets, jellies, and baked apples. Remember, though, that the tough ribs of mature leaves are not particularly digestible. Lemon verbena is extremely popular as a tea in France, where it's called *Verveine citronelle,* compounding the semantic confusion since it's not the calming herb *we* know as vervain (*Verbena officinalis*). A leaf steeped with black tea gives an interesting flavor.

Craft and home uses: Lemon verbena is a superb scent in soaps, aftershave lotions, and other toiletries for both men and women. A classic French fragrance called Eau de Verveine is still available in perfume stores. Since the leaves keep their citrus scent when dried, they are wonderful in potpourris and linen closets. I like to slip a fresh leaf in with a letter—it adds a herbal hello that often hastens a reply!

Medicinal uses: Although relatively little research has been done on lemon verbena as a medicinal plant, it has a place in the healing traditions of South America, North Africa, and other areas where it grows plentifully. A decoction of the leaves is given for colds, sinus congestion, and fevers, and it is thought to be calming in cases of nervousness, insomnia, and stress-related conditions. Its stomachic and antispasmodic qualities aid digestion and ease dyspepsia and cramps. Lemon verbena has proven antibacterial action and is being studied in the treatment of staph, *E. coli,* and other serious infections.

Aromatherapy: "True verbena oil," as it is called in the fragrance trade, is expensive and rare. It is light yellow to golden in color, and contains citral, geraniol, narol, and other constituents that give it a sweet, lemony aroma. For therapeutic use, avoid substitutes, commonly oil of "Spanish verbena" or "verbena Spanish" (*Thymus hiamalis*), or combinations of lemongrass, citronella, and lemon. Properties and uses of the true oil are similar to those described under Medicinal uses, above.

Lovage

Common names: Love ache, Love itch, Love parsley

Latin name: *Levisticum officinale* (formerly *Ligusticum officinale, Ligusticum levisticum*)

Latin and common family names: Umbellifereae/ Apiaceae (Carrot family)

Unrelated plants: Alexanders, *Smyrnium olusatrum;* Osha, *Ligusticum porterii*

Description: A big, robust perennial, lovage has large, dark green, deeply lobed leaves that grow on hollow stalks 2 to 3 feet high. From the center of the plant a thick flower stalk rises 4 to 7 feet, crowned with an umbel of inconspicuous, sticky, chartreuse flowers that attract bees. Seeds are flat, ridged ellipses, 1/4 inch long and light brown in color; their germinating power lasts about two years. The plant's roots are thick, fleshy, and aromatic.

Planting information and cultural directions: Lovage is sturdy and adaptable, growing exuberantly in rich, moist soil with full sun or partial shade and less vigorously in poor soil. In hot, sunny areas it does best if somewhat shaded. Completely hardy in the Northwest, lovage dies back in winter but comes up

year after year. The plants need an annual chilling period to survive. Roots must not be in standing water.

Propagation: In a hospitable environment, lovage self-sows readily. To encourage this, keep the soil at the base of the plants cultivated. The herb is easily grown from seeds, which are best sown when fresh in late summer. Large plants are produced more quickly from offsets sliced from the roots in early spring when the plant's reddish tips are just emerging. Be sure to keep them watered until they sprout healthy new leaves.

Year-round care: Lovage requires no special care. If grown in a moist spot, watering is unnecessary, but keep the plant reasonably weeded. When unharvested leaves turn yellow, you may wish to cut back the whole plant to encourage new growth. To keep your garden tidy, remove the leaves and seed stalk when the plant dies down.

Pests and diseases: This plant is not usually bothered by pests or disease. Aphids may infest leaves or seed heads, but insecticidal soap spray will take care of the problem.

Harvesting and preserving: Harvest lovage by cutting the stems back to the base of the plant. If dried too slowly, the leaves fade to an unappealing yellowish color. To prepare, remove and discard the thick stems and the fleshy midribs of the leaves, then dry the leaves in a dehydrator or very low oven (below 150°F). Dig lovage roots in late fall or early spring while the plant is dormant. Scrub, peel, and cut into chunks or thin slices, then dry or tincture them.

Garden uses: The beautiful deep green leaves of lovage, with their deeply cut texture, are the most ornamental part of the plant. Although the tall chartreuse flowers attract bees, they are not particularly showy. Because of its height and shade tolerance, this plant is perfect for the back of a border where something big and bold is in order. It is also a good candidate for an out-of-the-way place where herbs that require more sun will not thrive.

Culinary uses: The strong, intriguing flavor of lovage is reminiscent of celery with hints of allspice. Maggi, the Swiss seasoning concentrate, has a lovage flavor. In Europe lovage is a favorite for soups, stews, roasts, and savory dishes. Try grilling salmon with lovage butter, or add a few fresh leaves to a salad of spring greens or a tuna salad. It is far more interesting than parsley in spanakopita. To give tomato juice or aspic a new flavor, simmer it with a few stalks of lovage. The hollow stems make great "lovage straws" for sipping tomato juice or Bloody Marys on lazy summer afternoons. Roots and seeds are also edible but rarely utilized for culinary purposes.

Craft and home uses: "This herbe for hys sweet savoure is used in bathe," wrote Thomas Hyll in *The Gardeners Labyrinth* (1577). Considered a natural deodorant, lovage leaves are steeped in boiling water that is strained into the bath for cleansing and refreshment. Peppermint, sage, elderflowers, or other aromatic herbs may be added. Cooled infusions of lovage applied as facial waters improve the texture of the skin and are said to remove freckles.

Medicinal uses: The warmly aromatic character of this plant has been the basis of its use as a digestive herb since early times. An infusion of fresh seeds and leaves—or the formerly popular alcoholic "tonics"— help to relieve stomachaches, dyspepsia, and gas.

In Europe, lovage root is an important component of many diuretic preparations and treatments for urinary tract conditions. An infusion is drunk for flushing the kidneys and bladder to prevent stones from forming. It can be irritating, however, and should not be used if infection is present, or by pregnant women.

In the past, lovage has been classified with both the angelicas and the ligusticums. As pointed out by herbal writer Steven Foster in *Herbal Renaissance,* when the Chinese domestic supply of the important herb dong quai (*Angelica sinesis*) ran short, lovage root (known in China as European dong quai) made an acceptable substitute. Foster also notes similarities between lovage root and the Pueblo Indian herb osha (*Ligusticum porterii*), a strengthening tonic. The Pueblos call lovage "osha del jardin," or "osha of the garden."

Lovage root has medicinal properties similar to those of dong quai and osha. It is a strengthening tonic of particular value to women that helps to balance the menstrual cycle. It is taken to relieve the edema and cramps associated with menstruation, and to bring on late periods.

Aromatherapy: The essential oil contained in the lovage plant is responsible for the medicinal actions previously described, and is also antimicrobial, antiseptic, and generally sedative. The distilled oils of fresh leaves and stems, fresh roots, and dried roots contain varying proportions of pthalides (aroma bearers) and other components, including pinene, phellandrene, citronellol, bergapten, carvacrol, isovaleric acid, and engelic acid. The oils are used commercially in perfumery, cosmetics, and in flavoring liqueurs and tobacco.

Marjoram

Common names: Sweet marjoram, Knotted marjoram

Latin name: *Origanum marjorana* (formerly *O. hortensis, Marjorana hortensis*)

Latin and common family names: Labiatae/Lamiaceae (Mint family)

Varieties and cultivars: 'Erfo,' 'Large Leaf Marjoram'

Description: One of the most delightfully aromatic of herbs, sweet marjoram is an 8- to 12-inch plant with ¼- to 1-inch, velvety, oval, opposite leaves on branching stems. Unusual ball- or knotlike clusters of bracts form at the top of the stems, clasping tiny white flowers. The herb has an intense, sweet perfume that has been long been associated with happiness. The ancient Greeks called the plant "joy of the mountains." Its stems are tinged with red, and its roots are a shallow, fibrous mass. Seeds are reddish brown and very small. Within the last few years, large-leaved cultivars of sweet marjoram have been released, including 'Large Leaf Marjoram' and 'Erfo,' a taller, high-yielding strain.

The common and Latin names of marjoram and oregano can be misleading and keep changing; even the experts can't seem to settle on what's what. Some plants that are commonly called marjoram, such as wild marjoram (*O. vulgare* ssp. *vulgare*), are actually varieties of oregano that lack the perfume of sweet marjoram. On the other hand, Italian oregano (*O. x majoricum*) does have a similar sweetness although it is less intense. But there is nothing quite like the little knotted flowers of sweet marjoram, which distinguish it from its relatives. It is borderline hardy except in the mildest parts of the Northwest, and is usually grown as an annual.

Planting information and cultural directions: Like basil, sweet marjoram prefers sunshine and warm temperatures. To produce well it needs good garden soil with added compost or all-purpose fertilizer. Allow 6 inches between plants. Mulch with grass clippings or other material to control weeds. Sweet marjoram can be wintered over in a sunny window or heated greenhouse and returned to an outdoor location when danger of frost has passed. Three plants will generally produce enough for culinary use, but for marjoram aficionados who want extra for drying, six plants would not be too many.

Propagation: Individual marjoram plants grow slowly to harvestable size. Speed the process by sowing clusters of seeds indoors in February or March at 65°F or above. Seed can also be sown outdoors in April or May, but keep the tiny seedlings weeded or they will soon be overwhelmed. Or simply buy plants at your favorite herb farm or nursery in late spring and set them out when the garden soil has warmed.

Pests and diseases: Marjoram has never had a disease or insect problem in my garden.

Harvesting and preserving: Harvest sweet marjoram when the buds are just beginning to form. The little knots quickly become tough, so don't wait until plants are in bloom. Use any portion of the stalks that is green and tender, and strip the leaves from the rest. Sweet marjoram holds its flavor well when dried. Place sprigs in a dehydrator, or hang them in small bunches in a warm, airy place until brittle. Then rub off the leaves and store them in airtight containers.

Garden uses: Sweet marjoram does not spread in the garden like the less manageable oreganos, but remains compact and shapely with regular harvesting. Plant it toward the front border or in the kitchen garden. It is an excellent choice for strawberry pots and window boxes, especially when planted close at hand so you have only to reach for a leaf to enjoy its perfume.

Culinary uses: The saying "When in doubt, use marjoram" expresses this herb's versatility. It enhances casseroles, soups, omelets, cheese spreads, and salad dressings, and is marvelous with almost any vegetable, notably tomatoes, eggplant, carrots, and green beans. Try it in spaghetti sauce and Italian seasoning blends, and as the signature flavor of osso buco. Sweet marjoram is often rubbed on lamb, beef, or chicken before roasting. In Germany, its role in flavoring sausages earns it the name *Wurstkraut*. For best flavor, add this delicate herb shortly before serving; for variety, mince it with lemon juice.

Craft and home uses: In the language of flowers, sweet marjoram is the herb of happiness. It has been associated with weddings ever since garlands of it crowned the heads of bridal couples in ancient Greece and Rome. An herbal wedding bouquet should always contain a few sprigs of sweet marjoram. This is an herb of simple pleasures. There are many ways that it can make everyday living more enjoyable.

Medicinal uses: Although it is primarily a cooking herb, sweet marjoram also has medicinal uses. Taken as an infusion, it can soothe nervous tension, relieve stomach upsets, and forestall headaches if taken at the first indication. Antiseptic and antiviral, it is gargled for sore throats and hastens the healing of cold sores.

Aromatherapy: In the height of summer when the packing room at Silver Bay was full of fresh cut herbs, the "herb of happiness" provided the aromatic top note of a heady perfume. Even in time-crunch situations, it was impossible to feel negative emotions in that room. "Bottle it!" visitors would urge.

Essential oil of sweet marjoram is made up of more than forty components, notably cis-sabinene hydrate, which gives the herb its special fragrance. Linalool, carvacrol, ocimene, borneol, and the antioxidant rosmarinic acid are among the other constituents. Traditionally, sweet marjoram oil has been massaged on sprains, sore muscles, and rheumatic pains. If the marjoram oil available on the market does not possess the herb's characteristic scent, it is probably distilled from one of the oreganos.

Mint

Common name: Mint

Latin name: *Mentha* spp.

Latin and common family names: Labiatae/Lamiaceae (Mint family)

Species, varieties, and cultivars: Spearmint, *M. spicata;* 'Curly,' 'Crispy,' 'Kentucky Colonel,' 'The Best,' 'Moroccan Mint;' Peppermint, *M. x piperita*, 'Chocolate,' 'Mitchum Black,' 'Blue Balsam,' 'Chewing Gum Mint;' *M. x p.* var. *citrata*, ' Eau de Cologne,' 'Orange Mint,' 'Bergamot Mint,' 'Lavender Mint,' Apple mint, *M. suaveolens;* Pineapple mint, *M. s. suaveolens;* Corsican mint, *M. requienii;* many others

Description: Mints are usually recognized by their

refreshing aroma, square stems, smooth-pointed leaves, spikes of lavender or white flowers, and their habit of spreading rapidly by underground leafless stems (stolons). The plants are hardy perennials, most growing from 1 to 4 feet high, and they can easily take over even a large area. The tremendous variation among species and varieties of mints is reflected in the USDA collection, which numbers nearly 600.

Spearmint (*Mentha spicata*) has bright green, pointed leaves, white flowers, and a clean, light scent. 'Curly' or 'Crispy' mint is a spearmint variety with attractive pebbled, twisted leaves. Among other noteworthy spearmint cultivars, 'Kentucky Colonel' is fine flavored and perfect for mint juleps; 'The Best' is particularly aromatic and vigorous; and 'Moroccan Mint,' is excellent for teas.

Peppermint (*M. x piperata*) has dark green, pointed leaves with reddish veins and stems, lavender flowers, and a deeper mint scent. It is thought to be a hybrid rather than a distinct species; this is indicated by the 'x' in its proper name. Smelling a leaf of the peppermint cultivar 'Chocolate Mint' makes you think of Camp Fire candies. 'Mitchum Black' is a dark-stemmed, disease-resistant strain named after a famous growing area in England; 'Blue Balsam' has blue-tinged foliage and beautiful flowers; 'Chewing Gum Mint' doubles your pleasure with its fresh flavor and showy blooms.

'Eau de Cologne Mint,' 'Orange Mint,' and 'Bergamot Mint,' all variations of *M. x piperata* var. *citrata*, are all delightful but hard to tell apart. They have bronzy, rounded leaves, purple flowers, and a delicious citrus aroma. 'Lavender Mint' has similar characteristics. All

these varieties grow from 18 to 30 inches.

Apple mint (*M. suaveolens*) has large, hairy, rounded leaves, white flowers, a sweet menthol aroma, and can reach 5 feet tall in flower. Pineapple mint (*M. suaveolens* var. *suaveolens*) and variegated pineapple mint (*M. suaveolens variegata*) have smaller leaves that are green or variegated green and white. Their flowers are white and they have a mild fruity scent.

Corsican mint (*M. requiennii*) is quite different. It creeps along the ground, barely reaching 2 inches tall. Its tiny, light green leaves emit a powerful crème de menthe fragrance. Less hardy than most other mints, Corsican mint sometimes dies out in winter.

Planting information and cultural directions: Widely adaptable, mint will grow in any moderately fertile soil. It is most flavorful when grown in full sun, but is one of the few herbs that will also thrive in full shade. Ample moisture is an important requirement.

When different varieties of mint are grown in close proximity, they often cross-pollinate. Soon your spearmint has reddish stems and the apple mint leaves are pointed, and none of the mints are quite as they started out. It's better to plant one type in the front yard and another in the back, or separate them by some other means.

Oregon, Washington, and Idaho are major world producers of peppermint and spearmint. When the fields are being harvested, the air for miles around is so redolent of mint the effect is practically inebriating.

Propagation: Mint is one of the easiest herbs to propagate. However, many have sterile seeds or require cross-pollination by other varieties, so they don't produce offspring that duplicate the parent.

Consequently, you never know what to expect when you grow mint from seed. It's far better to buy starter plants with the characteristics you want, then propagate them vegetatively.

Mint plants can be divided almost any time of year. Tear them apart with your hands or clip them with pruners and replant. For larger numbers of plants, clip pieces of stolon that include a node, preferably with roots attached. Set them about 6 inches apart. They will soon produce top growth and start spreading. You can also root stem cuttings in sterile potting mix or even in a glass of water on your windowsill before planting them out.

Year-round care: Because mints can take over a garden quickly, it is prudent to plant them in pots or contained areas. Otherwise, cut back the roots with a sharp spade in spring and fall to keep the plants under control. In winter, when the plants die back to the ground, clip or mow the dead stalks to tidy up the garden. Early spring is an excellent time to trim back the beds and move plants.

Pests and diseases: Although insects seldom bother mints, on rare occasions garden webworms shred the leaves. Thuricide is an effective control, and must be applied while the caterpillars are in their feeding stage.

Mints are susceptible to soilborne viruses and rust. Light-colored patches on the leaves and stunted growth indicate virus, and orange to brown dots on the lower stems and undersides of leaves signal rust. You can harvest and use plant tips that are not affected by disease, but do not move plants to other areas or the problems will spread. For control, avoid fertilizing with fresh manure and clean up garden debris in the fall. Commercial mint beds are flamed with propane to burn back the earliest emerging shoots. Munscher and Rice, in *Garden Spice and Wild Pot Herbs*, recommend treating cuttings with hot water (115° F.) for 10 minutes before they are planted, in order to prevent *Puccinia menthae*, a rust that afflicts spearmint plants.

Harvesting and preserving: Pinch back mint tips for garnishes or as required to keep the stems bushy and delay flowering. Cut back plants to the ground when flowers begin forming, and they will produce a second and third crop. Hang the mint in bunches to dry—it will scent your entire house.

Garden uses: Because of their take-over growth habit, a place for mints must be selected with care. Confident that I could keep it under control, I planted 'Eau de Cologne Mint' in a fragrance garden, only to spend hours tearing it out two years later. The moral to this story: keep mints out of the flower or vegetable garden. Otherwise, try to contain them within cement edging tiles, or use metal or plastic tubs with worn-out bottoms or drainage holes. Varieties such as 'Blue Balsam,' variegated pineapple mint, and curly mint are very ornamental in whiskey barrels and other containers, especially when blooming.

Mints can solve garden problems as well as cause them. Give them a spot of their own, however shady and wet, and they will spread happily and provide abundant harvests.

Corsican mint, with its tiny leaves and spreading habit, makes an excellent ground cover. Plant it near a pond or between paving stones and enjoy the intense aroma released when you walk along the garden path.

Culinary uses: Few flavors are more refreshing than the clean, cool taste of mint, which is the most popular herb on the planet. You can travel around the world and find mint in all sorts of mouth-watering combinations.

Apple mint is a favorite in English cooking, traditionally served in new potatoes, peas, and, of course, mint jelly and mint sauce (mint in sweetened vinegar) with lamb. Fresh mint is teamed with basil and cilantro in Southeast Asian soups and other dishes. Cool cucumber and spearmint raitas are the perfect counterpart to fiery Indian curries, and dishes of fresh mint chutney are often served with meals. The Middle East is the origin of tabouli, a salad of bulgur and vegetables laced with mint and other herbs. Mint juleps may be the United States' contribution to the world treasury of mint recipes.

Fresh mint adds a lively note to fruit salads, punches, and desserts. Of course, mint with chocolate is a classic pairing. Spearmint and apple mint are generally preferred for kitchen use, while peppermint leaves are used in tea, and the oil flavors gum, confections, and breath mints, whether mild or curiously strong.

Any mint, fresh or dried, can be used for hot or iced tea. Spearmint, apple mint, orange mint, and peppermint are among the best. Hot, sweetened spearmint tea is the national beverage of Morocco, and quite salubrious in that arid climate. A little dried mint combined with chamomile, alfalfa, hibiscus, cinnamon, or other botanicals makes for interesting herbal tea blends. For inspiration on crafting your own blends, try some of the delicious mixtures on the market.

Crafts and home uses: Of mint, Gerard wrote, "The smelle rejoiceth the heart of man, for which cause they used to strew it in chambers and places of recreation, pleasure and repose, where feasts and banquets are made.' Dried mint leaves give potpourris a fresh aroma. A few drops of peppermint essential oil, diluted with water and misted, masks the odors of tobacco smoke, pets, and mildew.

Medicinal uses: There is a very good reason why peppermint-flavored mints are served after dinner. Peppermint's high menthol content (upward of 50 percent) and the balance of other constituents make it a remarkable medicinal herb. It is the most effective herbal antispasmodic and carminative, calming spasms of the digestive tract, easing stomach cramps and pains, and breaking up gas. Research published in the *British Medical Journal* indicates that an enteric (hard) coating on peppermint oil capsules allows the oil to reach the colon without being absorbed in the stomach, providing relief from irritable bowel syndrome. This is good news for patients who have been told there is no cure for the condition. The menthol in peppermint also destroys bacteria, parasites, and viruses in the stomach without harming beneficial intestinal flora.

Drinking a cup of peppermint tea causes internal warmth and promotes sweating, helping to chase away incipient colds and flu. An equal amount of elderflower, plus a little yarrow, enhances the effect.

Peppermint can also relieve nausea, morning sickness, and headaches, including migraines. Peppermint herb and oil are not to be confused with synthetic menthol, which can have toxic effects if ingested.

Aromatherapy: In addition to menthol, peppermint oil contains menthone, menthyl acetate, and menthofuran, plus azulenes, limonene, pulegone, cineole, rosmarinic acid, tannins, flavonoids, and other compounds. It is colorless to pale yellow and has a strong, camphorous aroma. The oil has many applications in aromatherapy. It is regarded as a mental stimulant that increases alertness and concentration. A few drops added to the bath have an invigorating and refreshing effect. Diluted in salves and liniments, it is rubbed on sore muscles.

Peppermint oil's antiseptic and numbing qualities bring emergency toothache relief, and some dentists apply it topically before injecting anaesthetic. The oil is used extensively to flavor toothpaste, mouthwash, gum, medicines, and many beverages and foods. It also scents shampoo, face masks, deodorants, soaps, and other body-care products.

Spearmint oil, which contains mainly carvone (50-70 percent), has similar but milder qualities and actions.

Monarda

Common names: Bee balm, Red bergamot, Scarlet monarda, Bergamot mint, Oswego tea

Latin name: *Monarda didyma*

Latin and common family names: Labiatae/Lamiaceae (Mint family)

Varieties and cultivars: 'Adam,' 'Cambridge Scarlet' (red), 'Croftway Pink' (pink), 'Prairie Night,' 'Blue Stocking' (purple), 'Snow White' (white)

Description: A stand of mature monardas in bloom, attended by hummingbirds and bumblebees, is a gorgeous sight. The distinctive pom-pom flowers come in vibrant hues that may include the old-fashioned scarlet as well as pale pink, lavender, luscious deep purple, and pure white. On closer inspection, you will find that the pom-poms are actually whorls of large, colored bracts with small, two-lipped, deep-throated flowers peeping out. They bloom atop 2- to 3-foot stems, often stacked two or three per stem.

Monarda is a hardy perennial with narrow, crinkled leaves tinged with red. The plant reveals its botanical kinship with the mints by its square stems, opposite pointed leaves, vigorous spreading habit, and preference for moist soils. It spreads by a mat of stolons, which extend from the center of the plant outward. The shiny leaves have a sweet citrus scent that would secure this herb a place in the garden even without the showy blooms. I love to brush against it while weeding or crush a leaf in passing because its aroma gives me the distinct impression that all is well with the world.

Planting information and cultural directions: Full sun, an open situation with good air circulation, and fertile, well-drained soils are what monarda likes best. It is a little unpredictable, however, and sometimes you need to try plants in two or three locations to see where they will thrive. In sunny parts of the region, it prefers partial shade. Dig the bed over and amend the soil with compost, then set plants about 2 feet apart. They will put out lots of growth from the roots in very early spring, but are less invasive than true mints.

Propagation: Monarda seeds are sometimes available, but since plants grown from seed are variable, it is best to start with a small plant or, if you happen to be in the right place at the right time, a root division from a neighbor or friend. The best time to divide the roots is while the rhizomes are still growing later-ally, usually until mid-April in our climate. Dig up the entire clump, or, if it is very large, dig it in sections using a sharp spade. Discard the worn-out centers, and with hand pruners slice the mat of rhizomes into smaller rooted pieces. Set them into the garden where they are to grow.

Year-round care: In late autumn, when plants die back for the winter, clip off the spent stems and cover the base of the plant with a 1-inch layer of compost or leaf mold. Winter protection is unnecessary, since the plants are quite hardy unless their roots are in standing water. If your monarda patch spreads more than you'd like, just chop the roots back to keep it in check.

Pests and diseases: The most common problem affecting monarda is mildew, which appears as a dusty white powder on the leaves. It usually occurs late in the season, especially after a rainy spell. Mildew resistance is bred into modern hybrids such as 'Adam' and the Zodiac series, but these often lack the intense fragrance of the standard red variety. To control mildew, try spraying the plant with a baking soda solution, using ¾ teaspoon baking soda per quart of water. Alternatively, cut the stems back to the ground, remove all affected leaves on the plant and on the ground, and destroy them. New growth will usually be disease free.

Harvesting and preserving: Ideally, leaves for tea should be harvested just as flower buds begin to form. If you can't bring yourself to sacrifice all the flowers, leave some stalks to bloom. Dry the leaves in small bunches, or strip them from the stalks and lay them on screens or dehydrator trays. To harvest flowers for dry-ing, cut stalks when the blossoms are at their prime. Bundle them in bunches of five to ten stems and hang them upside down in a warm, dry place out of the sun.

Garden uses: Look closely at photographs of ideal herb and cottage gardens, and you will often see monarda in bloom. Whether planted singly, in small groupings, or in glorious naturalistic drifts, this herb puts on a show from July through September. Its medium height, upright habit, and varied hues give it great versatility. It can provide vivid spots of color echoed through the landscape, or a gamut of colors in a single bed. Imagine purple-hued monardas lay-ered with salvia 'Victoria,' lavender, echinops, and buddleia. The dramatic reds stand out in Monet-inspired splendor with the bold primary hues of yel-low lilies, golden yarrow, and blue to purple delphiniums, contrasted with white feverfew. Clear pink monardas blend beautifully with pastel yarrows, dahlias, and foxgloves. Perhaps best of all, monarda is a star in any hummingbird garden.

Culinary uses: Two of monarda's common names refer to its primary use as a delightfully flavored tea. Native to the eastern United States, monarda was introduced by the Oswego Indians to the colonists, and as Oswego tea it became a patriots' brew after the Boston Tea Party. It is also called "bergamot," because its flavor resembles that of the citrus fruit that gives Earl Grey tea its special zest. Monarda is seldom available commercially, but it's easy to pick a few fresh leaves to infuse, or to dry some for winter. Enjoy the tea with lemon, honey, or milk, or com-bine it with mint or fruit juice. Tender leaves can also be chopped and added to fruit cups, or infused as a base for refreshing sorbets.

Removed from their bracts, fresh monarda flowers have a sweet flavor and are pretty and mild-tasting in salads, herb butters, and tea sandwiches, or for decorating cakes.

Craft and home uses: Bee balm's flowers are very decorative fresh or dried. They often start blooming around the Fourth of July in Northwest gardens, just in time for red, white, and blue bouquets with Queen Anne's lace, baby's breath, and delphiniums. They hold their bright color when dried and make unusual accents in dried wreaths, everlasting bouquets, and potpourris.

Medicinal uses: Monarda leaves contain thymol, an antiseptic oil. Native Americans had many uses for this plant—as a compress for problem skin, or a tea for colds, menstrual problems, and urinary tract disorders. The Shakers sold the dried leaf as a remedy for upset stomachs, vomiting, and flatulence. Current scientific evidence suggests that monarda may inhibit the *Herpes simplex* and related chicken pox viruses.

Nasturtium

Common names: Nasturtium, Garden nasturtium, Indian cress

Latin names: *Tropaeolum majus, Tropaeolum minus*

Latin family name: Tropaeolaceae

Varieties and cultivars:

Trailing: 'Glorious Gleam,' 'Tall Trailing,' Fragrant Giants,' 'Empress of India,' 'Jewel of Africa,' 'Moongleam,' 'Moonlight,' 'Sungold,' and others

Compact: 'Alaska,' 'Tip Top,' 'Tom Thumb,' 'Whirlybirds,' 'Peach Melba,' 'Butter Cream,'

'Strawberry Ice,' and others

Description: Cheery, adaptable nasturtiums deserve a place in container and garden herb plantings alike. These quick-growing annuals have flat, rounded leaves with radial veins like diminutive lily pads. The leaves grow profusely along brittle, succulent stems from a fleshy root.

Old-fashioned nasturtium flowers are trumpet-shaped and have five brilliant orange, gold, or red petals (sepals), the uppermost one ending in a tapering, nectar-bearing spur. Newer introductions may be fully double or semidouble and spurless; colors include cream, pale yellow, pink, mahogany, and other shades. Twin oval seeds are encased in a sheath at the end of flower stems. Nasturtiums reseed themselves lavishly.

The "vines" of trailing nasturtiums (*T. majus*) can easily reach 10 feet long, and may be trained to climb, cascade, or simply be allowed to spread. Popular varieties such as 'Fragrant Giants,' 'Tall Trailing,' and 'Glorious Gleam' have pointed spurs and brilliant blooms in many colors. The scarlet flowers of 'Empress of India' contrast with dark bluish green leaves to unusually lovely effect. 'Moonlight,' 'Moongleam,' and 'Sungold' are also quite beautiful, with pale to butter yellow blossoms and a vigorous trailing habit. 'Jewel of Africa' is a trailing variety with bright flowers and green leaves striped and splashed with cream.

Compact nasturtiums (*T. minus*) form low mounds with masses of flowers. 'Tom Thumb' is the smallest at 6 to 8 inches, with bright single blossoms. 'Tip Top' is a little bigger and is available in mixed colors or apricot. 'Whirlybird' is an excellent top-setting cultivar;

its spurless, multicolored flowers face upward. It blooms nonstop in a variety of shades. 'Alaska' forms a compact mound of bicolor green-and-white leaves and gold, salmon, orange, and mahogany flowers. Other delicious-sounding cultivars with lovely coloration include 'Peach Melba,' 'Butter Cream,' 'Strawberry Ice,' and others.

Planting information and cultural directions: Nasturtiums are very easy to grow, and bloom in full sun to full shade. When the weather gets hot they perform best in a shaded area. They like poor to average well-drained soil. Don't overfertilize or you will get too much foliage and few flowers. The plants flower freely through the summer months but are killed by the first hard frost.

Propagation and care: Growing nasturtiums from seed is a perfect project for children and beginning gardeners. The seeds are large and easy to handle, and also germinate promptly, especially if soaked in water overnight before sowing. Plant seeds indoors in March, or wait until early May and plant directly outside. The twin seedling leaves are round and flat, about the size of a quarter. Before long, flowers will be blooming—and if you choose a variety with spurs, there will be a sweet liquid to sample in the nectary base of each spur.

Year-round care: Extend the season by sowing nasturtiums in a sunny greenhouse in early spring or late summer. You can also root cuttings of your favorite plants in water and grow them indoors in winter. Watch out for aphids, though.

Pests and diseases: Aphids like nasturtiums and often congregate on the flower spurs and the undersides of leaves, especially in hot weather. In fact, nasturtiums are sometimes planted as decoys to divert aphids from other plants. Regular spraying with insecticidal soap will eliminate aphid problems.

Harvesting and preserving: Use nasturtium leaves and flowers fresh—they lose their flavor and texture when dried. Check closely for aphids, especially late in the season, and wash cuttings or flowers before using.

Flowers, leaves, and stems steeped in white wine vinegar make an excellent herb vinegar. Pickled flower buds and unripe seedpods are traditional caper substitutes, but it's hard to collect enough to fill a canning jar! Try adding a few to each jar when making dilled cucumbers or green beans.

Garden uses: Nasturtiums have much to offer as ornamentals and would be worth growing even without their other uses. They delineate or fill in areas quickly and have a long blooming season, in addition to the bonus of shade tolerance. At Silver Bay, I filled in shady spots with nasturtiums after spring bulbs finished blooming, sowing in May and again in July for continuous flowering.

Compact varieties are great for edging and lend the garden an air of gaiety when their full color range is used. Massed nasturtiums provide an eye-stopping display of color. Combine them with blue bachelor's buttons for added pizzazz, or narrow your palette and highlight one of the unusual new colors such as cherry rose, salmon, or cream.

Grow trailing varieties to cover the ground, scramble up a trellis, or spill over the edge of planters or hanging baskets. The public plantings at the British Columbia–Washington State border at Blaine,

Washington, include a happy profusion of nasturtiums cascading down a steep slope.

Culinary uses: The whole nasturtium plant has an agreeable peppery flavor reminiscent of watercress, and the blossoms are among the best edible flowers. As a garnish for salads and entrées, stuff them with goat cheese, herbed cream cheese, or tuna salad. Chop the flowers with the leaves to make colorful and tasty herb butter or cream cheese spreads for crackers and tea sandwiches. The leaves, especially variegated ones, also perk up mixed-greens salads and can replace lettuce in sandwiches. Take a tip from President Eisenhower, who added a handful of chopped nasturtium leaves and stems to his famous vegetable-beef soup during the last few minutes of cooking. Sprinkle chopped nasturtium "flecks of gold" over soufflés, eggs Benedict, and other egg dishes.

Medicinal uses: Nasturtiums are high in vitamin C and were taken aboard ships to prevent scurvy before it was discovered that lemons and limes were even more effective. The plant also contains glucotrapaeoline, a glycoside that hydrolyzes to antibiotic and sulfur compounds, and an essential oil (isothyocyanate or mustard oil), responsible for the plant's peppery bite.

Nettles

Common names: Stinging nettles, Nettles

Latin name: *Urtica* species

Latin and common family names: Urticaceae (Nettle family)

Varieties and cultivars: Stinging nettle, *Urtica dioica*; Coast nettle, *U. gracilis* var. *californica*; *U. gracilis* var. *lyallii*; Hoary nettle, *U. gracilis* var. *holosericea*

Description: Anyone who has hiked through the Northwest woods is familiar with stinging nettles, which have an arresting manner of making their presence known. As Nicholas Culpeper said in 1649, "They may be found, by feeling, in the darkest night." Their deeply notched, dark green leaves taper to a point like spearmint, but instead of releasing a pleasant scent when brushed, they deliver a burning sting that can cause redness and welts on the skin. Tiny hollow hairs on the plant release a toxin from raised sacs at their base that contains formic acid, histamine, acetylcholine, serotonin, and unknown substances. Appropriately, the first part of nettles' Latin name comes from *uros*, meaning "to burn."

Nettles are hardy perennials that creep on vigorous rhizomes. Their square, unbranched stems, which are 2 to 5 or even 6 feet tall, contain strong, pliant fibers. Clusters of wispy pale flowers, reminiscent of hazel catkins, hang from the leaf axils and are pollinated by the wind. Small, rounded seeds hang in clusters and drop when ripe. Nettles can form dense stands that are practically impossible to penetrate unless one is wearing armor.

The Latin name of the European species, *dioica*, means "two houses," referring to the arrangement of male and female flowers on different plants. According to Hitchcock and Cronquist, authors of *Flora of the Pacific Northwest*, the range of this variable species, which grows in moist areas from sagebrush desert to deep woods, may extend to the Northwest. It is the species usually described in herb books.

Hitchcock and Cronquist list several varieties of *Urtica gracilis*, the subspecies native to this region.

The explorer Menzies saw nettles growing at Birch Bay; the plant was called *qwunqwu'n* ("it stings you") by the Chehalis tribe, and *padakokoxl* ("it blisters") by the Quileute. In these varieties, which have the same properties as *U. dioica*, male and female flowers appear on the same plant. *U. gracilis* var. *lyallii* is the variety most common west of the Cascades throughout the region and in western Montana. Its leaves are broad, the length rarely exceeding twice the width. I've measured leaves 8 inches long without the stem, and this size is not unusual. They are sparsely hairy and bristly but still sting like heck.

Urtica gracilis var. *holosericea*, the hoary nettle, is another variety in the region. Its leaves are at least three times as long as they are broad, very hairy, and ash colored. The hoary nettle is common in the southwestern United States, but is occasionally present in eastern Washington, Oregon, and Idaho. The coast nettle, *U. gracilis* var. *californica*, is also grayish and hairy, especially on the underside of the leaves. It appears mainly in California and occasionally east of the Cascades as far north as central Idaho and Okanogan County, Washington.

Despite their waspish ways, nettles are among the Northwest's most valuable wild plants. Prehistoric Europeans and Native Americans, as well as present-day herbalists, have recognized the herb's varied attributes and its surprising range of uses.

Planting information and cultural directions: Because of their stings and invasive tendencies, nettles are seldom cultivated. Most gardeners work hard to get rid of nettles, which can get out of control and be very persistent. In rural areas, nettles are not hard to find, commonly appearing along roadsides and trails, and in ditches and barnyards. In cities, look for them in naturalistic parks and in areas where the ground has been disturbed.

At certain times and places, nettles have been cultivated on a large scale, producing three or four harvests each season. Plants grow in full sun to part shade; yields are highest when nitrogen is added to a rich, moist soil.

Propagation: Don your gloves and dig up a clump of nettle roots in spring, when the ground is moist and the young green tops are just beginning to emerge. Transplant the clump to the chosen site (keep those gloves on) and water it regularly until new roots are established. Nettles can also be started from cuttings taken in late spring, or from seed collected in late summer.

Pests and diseases: Holes in the leaves of wild plants are evidence that something devours them, but in general nettles are healthy plants. The leaves themselves are made into a natural spray to deter garden pests.

Harvesting and preserving: Harvesting young nettles is a rite of spring. If I don't have time to go out into the woods to gather them, I know that my life has become too busy. I am renewed by the sound of birdsong and the scents of moist earth and fresh growing things—especially the earthy perfume of young nettles. They are at their finest from the time their tender tops emerge until they are about 8 inches tall. Suit up in rubber gloves and boots, long-sleeved shirt, and long trousers, grab a plastic bag, and you're ready to harvest them. Pinch off the tender tips and two to three sets of leaves for the most delicate greens.

As the season progresses, the plants become taller and more stemmy. Keep picking the top sets of leaves, but leave stringy stems behind. Pinching back the plants encourages new growth, allowing multiple pickings. Stored in a plastic bag in the refrigerator, nettle tops will keep for about two weeks. Stop harvesting when plants begin budding, usually in May. Older leaves contain high oxalic acid concentrations and mineral crystals that are irritating to the kidneys.

Nettle leaves are easy to dry, and can be eaten as a seasoning and a health supplement. When dry they have no sting, and you can crumble them directly into soups and stews. Strip the leaves from the stems and lay them on screens or old sheets spread over an unused bed until they're crisp.

Garden uses: Native Americans noted that places where nettles grew wild made the best gardens. They are indicators of fertile soil, and some gardeners consider them excellent companion plants. Scientists at Sweden's University of Lund demonstrated that a boiling-water infusion of nettles makes a potent liquid fertilizer that increases the overall vigor of plants, as well as their resistance to disease and insect attacks. Alternatively, fill a 5-gallon bucket halfway with nettles, cover them with water, put a lid on the bucket, and allow them to steep for a week or two. Dip out the tea and drench plant roots with it, or strain and use as a foliar spray for speedy absorption. Some gardeners use this "nettle tea" as an organic fungicide and bug spray. Nettles also act as a compost activator, speeding the breakdown of organic material while adding nutrients to the fin-ished product. Nettle humus is rich and crumbly. Just make sure that no ripe seeds make it into your compost pile.

If you decide that the benefits of growing nettles outweigh their drawbacks, try to situate them where they won't spread through garden beds or sting the unwary. If eradicating them is your goal, mow them frequently until the plants are exhausted.

Culinary uses: Cooked as leafy greens, nettles are delicious, full flavored, and very good for you. They are exceptionally high in chlorophyll and contain vitamins A, B complex, C, E, and K_1. They also supply iron, calcium, phosphorous, potassium, silica, manganese, and trace minerals, plus folic acid, high-quality protein, tannins, and dietary fiber. Cook them in a basket steamer or a small amount of water for about 15 minutes, until they lose their fuzziness and sting. For variety, season them with lemon juice, soy sauce, butter, salt and pepper, nutmeg, garlic, cayenne, sesame seeds, or pine nuts.

Those who find nettles a bit strong may prefer them in one of the many versions of nettle soup, whether creamy, egg drop, or hot-and-sour style. They can substitute for spinach in frittatas, lasagne, spanakopita, and casseroles, and they're good in potato pancakes. Scramble them with eggs for green eggs and ham à la Dr. Seuss.

If you have a juicer, extract the juice from raw nettles and add it to health drinks as you would wheat grass to spike up the nutrient level. Beer made with nettle tops is a time-honored remedy for anemia and rheumatic pains. However you prepare them, rest assured that you are serving up a terrific nutritive tonic.

Craft and home uses: Accounts of the domestic use of nettles over the centuries make fascinating reading. Their long-standing reputation as a beauty aid derives primarily from their astringent, stimulant, and nutritional qualities. Externally, the young leaves benefit the skin in facial steams and baths, and a vinegar infusion or tincture of nettle leaves or roots is rubbed into the scalp to clear up dandruff and stimulate hair growth. Eaten fresh or taken in tincture form for several weeks, their abundant minerals promote thick, lustrous hair, strong nails, and clear skin. Erna Gunther notes in *Ethnobotany of Western Washington* that Chehalis and Skokomish girls boiled nettle root for a hair wash.

A remnant of nettle cloth was found in a Danish burial mound dating from the Bronze Age (5000 to 2000 B.C.). Until the early 1900s, the plants were cultivated in Scotland, Norway, and other northern countries, and the fibers were made into sturdy canvas and rope, as well as velvet, plush, and a fabric resembling silk. Eventually, flax supplanted nettles as the raw material for linen because it was less expensive to grow. More information on European use of nettles can be found in Maude Grieve's classic, *A Modern Herbal*.

Here in the Northwest, native peoples throughout the region peeled and dried nettle stems and rolled them on the thigh to make strong two-ply twine. The Lummi, Snohomish, and Skokomish used this twine for duck nets. It's fun to imagine nettles, like hemp, making a comeback as a source of fabric and fiber.

Medicinal uses: Herbalists regard nettles as among the premier nourishing, tonic, and blood-building herbs. With their well-balanced, easily absorbed nutrients, nettles support overall health and optimum function of major bodily systems. Noted herbalist Christopher Hobbs says nettles "keep us young"; David Hoffman, author of *The Holistic Herbal*, affirms that they are "good for everything." They are also regarded as specific remedies for several ailments. As with the constituents of their stinging toxins, the exact makeup and mechanisms of nettles' healing abilities are not completely understood.

Urtication, or burning, is one of the most ancient treatments for rheumatism, impotence, and paralysis. In many cultures of Europe as well as among Northwest Indian tribes, sufferers were whipped with whole stems of nettle; the burning stings were thought to stimulate healing or at least provide a distraction from the original pain. Infusions taken internally or rubbed on the body were alternative, less severe treatments. The histamines and acetylcholine in the toxin are now known to be potent vasodilators. In Europe, nettles were also eaten or sipped to break down what we now call uric acid, relieve arthritis, gout, and eczema.

In both traditional and contemporary herbal medicine, nettles are regarded as a great herb for the blood. Chlorophyll, iron, and other nutrients build hemoglobin and are beneficial in anemia, chronic tiredness, and recovery after illness or blood loss. Nettle is also known as a hemostatic and astringent that can lessen heavy periods, internal hemorrhage, and hemorrhoids. The Quinault tribe used peeled nettle bark to stop nosebleeds; the dried leaf powder has the same effect. Of course, you should consult a competent medical doctor—M.D. or N.D.—if the symptoms mentioned above are severe or lasting.

Nettles have long been considered a blood purifier, a term not currently in vogue that describes the
herb's ability to speed up metabolism, improve circulation, reduce plaque buildup in arteries, and support
the liver in its cleansing and digestive functions.
Nettles' internal cleansing actions can also help clear
up eczema, acne, boils, and other skin problems. The
Physicians' Desk Reference for Herbal Medicine, validates
nettles' traditional use for urinary tract infections and
kidney pains and stones. It has diuretic and gently
laxative effects.

Allergy sufferers may find that nettles can help
relieve their symptoms. In one study, a majority of
patients with allergic rhinitis (hay fever) treated with
freeze-dried nettles showed improvement. Nettles
also bind immunoglobulin G, responsible for many
food allergies. Traditionally, nettles are considered a
specific remedy for adults with asthmatic allergies.
They also speed healing of chest coughs, bronchitis,
and stubborn chest congestion.

A recent application of nettle is in the treatment of
symptoms of prostatic enlargement (benign prostate
hyperplasia or BPH). Although it does not reduce the
enlargement, a decoction of nettle roots does reduce
the incidence of nocturia (getting up in the night to
urinate) in early, less severe stages of the condition,
as substantiated by scientific studies.

Caution: Use only nettles that have not been
sprayed with herbicides—that is, avoid gathering
them near roadsides. In rare cases, allergic reactions
after ingestion of nettles have occurred. Use of nettles is not recommended where there is fluid retention caused by a weakened heart or kidney condition.

Oregano

Common names: Organy, Origano
Latin name: *Origanum* spp.
Latin and common family names: Labiatae/
Lamiaceae (Mint family)

Varieties and cultivars: Italian oregano or Hardy
sweet marjoram, O. x *majoricum*; Pot marjoram or rigani, O. *onites*; Greek or Turkish oregano, O. *vulgare* ssp.
hirtum, also called O. *heracleoticum*; Wild marjoram, O.
var. ssp. *vulgare*; varieties: 'Aureum' (Golden creeping
marjoram), 'Dr. Ietswaart' (Golden oregano), 'Jim
Best,' 'Herrenhausen,' 'Silver Anniversary'

Description: The many varieties of oregano are
part of a large, somewhat perplexing genus that also
includes marjorams; over the years there have been
many attempts to clarify its seemingly hopeless confusion of names. What is generally recognized as the
oregano of the kitchen is a 12- to 18-inch perennial
with shallow creeping roots and small, dark green,
opposite leaves on many reddish stems. Clusters of
small white, pink, or purple, upward-facing flowers
emerge from overlapping bracts at the stem tips.
Some varieties produce abundant seed that scatters in
the garden, resulting in new plants that may or may
not duplicate the parent plant.

The strong, hot flavor that has made this herb so
popular comes mainly from its flavor constituent carvacrol. I always advise my customers to taste a leaf
before choosing an oregano plant, because there is so
much variation. Dr. Art Tucker of Delaware State
College, and Elizabeth Rollins, former president of
the Herb Society of America, are making some head-
way in sorting out the classification of oreganos. The

following descriptions are based on their work. The most pungent-flavored variety, the "pizza herb," is Greek or Turkish oregano (*O. vulgare* ssp. *hirtum*). It has white flowers and green bracts. Italian oregano, also called hardy sweet marjoram or winter marjoram (*O.* x *majoricum*), is a hybrid between sweet marjoram (*O. majorana*) and *O. vulgare* ssp. *virens*. Its flavor is sweeter and less hot, more like sweet marjoram, but it is not reliably winter hardy. Pot marjoram or rigani (*O. onites*) from Crete has a peppery flavor. Wild marjoram (*O.* var. ssp. *vulgare*) has purplish bracts and pink flowers. It is readily grown from seed and often sold as oregano, but its flavor is just plain blah.

A variety of exciting cultivars of wild marjoram reveal the ornamental possibilities of the genus Oregano. 'Aureum' or 'Creeping Golden Marjoram' was illustrated by Parkinson in 1629. It has chartreuse leaves, as does the petite and crinkly 'Golden Oregano,' also called 'Dr. Ietswaart.' 'Jim Best' is a more recent introduction with green leaves splashed with gold. 'Silver Anniversary' is an excellent hardy and low-growing variety with green-and-white variegation. 'Herrenhausen' boasts leaves and stems tinged with burgundy and showy flower heads in the same dark hue, which hold their color when dried. Like their parent plant, these varieties have little flavor.

Planting information and cultural directions: Oregano tolerates poor soil, drought, harsh sun, high temperatures, and freezing cold. Give it well-drained soil and a sunny location and it can multiply prodigiously. Oregano's ability to thrive in arid conditions makes it a natural choice for hot, dry areas.

Although culinary oreganos have their place in kitchen gardens, beware of their spreading habit.

Propagation: Attempting to determine which oregano has the characteristic flavor, Dr. Tucker planted seeds he found in a bottle of dried oregano from the grocery store. Up came short and tall oreganos, oreganos with different sizes and colors of leaves, oreganos with various flavors, plus hairy spearmint, pennyroyal, a scentless lemon balm, and a few grasses. As he demonstrated, it *is* possible to grow oregano from seed, but good results are more predictable with cuttings or root divisions.

Use a sharp spade or knife to divide 2- or 3-year-old plants in spring or fall. Oregano air-layers readily, and almost any stem with roots attached will grow quickly into vigorous new plants.

Year-round care: Keep grasses, dandelions, and other weeds out of your oregano plants, especially when they are just emerging from dormancy. Cut plants back severely once or twice each season for a neat appearance. After they die down for the winter, remove the dead stems with hand pruners or a string trimmer.

Pests and diseases: Oregano is not usually susceptible to insect damage, and diseases are seldom a problem. You may, however, find slugs hiding in cool places at the base of the stems, just waiting to crawl out and devour other, more palatable plants growing nearby.

Harvesting and preserving: Pick oregano for the table anytime during the growing season. Use the tender tips or strip the leaves from woody stems. As the flower buds begin to form, cut plants back to the ground, fasten the cut bunches with rubber bands, and hang to air-dry. Oregano is easy to dry and keeps its flavor better than most other herbs. If your oregano blooms, do not despair—the leaves are still very pungent.

Garden uses: Pretty but hard-to-find Golden Oregano ('Dr. Ietswaart') and 'Silver Anniversary' are both choice low-growing ornamentals. They are well-behaved creepers, suitable for pots and small areas where the texture and color of their foliage can be appreciated. Creeping golden marjoram is more readily available and its bright color contrasts dramatically with darker leaves, especially bronze and purplish shades. It creates bright, gently curving mounds, draping downward in a rockery, although it will try to take over. 'Herrenhausen' is quite striking with its dark stems and flowers. Greek and common oreganos in bloom are usually surrounded by a busy contingent of bees.

Culinary uses: Oregano became popular in the United States after World War II, when GIs returned home with a taste for it, and some brought Italian brides who knew wonderful ways to cook with it. Pizza, spaghetti sauce, and pasta salads just do not taste right without oregano. It is also an essential ingredient in salsa, chili, and many Mexican dishes. Oregano's robust flavor enhances chicken, meat loaf, and soups. It's great with Greek salads, zucchini, roasted red bell peppers, and other vegetable dishes.

Craft and home uses: You can hang varied bunches of dried oregano in the kitchen for decoration, or combine them with other herbs, peppers, and garlic in edible wreaths. Florists use the flowers fresh or dried in arrangements.

Medicinal uses: Wild marjoram (*Origanum* var. ssp. *vulgare*) has been used as a folk medicine for centuries. Its composition varies considerably depending on where it is grown, but includes carvacrol (40 to 70 percent), thymol, and other compounds, along with tannins, resins, and bitter principles. It possesses antiviral, antiseptic, and expectorant properties, and is effective as a tea or inhalant for upper respiratory tract problems, including colds, bronchitis, and flu. It reduces muscle spasms and has a beneficial effect on the digestive tract, easing stomachaches and menstrual cramps.

Wild marjoram is applied externally as a poultice or liniment to swellings and rheumatic joints. It can also be added to a stimulating bath that reduces muscular aches and combats skin infections.

▊ Parsley

Common names: Curled parsley, Italian parsley

Latin name:

Curled: *Petroselinum crispum* var. *crispum*

Italian: *Petroselinum crispum* var. *neapolitanum*

Latin and common family names: Umbelliferae/Apiaceae (Carrot family)

Varieties and cultivars:

Curled: 'Moss Curled,' 'Triple Curled,' 'Darki,' 'Krausa,' 'Pagoda'

Italian: 'Catalogno,' 'Italian Giant,' 'Gigante d'Italia'

Description: Parsley is a basic herb, familiar even to people who claim to know nothing about herbs. It is such a favorite that many seed catalogs include it with the vegetables or devote a special section to it. Parsley forms a rosette of deep green leaves about 12 inches tall during its first year. The leaves emerge from the center, unfurling gradually. Stems are 6 to 8 inches long, paler green, and ridged. The white, fleshy root tapers like a parsnip.

The second year, a branched seed stalk rises to about 3 feet, topped with umbels of small yellow flowers. When pointed brown seeds ripen, the plant's life cycle is complete. Occasionally, plants go to seed in their first year, especially if they become dried out in hot weather. Pull out these rogues and replace them with young plants.

Curled parsley is the type most often seen in the grocery store or as a garnish. Its tightly curled, serrated leaves are bright green. 'Moss Curled' and 'Triple Curled' are standard varieties; newer on the market are 'Krausa,' a Dutch garnishing variety with a fine flavor; 'Pagoda,' which forms dense, uniform mounds; and others. Italian parsley is similar in all respects except that its leaves are flat, dark green, and deeply lobed, not curled. The plant grows larger than curled parsley and is more tolerant to cold temperatures. Some cooks prefer its stronger, sweeter flavor. 'Catalogno,' 'Italian Giant,' and 'Gigante d'Italia' are some selected cultivars.

Planting information and cultural directions: Parsley is not hard to grow, but appreciates rich soil with ample moisture. Improve the soil by working in compost, worm castings, composted manure, or other organic matter, and your plants will reward you with luxuriant production. Parsley flourishes in full sun or partial shade. For many gardeners, three or four plants of this herb are enough, but those who use it as a culinary staple may need an entire row.

Space plants about 10 inches apart.

Propagation: Before planting, soak parsley seed overnight, then sow indoors in February or March for early plants. Seeds germinate slowly; folk wisdom holds that parsley must go to the devil and back seven times before it can sprout. The first leaves are narrow and pointed; subsequent leaves are characteristically curly or lobed. Transplant young seedlings carefully in early spring for best results.

Seeds can be sown directly in the garden in March or April, though I don't recommend it because fast-growing weeds can easily overtake young plants. If you don't sow seed early, it's probably best to buy a few plants, but make sure they are not root-bound in their pots. Parsley reseeds abundantly; some gardeners never bother planting it yet always have plenty.

Year-round care: Left outdoors, parsley winters over easily in the Northwest. Plants go dormant in very cold weather, but resume in early spring. For year-round harvest, pot up a few plants in October or November and bring them indoors. The leaves may die back, but new ones soon replace them. You can prolong the life of your parsley by breaking off the seed stalk when it appears, but eventually the plant will go to seed and then the leaves develop a strong, bitter flavor.

Pests and diseases: Parsley is seldom affected by insect pests or diseases. Root rust can be a problem, but has never affected my plants.

Harvesting and preserving: When picking parsley, grasp one of the lower stalks and pull it gently downward while giving a little twist. The stalk comes away where it meets the plant, leaving no piece behind to rot. Use this method consistently, and picking will be easier and cleaner. Parsley can be picked through the winter in mild-weather areas or protected spots, providing an almost year-round harvest.

To keep parsley fresh, place whole stems in a glass jar with a small amount of water in the bottom and refrigerate. Dried parsley is handy to have in the pantry, but the herb turns yellow if hung in bunches to dry without extra heat. In early fall, before cold temperatures slow leaf growth, I fill a garden basket with parsley; wash, spin, and chop it well; and spread it on rimmed baking sheets to dry in the oven on low heat, keeping the door open a crack. It needs stirring once or twice to ensure even drying. You can also dry parsley in the microwave or dehydrator. Keep it in tightly sealed containers because it reabsorbs moisture easily; store it away from light to preserve its bright green color.

Parsley also freezes well. Prepare it as for oven-drying, but place the baking sheets in the freezer. Or, purée it in the blender with a little water and freeze it in ice cube trays. Once frozen by either method, transfer the parsley to glass jars with tight lids for freezer storage.

Garden uses: Since the days of the ancient Greeks, parsley has been used as a border plant. It can make a lush yet tidy edging of refreshing deep green around the entire garden or along a path. It is a must for kitchen gardens, and excellent in planters and window boxes. It remains compact for the first year, but grows very tall in the second year. Remove it unless you like its airy, branching appearance. Beneficial insects love the flowers.

Culinary uses: Be sure to eat that parsley that garnishes your restaurant meal—it may be the most nutritious thing on the plate! Rich in vitamins C, A, and B complex; iron; calcium; manganese; and phosphorous, parsley also contains abundant chlorophyll, fiber, and up to 22 percent protein. It has a fresh, versatile flavor that is excellent in dips and spreads, soups, quiches, tabouli, falafels, salads, and any savory dish. Parsley and new potatoes is an early-summer treat; the herb also enhances tomatoes, peas, zucchini, and other vegetables. A chef's tip to enliven dried herbs: mix them with freshly minced parsley and allow the flavors to meld for a few minutes. When parsley is added during the last minutes of cooking, color and nutrients are retained at their peak.

My family tested parsley's reputation as a breath freshener after eating an aïoli sauce made with twelve cloves of raw garlic (also an experiment—not recommended). We each chewed two large sprigs of parsley at the end of the meal and, by golly, it really seemed to work. We couldn't detect garlic breath on each other later, but it's possible that our whole house was saturated with the odor. When serving garlicky dishes, try placing a small bowl of chopped parsley on the table for diners to help themselves.

Medicinal uses: As well as being a storehouse of nutrition and a general tonic, the leaves, roots and seeds of parsley have medicinal properties. The herb stimulates the production of gastric juices, improves digestion, and eliminates gas. An infusion of the seeds is recognized as an effective diuretic, eliminating excess water from the body, and as an antiseptic particularly useful in treating urinary tract infections and eliminating kidney stones. A tea of the roots is milder but contains flavonoids that assist this action.

Traditionally, parsley is an emmenagogue that induces menstruation. However, drinking the tea in medicinal doses, ingesting the seeds, or eating large amounts of the leaves is not recommended for pregnant women because the herb also stimulates uterine contractions that can lead to miscarriage.

Rose

Common name: Rose

Latin name: *Rosa* spp.

Latin and common family names: Rosaceae (Rose family)

Varieties and cultivars:

Wild roses: Wild rose, Dog rose, *R. canina;* Nootka rose, *R. nutkana;* Peafruit rose, *R. pisocarpa* 'Gray;' Sweetbriar, Eglantine, *R. rubiginosa* or *eglantaria*

Cultivated roses: Apothecary's rose, *R. gallica* 'officinalis;' Damask rose, *R.* x *damascena;* Rugosa rose, *R. rugosa*

Description: Surely the most universally beloved of flowers, the rose also has a long history of herbal uses. There are so many types and varieties of roses that learning them all is a life study—in fact, some experts estimate the number of varieties at more than 10,000! But it is the wild and the very old roses, highly fragrant and bearing many or large hips, that are prominent in herbal traditions and current use.

Hitchcock and Cronquist list eight species of wild roses in their monumental work, *Flora of the Pacific Northwest.* Among these are *R. canina,* the wild rose or dog rose from Europe, which blooms from May to June (as do other roses). It is characterized by five clear pink, delicately fragrant petals, five sepals, and a ring of stamens like golden filaments. Its leaves are elliptical with toothed margins, opposite in pairs of five to seven, smooth on the underside, and unscented. Arching stems to 6 feet tall are covered with straight thorns. Hips are rounded and bright red when ripe. The Nootka rose, *R. nutkana* var. *nutkana,* is a beautiful variety with larger flowers and hips; it has sticky glands on the underside of the fragrant leaves and the main leaf axis. The sweetbriar or Eglantine rose (*R. rubiginosa* or *englanteria*), brought to the Northwest by pioneers and naturalized in some places, has small, light pink blossoms and clusters of elongated hips. The flowers are fragrant, and the leaves smell like fresh apples. It grows vigorously to 8 feet. Floral designers prize the Peafruit (*R. pisocarpa* 'Gray'), which is distinguished by clusters of tiny, bright red hips.

Two very ancient cultivated roses merit inclusion as herbs because of their importance in medicine, perfumery, and aromatherapy. *Rosa gallica,* known as the Apothecary's rose, originated in Persia before the twelfth century B.C. and is the forerunner of most garden roses. It is a beautifully fragrant rose, with deep pink to red semidouble flowers. Its canes are about 3 feet tall, almost thornless, and spread by suckering. Its offspring, *Rosa damascena,* the Damask rose, is the most significant rose in the production of the fabulously fragrant attar or oil of roses. Its flowers are velvety, purplish pink, and semidouble. This rose grows 4 to 6 feet tall and is slightly less hardy, to around 15°F.

Crosses between the Apothecary's rose, the Damask rose, and the roses imported from China during the eighteenth century resulted in the myriad seedlings, sports, and crosses made before the first hybrid tea rose was developed in 1876, and now collectively known as Old Roses.

Rugosa roses are garden stalwarts. Cold-hardy and disease free, their leaves are heavily crinkled, dark green to purplish, and their canes quite thorny. Flowers range in color from white through pinks to deep magenta, single to semidouble, and are often followed by round, fleshy hips as large as 2 inches across. Plants tend to grow large and often naturalize, particularly near the sea.

Planting information and cultural directions: Roses grow best in an open situation that has free air circulation yet is not too windy. Full sun is ideal, but most varieties will tolerate dappled shade. Soil should be well drained and neutral; a naturally fertile loam or ordinary soil enriched with organic matter such as compost, manure, worm castings, or leaf mold is ideal. Wood ash, which contains potash, needed for healthy growth and good flowers, is an excellent soil amendment.

Propagation: Softwood cuttings are the easiest way to propagate most roses. In late spring to summer, take cuttings 6 to 8 inches long from the current year's growth, which will be green in color rather than brown. When the stem snaps cleanly as you bend it, the wood has matured to the right point. The time-tested folk method is to stick the cuttings in the ground where they will be partially shaded, and place a quart fruit jar over them, pushing it into the ground to make a mini-greenhouse that provides extra humidity. Cuttings should take within 2 to 4 weeks; you can tell when new growth appears. Leave the glass jar over

the cutting until enough roots have developed to sustain the plant, usually by the end of the season. Then pot the cuttings and keep them in a cold frame, or simply plant them where they are to grow.

Rosa gallica and many wild roses spread gradually by sending up suckers, which are easy to dig and propagate (see Suckering, Chapter 1). Roses are also propagated by taking hardwood cuttings (see Hardwood Cuttings, Chapter 1). It is possible but not easy to start roses from seed, and only species roses will come true from seed, not hybrids. For details, consult *Plant Propagation: Principles and Practices* by Hartmann and Kester.

Year-round care: In January or February, cut back the top third from strong shoots of *gallica* and Damask roses for best flower production, and remove weak shoots and crossing branches after blossoms fade. Wild, sweetbriar, and rugosa roses are largely self-sufficient once established, and require only occasional pruning to maintain the size and shape desired. Water roses regularly during the dry months, using soaker hoses or other ground-level methods rather than overhead sprinkling, which can promote disease. Old Roses respond well to annual spring fertilizing with organic materials such as bonemeal, alfalfa meal, and compost. For even better results, give the plants a monthly dose of tea made by soaking 1 cup of dried manure or compost in 2 gallons of water for two days.

Pests and diseases: One of the real beauties of the roses I've described is their resistance to the diseases and pests that plague so many of the newer hybrids.

To keep plants healthy, start with good sanitation,

cleaning up all fallen leaves and debris when you prune in January or February. Look for cane lesions and remove them too. Do not compost this material; burn it. To head off rust, black spot, and powdery mildew keep potassium levels high by using wood ash or other fertilizers. If any of these fungus diseases strikes, pick off diseased leaves or cut back diseased parts, then spray the plants with a solution of 1 tablespoon of baking soda dissolved in 1 gallon of water. Planting garlic around your rosebushes really does seem to deter aphids, but if they attack, timely applications of insecticidal soap should take care of the problem. Pick off caterpillars by hand, or spray affected plants with Bt (*Bacillus thuringiensis*, see Organic Pest and Disease Management, Chapter 1).

Harvesting and preserving: How and when you harvest rose petals depends on what you plan to do with them. For potpourri, rose beads, and other craft projects, pluck newly opened flowers, twisting off the calyxes as you go along. Make sure that the petals are dry or they will turn brown. Spread them out on newspapers, screens, or dehydrator racks, and turn them occasionally to make sure they dry evenly.

For high-quality medicinal preparations, select plump, unopened buds and remove the calyxes, leaving the conical bundle of petals intact. Cut off the white part at the base of the petals, then make up the preparation of the whole fresh bundles, or dry them quickly without separating the petals. Dried petals must be stored in airtight tins or they will reabsorb moisture from the air and lose their color.

Rose hips are ripe when they turn bright orange or red but are still firm. Rub off sepals, spread the hips on trays, and dry them in a warm place for best color.

Garden uses: From late May through June, Old Roses in bloom can make the garden a heaven on earth. Mature bushes are covered with blossoms that waft their sweet perfume through the air. Wild roses adorn the roadsides.

These rosebushes combine well with longer-blooming rose varieties, herbs, foliage plants, shrubs, and other flowers that extend the flowering period and provide continuous garden displays. Many rose gardens are formal in design, the plants in neat rows or beds edged with compact plants such as germander, dwarf sage, santolina, or boxwood. Some gardeners prefer an informal, cottage-garden look, with roses as occasional features, interspersed among lilies, delphiniums, daisies, baby's breath, phlox, and other time-honored favorites.

Roses can also be important elements of herb gardens combined with lavenders, feverfew, anise hyssop, rosemary, and other tall herbs. Sweet woodruff, creeping thymes, and cheerful violas are some low-growing options that can enhance the beauty of your roses.

The Apothecary's rose, grafted on nonspreading rootstock, is a good container plant, while the tough sweetbriars and rugosas make fine hedges, whether carefully clipped or allowed to grow to their full height.

Culinary uses: In centuries past, roses were valued more for cooking, perfumery, and medicine than as beautiful garden flowers. *Rose Recipes from Olden Times* by Eleanour Sinclair Rohde is a charming book of recipes for rose conserves, "sirops," vinegars, "oyles," and scented mixtures, all collected from antique herbals. Nowadays, the culinary merits of the rose seem to be most appreciated where roses are grown on a commercial scale. Rose preserves from Bulgaria and Turkey can be found in import shops. Turkish delight, similar to the familiar Northwest confections Aplets and Cotlets, is flavored with rose water, as is *lassi*, a yogurt-based drink of India. In the Middle East, a splash of rose water is added to lemonade for a very refreshing beverage. At Silver Bay Herb Farm, pastry chef Steve Whippo once served a Rose Tea at which every dish contained roses in some form, from rose tea-sandwiches to rose hip jelly. His White Chocolate Rose Petal Cheesecake was the piece de resistance; see page 60 for recipe.

Rose hips are very high in vitamin C and have a full and pleasantly ascorbic flavor. The rugosa varieties have the fleshiest hips, but hips from wild roses and sweetbriars are fine, too. Rose hip soup, a sieved purée of rose hips thickened with potato flour, is popular in Scandinavian countries.

Craft and home uses: The hedonistic Romans of old loved roses and used them extravagantly in wreaths and garlands, strewed them on their banquet floors, and showered them down on partygoers. At a party given by one Heliogabalus, several of his guests were suffocated by an overly lavish shower of rose petals!

Compared to this, having a few "rose jars" or pot-pourri crocks around the house seems positively timid. Still, it's satisfying to harvest rose petals and preserve their scent, and those inclined will find pot-pourri recipes in this and other herb books. Rose or rosary beads fashioned of cooked rose petals are fun to make, too.

Roses are mainly grown for perfumery and cosmetics. The precious attar of rose, distilled from the petals, is used to scent fine lotions, creams, and soaps. Rose water, a hydrosol produced in the distilling process, has a lighter scent of rose and is mildly astringent. It is wonderfully refreshing misted on the skin after a shower or while traveling during hot weather. A compress of rose water is soothing to the eyes, especially after crying or using the computer too long. Rose oil and water are moisturizing to the skin, as in grandma's rose water and glycerine lotion.

To make an approximation of rose water, place freshly picked or dried rose petals in a stainless steel or enamel pan, barely cover them with distilled water, bring them slowly to a boil, then simmer them for 15 minutes. Strain and use in beverages or as a wash for the face and eyes.

Medicinal uses: Roses, specifically *R. gallica*, were included in the pharmacopoeias of the United States and Britain until the 1930s. Syrup of roses was recommended as a mild astringent and tonic, helpful for sore throats. Now it is generally agreed that all Old Roses in deep shades of rose and red have medicinal qualities, since the beneficial constituents of their petals are linked with their color. A tea of rose petals is thought to be cooling, diuretic, and tonic, gently stimulating and cleansing the liver and gallbladder and relieving associated digestive problems. In Chinese medicine, *R. rugosa* petals are prescribed for regulating *chi* (energy) and other actions.

In addition to their high vitamin C content (sixty times more than oranges), rose hips are rich in vitamins

A, B$_1$, B$_2$, E, K, and P. Rose hip tea is good tasting and highly nutritive, and can be drunk freely as a restorative tonic and to prevent colds and flu. To make the tea, simmer 3 teaspoons fresh or 1 cup dried rose hips in 1 cup of water for 10 minutes. Use it immediately or steep the hips for up to 24 hours for maximum flavor. Be sure to strain out the seeds and their prickly hairs before drinking the tea.

Aromatherapy: Attar of roses, distilled from rose petals, is one of the costliest essential oils. It takes 10,000 petals to produce a pound. Much of this oil is used in perfumery, but it is also significant in aromatherapy. In the words of Marguerite Maury, author of the *Guide to Aromatherapy*, "the rose procures us one thing above all: a feeling of well-being, even of happiness." It seems natural that the luscious aroma of Old Roses would help to ease cares, and, indeed, rose oil is used to treat stress, anxiety, depression, grief, and insomnia. It is nontoxic, nonirritating, antiseptic, and healing to the skin. A word of caution: inexpensive "rose oil" is a synthetic product and does not have healing properties.

Rose Geranium

Common name: Sweet-scented geranium

Latin names: *Pelargonium graveolens, P. radens*

Latin and common family names: Geraniaecae (Geranium family)

Varieties and cultivars:

P. graveolens: 'Charity,' 'Cinnamon Rose,' 'Lady Plymouth,' 'Grey Lady Plymouth,' 'Lilac Rose,' Rober's Lemon Rose,' 'Old Fashioned Rose,' 'Rose of Bengal,' and others

P. capitatum: 'Attar of Roses'

P. radens: 'Dr. Livingston' or 'Skeleton Rose,' and others

Description: Start your exploration of the addictive scented geraniums with the rose varieties. These tender perennials, native to South Africa, are prized for their wonderful rose scent more than their blossoms. Their deeply lobed, veined leaves are 1 to 3 inches long and contain high quantities of essential oil with a powerful rose aroma. The oil is produced in glands situated at the base of tiny leaf hairs. The small, five-petaled pink flowers, often tinged with burgundy, appear in terminal clusters. Each flower produces five small, brown seeds that remain viable for up to three years. The jointed, succulent stems become brown and woody with age. Mature plants grow at least 3 feet tall and can live for many years with winter protection.

The 'Old Fashioned Rose' variety is probably the most popular of all scented geraniums. People are often astonished when they first smell the intense rose odor of its leaves. It grows fairly large and has an upright habit.

Years of breeding have resulted in more than fifty other rose geranium cultivars, each having a different leaf shape and scent. 'Attar of Rose' has broader, three-lobed leaves and a marvelous rose fragrance equal in intensity to 'Old Fashioned' but deeper in character. 'Lady Plymouth,' a beautiful offspring of 'Old Fashioned Rose,' has similarly shaped leaves outlined and flecked with white; its sport, 'Gray Lady Plymouth,' is even prettier. 'Charity' is a lovely plant with gold-edged leaves and a dense growth habit.

'Rose of Bengal' is a petite plant with larger blossoms that are almost as showy as a Martha Washington type. The scent of roses is mingled with other aromas in 'Rober's Lemon Rose,' one of my personal favorites. Deeply incised leaves distinguish both 'Dr. Livingston' and 'Skeleton Rose' (*P. radens*), a rangy grower, and floriferous 'Crowfoot Rose' (*P. capitatum*).

These and other scented geraniums—which smell like anything from peppermint and lemon to musk and apple cider—are an altogether fascinating group of plants. Be forewarned—you always want one more variety.

A brief botany refresher may help to straighten out the nomenclature of these plants. Scented geraniums are properly called pelargoniums, and are members of the genus *Pelargonium*, one of four genera (plural of genus) and 250 species belonging to the Geranium family (Geraniaceae). The familiar, vivid garden geraniums are also pelargoniums. Pelargonium comes from the Greek word *pelargos*, or "stork," from the long pointed seedpods that look like a stork's bill.

Planting information and cultural directions: Give rose geraniums good, well-drained soil and full sun, or partial shade where summers are sunny and hot. Work some compost and organic fertilizer into the soil before planting and your plants will flourish. These drought-tolerant plants like to dry out completely between waterings. Like other geraniums, they rarely survive winters outside. In September or October, when nights grow cold, bring them into a frost-free area such as the house, garage, or cool greenhouse.

Rose geraniums make excellent container plants. Although they get big, they don't mind being root-bound. Even apartment dwellers can enjoy the fragrance of scented geraniums year-round by growing them in a sunny window. Outdoors they can be left in pots and sunk into the ground, but will grow much larger if planted in large tubs or directly into the garden.

Propagation: To propagate, take stem cuttings from soft growth in early spring and fall. Cut directly across a node or just under a node, strip off the lower leaves, and place the cutting in a mixture of sand and perlite. At 70° to 80°F, cuttings root in four to six weeks. A source of bottom heat is helpful but not crucial. See Herbaceous Cuttings, Chapter 1, for information.

Since *P. graveolens* is a species rather than a hybrid, its seed reliably replicates the parent plant. You can harvest seed from your own plants, and it is available through some mail-order catalogs. Sow it shallowly in pots of seedling mix, cover pots with plastic wrap, and set them in a sunny window. Once the seed germinates, remove the plastic wrap. Transfer seedlings to individual pots when they are about 3 inches tall.

Hundreds of scented geranium varieties have been produced by hybridization between species. If you'd like to try your hand at this and possibly come up with a fantastic new scented geranium, consult *Scented Geraniums* by Jim Becker and Faye Brawner.

Year-round care: Pinch flowers back to encourage bushy growth on your rose geraniums. Shape your plants as you harvest the leaves, cutting or pinching them back to a leaf node. Monthly applications of diluted fish fertilizer or compost tea are beneficial but not imperative if you have enriched the soil.

When you dig plants in the fall, cut them back by a third (use or root the trimmings). Store them in dampened peat, singly in pots, or together in a large tub. Water only enough to keep them alive through the winter, about once a month. When new growth begins to form, usually in February, prune the plants back by at least half to keep them compact. Water more frequently as the plants come out of dormancy. Gradually harden them off and set them outside mid-May to June when the weather is warm and settled.

If a busy schedule prevents you from bringing in your scented geraniums for the winter, don't be too hasty to pitch out the "dead" plants in spring. They are alive as long as their stems are firm and their roots are light brown. Leave the plants where they are, water them occasionally, keep an eye on them, and don't be surprised if you get lucky. New leaves may sprout from the roots when the weather warms in May or June, and plants can recover completely.

Pests and diseases: Aphids and spider mites can be a real problem on rose geraniums, especially when they are in an enclosed area. Spraying insecticidal soap as needed should keep pests in check.

Harvesting and preserving: Use the leaves fresh, hang them in bunches, or dry them in a dehydrator and store for later use.

Garden uses: In the garden, rose geraniums contribute luxurious fragrance and beauty. Position them where they are accessible, lining a path or beside a well-used garden bench. Or grow them on a deck or patio where you can reach out easily and crush a leaf. Large planters of rose geraniums make an entryway memorable, and they look good grouped with roses and other fragrant flowers. These quick growers are great for filling in empty places. Sometimes I set out pots containing large scented geraniums to hide gaps where sage or other herbs have been cut back—and presto! a lush garden.

Culinary uses: Rose-scented geraniums have an exotic flavor similar to rose water that is especially delicious in desserts. When baking a white, angel food, or pound cake, line the bottom of a greased pan with leaves (bottom side up) before pouring in the batter. Remove the leaves before serving.

Layer the leaves with sugar in a tightly covered container and allow them to age for a week or two. Remove the blanched leaves carefully and save them for garnishes. The aromatic sugar is wonderful in muffins and scones, whipped cream, frosting on sugar cookies, or sprinkled on cakes and other baked goods. If you can't wait, combine the leaves with sugar in a blender and grind to a fine texture. Or, steep the leaves in warm sugar syrup to enhance lemonade, Earl Grey tea, and other beverages. Rose geranium latte, anyone?

Rose geranium and fruit is a combination made in heaven. Small amounts of rose geranium sugar or syrup—or finely chopped leaf—bring out nuances of flavor in strawberry, rhubarb, apricot, peach, or blackberry dishes. Add a rose geranium leaf to each pint jar when making apple or crabapple jelly or jam with the fruits mentioned above.

Craft and home uses: Because scented geranium leaves hold their fragrance when dried, they have been used for centuries to scent the home and body. Combined with rose petals, lavender, and other fragrant herbs, they are a classic ingredient in potpourri, sachets, and sweet bags.

The fresh leaves are wonderful in herbal tussie mussies and other bouquets. At Silver Bay we included rose geranium leaves in brides' bouquets and grooms' boutonnieres. Besides their long association with love, they imparted a fragrance unmatched by anything from the florist.

Like the well-known insect repellent citronella, rose geranium contains a large percentage of citronellol. What more delightful way to repel insects could there be than squeezing a rose geranium leaf or burning a candle containing its fragrant oil at your picnic table? A rose-geranium-scented room spray is deodorizing as well (for recipe, see Herbal Craft Recipes in Chapter 4).

An excellent skin herb, rose geranium is an ingredient in soaps, creams, bath salts, and other cosmetic products. Its cleansing, antiseptic, and mildly astringent qualities make it a remedy for acne and dermatitis. Its renewing, normalizing character helps dry, oily, and mature skin. Steep a handful of leaves in boiling water for a few minutes to make facial steam or sweet washing water. Rose geranium essential oil is an ingredient in quality perfumes for men and women, including Gucci No. 1, L'Aimant, Sandalwood, and Paris.

Medicinal uses: In folk usage, rose geranium leaves have been used stop bleeding, and Italian studies verify that they have styptic properties. However, the majority of therapeutic applications of this herb involve its essential oil.

Aromatherapy: The oil that is steam-distilled from the leaves of *P. graveolens* is among the most widely used in aromatherapy. It contains primarily geraniol and citronellol, the main fragrance components of attar of roses.

"Geranium" or "geranium rose" oil, as it is usually called by aromatherapists, both soothes and revitalizes. Gentle and nontoxic, it is believed to have a positive and balancing effect on the emotions and the body, particularly the skin, circulation, nervous system, and adrenal cortex. It helps to allay nervous tension, stress-related conditions, and depression. It normalizes the menstrual cycle, and is used to treat PMS, menopausal imbalance, and endometriosis. Add a few drops to your bathwater or to a carrier oil for gentle relaxation and refreshment.

Rosemary

Common names: Rosemary, Dew of the Sea, Incensier

Latin names: *Rosmarinus officinalis, R. prostratus*

Latin and common family names: Labiatae/Lamiaceae (Mint family)

Varieties and cultivars:

Rosmarinus officinalis: 'Alba,' 'Albus,' 'Arp,' 'Gorizia,' 'Hills Hardy,' 'Majorca Pink,' Miss Jessop's Upright,' 'Mrs. Howard's,' 'Red Flowered,' 'Spice Islands,' 'Tuscan Blue,' and others

Rosmarinus prostratus: 'Huntington Carpet,' 'Irene,' 'Santa Barbara,' 'Mozart,' 'Severn Sea,' and others

Description: Rosemary, the herb of remembrance, is an aromatic evergreen perennial, prized for its culinary, medicinal, ornamental, and symbolic qualities. Its dark green, glossy leaves are opposite, narrow and pointed, white on the underside, and have a strong piney fragrance. Its flowers, borne in clusters along the stems, are usually blue, less commonly pink, red, or white, and like others in the mint family look like little orchids. In the Northwest, they usually bloom in April and May. Four small brown seeds form in the calyx of each flower.

Upright rosemary varieties form woody shrubs up to 6 feet tall. Several large branches grow from a single trunk, which becomes gnarled and woody with age. Roots are brown and wiry, spreading and relatively shallow. Prostrate varieties creep and trail along the ground at only 6 inches in height.

Rosemary has been cultivated since ancient times, and there are many fine varieties available. *R. officinalis* or common rosemary is the standard against which all others are measured. 'Arp' and 'Hills Hardy' are broad-leaved, extra-hardy varieties that survive temperatures of about 15°F. 'Gorizia,' a fast-growing bush, has large, light blue flowers with darker blue markings. 'Spice Islands' has dark blue flowers, very broad leaves that are green on the undersides, and an excellent flavor. 'Miss Jessop's Upright' is a strong-growing, free-flowering variety that forms a neat bush suitable for hedges. 'Tuscan Blue' is notable for narrow leaves, thick columnar growth, a sweet rosemary flavor, and bright blue flowers. 'Alba' has white flowers, 'Majorca Pink's' are amethyst, and 'Red Flowered' rosemary, a rare and tender variety from Portugal, is spectacular in bloom. 'Severn Sea' and 'Mrs. Howards' are distinguished by their attractive semiprostrate habit; plants grow about a foot tall, then cascade gently downward.

Of the prostrate varieties, the vigorous 'Santa Barbara' is most widely available; 'Irene' has deep blue flowers and spreads 18 to 36 inches a year. The long-blooming flowers of 'Mozart' are cobalt blue.

Planting information and cultural directions: Native to the Mediterranean, rosemary thrives in dry, well-drained soil. Give your plants full sun for as much of the day as possible. For best results in acid soils, work in about ¼ cup of agricultural lime when planting and again each spring.

Watering rosemary can be a little tricky. Herbalists say "a dry rosemary is a dead rosemary," yet plants also die if they are watered too much. Ordinarily, plants in the garden need watering only during prolonged dry spells.

Rosemary is an excellent container plant. It likes a good potting soil with compost and a little lime added. Container-grown rosemary should be watered when the top 2 inches of soil dry out.

Some people prefer to grow plants indoors, at least during the winter. If possible, place the plants in a well-lit area that remains relatively cool. Daily watering may be necessary in the dry atmosphere of a centrally heated home, but take care that the roots do not stand in water.

Propagation: Rosemary can be grown from seed, although germination is erratic and seedlings grow slowly, even with bottom heat. The first leaves are oval; true leaves are long and narrow. Most gardeners get better results by purchasing plants or by taking cuttings in midsummer. Another method is to layer an established rosemary by scraping a little bark from the underside of a branch, then pegging it to the ground. Sometimes plants layer on their own. When roots form, cut the new plant from the parent and replant it.

Year-round care: Outdoors, rosemary is an almost maintenance-free herb. Whatever pruning or shaping you may wish to do can be accomplished by judicious harvesting. Mature rosemary can compete with most weeds, but do keep grass away from your plants.

Until it has a well-established root system (two to three years), rosemary will not reliably survive Northwest winters. Most varieties should be potted up and wintered in a garage or cool greenhouse when they are small. Larger plants usually survive to 20°F but may lose some branches. To protect them, mulch the roots with dry leaves, straw, or other materials, and if you want to be especially solicitous, throw an old blanket over the plants when nighttime temperatures drop to the teens. Rake off the mulch in early to mid-March. Trailing rosemary is even less hardy than the upright form, and survives winter outdoors only in the most protected locations.

Pests and diseases: Rosemary seldom has insect or disease problems. Leafhoppers can yellow plants outdoors and spider mites sometimes attack plants grown inside; use insecticidal soap sprays for control.

Harvesting and preserving: For the finest dried rosemary, pick new growth on pale stems that are tender yet firm. Fasten small bunches with rubber bands and hang them in a very warm, airy place. July and August are the best months for harvesting, after the blossoms and calyxes have dropped and new shoots up to a foot tall are in their prime. Although rosemary is evergreen, it goes dormant in the winter. Harvest your plants only lightly during this season, especially when they are young, so that harvesting does not outstrip their ability to regenerate and grow

larger. If you cut woody stems, strip off the leaves and use them for cooking; discard the stems.

Garden uses: With its handsome evergreen foliage, delicate blossoms, and strong vertical lines, rosemary is an asset in garden design. A pair of rosemary plants placed beside a gate or other entrance extends a special welcome to visitors. A tall plant makes a handsome focal point in the center of a formal herb garden and grows more quickly than a bay tree. Rosemary in whiskey barrels or large clay pots can also add interesting height and texture. Prostrate varieties are lovely cascading from planter boxes or hanging baskets, and also soften the edges of concrete steps and rock walls.

Although a gardener must be patient, a hedge of mature rosemaries is worth a few years' wait. Clipped, such a hedge provides a beautiful edging; allowed to grow tall, it is a splendid garden divider or screen, all the more appealing if a nearby bench allows enjoyment of the plants' fragrance and honeybees busy amid the tiny flowers.

Culinary uses: The warm, resinous, yet sweet flavor of rosemary makes it an extremely versatile culinary herb, enhancing everything from meats, soups, and pasta dishes to vegetables, beverages, and desserts. It is excellent with pork, lamb, and beef. Try grilling lamb, fruit kebabs, or new potatoes on rosemary skewers (first soaked in water) for an impressive presentation, or place the fresh or dried herb over the coals when grilling meat or poultry. Rosemary is the signature flavor of minestrone soup and indispensable in many other Italian specialties. Split pea soup, fried potatoes, carrots, fresh orange slices, herb vinegars, lemonade, biscuits, and shortbread are also delicious with rosemary.

Craft and home uses: Both upright and prostrate rosemaries are good choices for topiaries. It's fun to train them to resemble small, bushy trees or to use wire or wooden forms to create cones, hearts, and other fanciful shapes. Rosemary has long been associated with Christmas, and potted plants are fine miniature Christmas trees.

"See thee much rosemary, and bathe thee therein to make thee lusty, lively, joyful, likeing and youngly," instructed William Langham in *The Garden of Health* (1579). Rosemary has traditionally been associated with youthfulness and vitality, and has a long history as a beauty and bath herb. A handful steeped in boiling water and strained into the bath improves circulation and relaxes aching muscles. Legend has it that Queen Elizabeth of Hungary (ca. 1370) added a rejuvenating distillation of rosemary with citrus and herbs to her bath. It not only healed the elderly queen's paralysis, but kept her so "youngly" that a twenty-seven-year-old man proposed to her. This "Hungary Water" was the forerunner of Eau de Cologne. Modern perfumes that incorporate the fresh scent of rosemary oil include 4711, Tsar, and Eau de Cologne Imperiale.

Beneficial to the hair and scalp, rosemary is an ingredient in shampoos and hair rinses (especially for brunettes) and in formulas to stimulate hair growth and prevent dandruff. It is also popular in soaps, lotions, creams, and deodorants.

Rosemary gives an herbal scent to potpourris, blending well with citrus, lavender, mint, and other herbs. Along with tansy, southernwood, cedarwood, clove, and other strongly aromatic botanicals it is an ingredient in insect-repellent mixtures.

Rosemary is the primary wedding herb because it stands for remembrance and faithfulness. Traditionally, brides have carried it in their bouquets, worn garlands of it in their hair, and gave it to wedding guests so they would hold the couple in their thoughts.

Medicinal uses: While most familiar as a cooking herb, rosemary has also earned respect as a medicinal herb over the centuries, especially in connection with memory. Roman students wore crowns of it during exams, Gerard claimed that "Rosemary comforteth the braine, the memorie, the inward senses," and Shakespeare's Ophelia evoked the herb "for remembrance." Modern research shows that the herb does improve circulation and stimulate the brain. In Europe, a rosemary infusion is added to the bath for this purpose and to promote the healing of wounds. The herb is steeped in wine and taken internally as an aid to circulation, and made into creams and liniments to relieve rheumatic pains. It is current in the *British Herbal Pharmacopeia* for "depressive states with general debility and indications of cardiovascular weakness."

Rosemary ranks with peppermint, lemon balm, chamomile, and valerian as one of the best herbal antispasmodics, acting on the digestive system to ease pains and cramps, expel gas, tone the stomach, and stimulate the liver and gallbladder. It also shows promise as a cancer-fighting herb. Rosmarinic acid, an important constituent of rosemary, has powerful antioxidant and preservative qualities.

Aromatherapy: Essential oil of rosemary was first distilled in about A.D.1330 and has been used therapeutically ever since. This highly aromatic, colorless, or pale yellow liquid has more than fifty constituents, predominantly cineole, alpha-pinene, camphor, borneol, and rosmarinic acid. Chemists have identified six distinct rosemary chemotypes; they vary in character and aroma depending on the proportions of these and other substances.

Rosemary oil is antibacterial, antiviral, antifungal, and anti-inflammatory. Aromatherapists value it as an invigorating stimulant to the nervous system and as an overall reviving tonic. For a stress-relieving massage oil that gently tones and stimulates the entire body, add 5 to 10 drops of rosemary oil to 2 teaspoons of grapeseed oil. A little of this diluted oil rubbed on the temples may allay headaches, uplift the spirits, and promote clear thinking. Instead of a cup of coffee to perk you up in the morning, try adding 10 drops to your morning bath, especially if you wake up with a hangover.

Sage

Common name: Sage

Latin name: *Salvia officinalis*

Latin and common family names: Labiatae/ Apiaceae (Mint family)

Varieties and cultivars: Pineapple sage, *Salvia elegans*; Common sage, *S. officinalis*; 'Berggarten,' 'Golden' or 'Aurea,' 'Holt's Mammoth,' 'Purpurascens' (purple), 'Tricolor,' and others

Description: There are many members of the salvia clan, including the ubiquitous bedding types. All have ornamental value, but those considered herbal are also useful for cooking or medicine. Sage comes with leaves of gray-blue, purple, gold and green variegation, and green, white, and pink-purple variegation.

Common sage is a hardy and often long-lived perennial that grows to about 3 feet high. Its grayish green, pebbled leaves are "like in roughness to woollen cloth threadbare," according to the herbalist John Gerard (1597). They remain on the plant year-round. Left to grow untended, the stems become long and woody with leaves mainly at their tips. In June and July, purple flowers like tiny snapdragons bloom in whorls along terminal spikes. Look into the toothed, bell-shaped calyx after the flowers drop and you'll see the round, dark brown seeds forming.

'Berggarten' is a fine-flavored, broad-leaved sage that quickly grows into a huge mound. The good flavor and large leaves of 'Holt's Mammoth' make it popular among commercial growers. Purple sage, also called Red sage, is distinguished by its purplish leaves. Golden sage has pretty light green and gold variegation, is mildly flavored, and grows to 2 feet. 'Tricolor' is similar in flavor and growth habit, but its colorful leaves are streaked with pink, white, and purple. 'Mildred Faye's Rainbow,' an exciting new selection, may be the most beautiful of all. Pineapple sage (*S. elegans*) is quite different, with thin, smooth green leaves and a sweet pineapple scent; showy red flowers attract hummingbirds to the garden. It cannot tolerate cold and must be taken in during the winter.

Planting information and cultural directions: Sage thrives in almost any well-drained soil with abundant calcium, preferring a sunny spot, though it also does well in dappled shade. It is hardy, drought resistant, and very easy to grow.

The smaller-growing sages are an excellent choice for containers. Give them quick-draining potting mix and take care not to overwater them. Consider grouping them with lavender, thyme, and other herbs with similar drought tolerance.

Propagation: Common sage is easily grown from seed, although seedlings may be different from the parent plant. Start seeds indoors in March; for best results sow them shallowly and keep them at 60° to 70°F until germination occurs. Transplant seedlings to individual pots or directly outside, spacing them about 6 inches apart, then thinning to 18 inches apart as they grow. Sage occasionally reseeds.

Cuttings are easy, and you can also peg down branches until they root. Look under your plants in midsummer and you may find branches that have layered on their own. Pineapple sage roots readily from cuttings, even in water. 'Berggarten' seldom flowers in our climate and must be propagated from cuttings.

Year-round care: Most sage is hardy enough to survive Northwest winters without protection. To renew plants that are getting leggy, cut them back to about 5 inches high in early spring (usually March) when they are beginning to break dormancy. Fertilize them generously with All-Purpose Fertilizer Mix (see Fertilizing, Chapter 1) scratched in around the roots. New growth will soon begin from the base of the plants, and before long they will be beautifully bushy and compact. I first tried this technique on some straggly old plants I expected to replace anyway, and liked the results so much I've done it ever since.

Pests and diseases: Insects usually stay away from sage. Mildew, the most common disease problem,

looks like a white powder on the leaves and strikes when humidity is high and air circulation is poor. To avoid it, try spacing plants farther apart and spraying them with a solution of ¾ teaspoon of baking soda per quart of water.

Harvesting and preserving: Harvest your sage plants twice each season, just before they bloom and a month or so later. Cut the new growth on a dry day, bunch the stems, and fasten with rubber bands. Hang the bunches to dry in an airy room. Alternatively, use a food dehydrator for drying. When the leaves are brittle, store them in air-tight containers; rub them to a powder by hand or with a mortar and pestle before using.

Put up a few bottles of sage vinegar, spiked with shallots and lemon zest, when your sage is at its peak. You'll appreciate it later in marinades and dressings that are especially delicious with poultry or baked onions.

Garden uses: As a landscaping herb, sage offers year-round good looks, go-with-everything foliage, and flowers that attract bees and hummingbirds to the garden. Its rounded shape contrasts nicely with vertical growers such as fennel, and its medium height makes it suitable in many situations. Because leaves remain on the plant year-round, sage helps define the structure of a garden in winter as well as summer.

Massed together, sage plants of various colors make an interesting garden vignette. Purple sage is often utilized by landscape designers to set off pink, yellow, and orange shades. The brilliant red blossoms of pineapple sage bloom late in the season, but the unexpected splash of autumn color in herb gardens or planter boxes makes it well worth the wait.

Culinary uses: Fresh sage has a far more delicate flavor than dried, and it is a shame to relegate it to stuffing mixes for poultry. Used with a light hand, it can be delightful in breads, cheese spreads, and in pasta, poultry, or pork dishes. Italian cooks use it with liver and veal; in England it is favored with cheeses, sausages, and "savoury dishes." For a new twist on the sage-and-turkey theme, grind the fresh herb with turkey for low-fat grilled burgers.

Sage also makes a pleasant and healthful tea, much favored on the island of Crete, where the herb grows wild. Fresh sage tea, steeped for 5 minutes, is more subtle than the assertive brew made with dried sage. Herbalist Carol McGrath of Victoria, British Columbia, demonstrates the striking difference in flavor to her students by offering them tea from both fresh and dried sage. Lemon and honey enhance the flavor.

Craft and home uses: Bunches of dried sage, with their gray-green color and twisted leaf shapes, make homey kitchen decorations. They also look good in herbal wreaths and everlasting bouquets.

Like rosemary, sage is reputedly beneficial to the hair and scalp. With its astringent qualities, a strong sage infusion helps to reduce oiliness and control dandruff. Hair that is beginning to gray can be darkened with a sage rinse, though as one of my customers pointed out, "It works, but you have to keep using it."

Medicinal uses: An ancient Latin saying, *"Cur moriatur homo cui Salvia crescit in horto?"* translates as "Why should a man die when sage grows in his garden?" No one has come up with a definitive answer to this question, but the ancients' high esteem for sage is also reflected in its name, *Salvia,* which means "to save" or "in good health."

Sage contains vitamins A, B complex, and C; calcium; iron; and potassium. As early as 1600 B.C., sage was used in Crete to clear the throat. The tea is still used as a gargle for sore throats, laryngitis, tonsillitis, and sores in the mouth. Its potent antibacterial and antiviral actions make it an effective remedy for colds, flu, and respiratory tract infections.

Sage tea also has the unusual ability to inhibit perspiration, helping to prevent night sweats. It takes effect two hours after it is drunk. The herb is an ingredient in deodorants for external use. It also decreases production of saliva and breast milk. Its estrogenlike components may have a role in the latter effects, and in its use for problems relating to menstruation and menopause.

According to the 1999 *Physicians Desk Reference for Herbal Medicine,* lab studies with animals show that sage has an antispasmodic effect on the central nervous system. The herb is recommended for dyspepsia, hypertension, and stress-related digestive upsets. The recent discovery of its strong antioxidant properties supports the old folk wisdom that links drinking sage tea with longevity. Sage tea may not be an elixir of immortality, but in the words of Sir John Hill (1755), sage "maketh the lamp of life, so long as nature lets it burn, burn brightly."

Aromatherapy: Thujone and cineole are the main constituents of the pale yellow essential oil distilled from garden sage leaves, along with camphor and pinene, estrogenic and bitter compounds, tannins, and rosmarinic, ursolic, and other acids. As with many essential oils, its character and aroma vary widely depending on the plants' growing conditions. It is used in perfumery for its camphor-eucalyptus aroma. The oil is antiseptic, antiviral, antioxidant, astringent, and antispasmodic; however, in the opinion of Robert Tisserand, Julia Lawless, and other well-known aromatherapists, it is not safe for home use. Clary sage (*Salvia sclarea*), a related species, is less toxic and has various applications in aromatherapy.

Caution: Sage products or sage in therapeutic doses should not be taken during pregnancy. A moderate amount of sage in the diet for seasoning purposes is not enough to be harmful.

Salad Burnet

Common names: Burnet, Lesser burnet

Latin names: *Sanguisorba poterium* (formerly *S. minor* or *Poterium sanguisorba*)

Latin and common family names: Rosaceae (Rose family)

Description: Salad burnet is an often overlooked herb, unassuming yet lovely in the garden and elegant in the kitchen. Its most striking features are its small, delicately notched leaflets in opposite pairs on arching 6- to 8-inch stems. As described in Turner's *Newe Herball* (1551), "it has two little leives like unto the wings of birdes, standing out as the bird setteth her wings out when she intendeth to fly." The leaves form neat mounds about a foot high and of equal circumference. Tough, wiry roots reach 12 to 18 inches into the soil. As the weather warms, numerous rose-tinged stems rise up to 2 feet. They are topped with unusual green heads shaped almost like redwood

cones, from which small, bright red flowers open in tiers. Seeds are small, hard, angular, and light brown in color, with a burrlike texture.

Planting information and cultural directions: This long-lived evergreen perennial will grow in ordinary to dry soil with good drainage. It prefers a sunny spot but will tolerate partial shade. Plants are very cold-hardy but cannot survive either "wet feet" in winter or extremely hot temperatures.

Propagation: Salad burnet is easy to propagate from seed sown indoors or directly in the garden in early spring. If left alone, plants in the garden often reseed, producing a cluster of plants in close proximity.

Pests and diseases: Pests and diseases of all kinds seem to leave salad burnet alone.

Year-round care: After blooming, salad burnet plants lose their gracefulness. The long stems turn brown, fall over, and look disheveled. Cut them back to the ground, and compact new growth will soon appear.

Harvesting and preserving: This herb is best used fresh. Pinch or clip the stems near the base. For salads, choose the youngest leaves from the center of the rosette, as these are most tender and mildest in flavor.

Garden uses: Cold-hardy and dependable, salad burnet's gentle mounds of green provide pleasing texture in the garden year-round. It stars in winter and early spring, when other perennials are dormant. Observing the newly emerging stems with their half-folded leaves glistening with dew or touched by frost, we can forgive the plant's tendency to become rangy later on. It is a good choice for edging and for large planters as long as it is kept pruned.

Culinary uses: Many cooks have yet to discover

this herb, obviously named for its former popularity as a salad ingredient. The young leaves have a mild cucumber scent and flavor; older leaves have a bitter tinge that is not unpleasant. Salad burnet leaves can be harvested every month of the year, and are most welcome during the winter and early spring. They are delicious combined with other early greens and herbs, such as chives, parsley, arugula, and corn salad, in the first salads from the garden.

Try salad burnet with pears, walnuts, Gorgonzola, and butter lettuce for an herbed version of a salad that always pleases. Add chopped leaves to creamy dressings, homemade mayonnaise, or cream cheese spreads, and keep your guests guessing which herb you used. Add a nuance of flavor to cucumber sauce for salmon with chopped salad burnet leaves, which make an elegant garnish as well.

Highly esteemed among herbalists is delicate salad burnet vinegar, which captures the herb's cucumber flavor while smoothing out its bitterness, and takes on a beautiful pink color from the stems. It is a natural for marinating cucumbers or dressing any green salad.

Medicinal uses: Herbalists from Pliny to Parkinson recommended Lesser burnet, as it was known, to stop bleeding, heal wounds, and reduce fevers. The plant contains vitamin C, essential oil, and tannins, and has astringent and hemostatic actions. It is employed in treating hemorrhoids, diarrhea, excessive menstrual bleeding, and wounds. Interestingly, in Chinese medicine, a tea of the root is similarly used to stop bleeding, for hemorrhoids, dysentery, and external sores.

Sorrel

Common names: French sorrel, Garden sorrel, Sourgrass, Greensauce

Latin name: *Rumex acetosa*

Latin and common family name: Polygonaceae (Knotweed family)

Varieties and cultivars: French sorrel, Garden sorrel

Related plants:

R. scutatus: Buckler leaf sorrel, true sorrel

R. acetosella: Sourgrass, Sheep sorrel, Wild sorrel

Unrelated plants: *Oxalis acetosella,* Wood sorrel, oxalis

Description: Sorrel is easily recognized by its long, crinkly, arrowhead-shaped leaves and its refreshingly sour flavor. This tartness comes from oxalic acid and oxalate salts, also present in rhubarb and the shamrock-leaved weed *Oxalis acetosella* (wood sorrel). The leaves grow in a cluster about 2 feet tall and a foot across, on long branching stems from a long root system. The plant's height increases to 3 or 4 feet as it sends up tall seed stalks with opposite leaves and airy panicles of greenish yellow flowers. When ripe, the small triangular seeds are a warm russet brown, reminiscent of sorrel's wild relatives, green and yellow dock. French sorrel varieties have been selected over the years for large, tender leaves and good flavor. Garden sorrel is less refined.

To confuse matters, Buckler-leaf sorrel is also called "French" or "true" sorrel. It has smaller, triangular-shaped leaves that have a silvery cast. According to some writers it has "a more grateful acidity," or milder flavor, which is preferred by French cooks. Sheep sorrel (*R. acetosella*) is a miniature version, with tangy leaves up to 2 inches long, which creeps through the garden uninvited.

Planting information and cultural directions: An extremely hardy perennial, sorrel is easy to grow in almost any situation except full shade. Plants produce the best leaves in full sun and moist, rich, acidic soil conditions (the presence of sheep sorrel as a weed is an indication of an acid soil). Sorrel is a sturdy plant that can tolerate drought and will grow with little tending, although it produces greater quantities of large, juicy leaves when steadily watered. It is a fine choice for a large individual pot or an herb planter, provided the soil depth is at least 1 foot, and it can also be grown indoors. Sorrel plants tend to deplete the soil and become less productive after three or four years, so it is best to move or renew plantings at that point.

Propagation: Since home gardeners seldom need more than two or three sorrel plants, it's easiest to buy young starts. Alternatively, sow seeds indoors in March and set out seedlings when they are about 3 inches tall. Plant a few extras in case of sneak attacks by slugs. For an abundance of sorrel, sow seeds about ½ inch deep in a row in early spring, then thin the plants to about 1 foot apart. Cultivated sorrels self-sow if allowed, and can become almost as pesky as the invasive sheep sorrel.

Year-round care: Once your sorrel plants become established, you don't need to do anything more than weed them occasionally, harvest the leaves, and cut back seed stalks to maximize leaf production and keep plants looking trim. If you let the plants go to seed, cut back the stalks and harvest the seed unless you want little sorrel plants popping up here and there. To extend the growing season, cover sorrel plants with spun-bonded polyester row covers, cloches, or cold frames as cold weather approaches.

Pests and diseases: Slugs and snails are fond of sorrel, and chew unsightly holes in the leaves or leave trails across them. Patrol your sorrel plants morning and evening and in damp, cool weather, looking especially for the tiny gray slugs, which can do great damage before being noticed. If the leaves curl, check for mites, which can be controlled with insecticidal soap.

Leaf miners can also be a problem, as evidenced by their tunnels through the leaves. The winged adult fly is gray with black hairs; in June it lays its eggs under the surface of the leaves. Within days, green or whitish grubs hatch and begin eating. Because they are protected inside the leaves, contact insecticides can't reach them. Pick affected leaves and burn them.

Harvesting and preserving: Sorrel can be harvested from the time the leaves come up in early spring until the killing frosts of early winter. Select fully grown leaves that are still young and tender, cutting or snapping them individually at the base of the stems. You can also cut handfuls of leaves or even whack off all of them at once, but some will be more tender than others and your overall harvest will be less abundant. Sorrel is seldom available in markets or spice shops, and is definitely best fresh from your garden. It loses flavor when dried, but freezes well in prepared dishes.

Garden uses: Sorrel deserves a place in any kitchen herb garden or edible ornamental landscape. The unusual shape and green to rosy hues of the leaves and flowering stems are attractive. It can even be used as an edging plant; as long as you cut back the seed stalks as they appear, it remains fairly neat and compact.

Culinary uses: Like the ever-useful lemon, sorrel has an acidic bite that complements bland or fatty foods. Many recipes from France and other European countries highlight this attribute, pairing sorrel sauce with oily fish, duck, pork, and eggs. Perhaps the most popular use for this herb is sorrel soup, which can vary from the delicate French *soupe aux herbes* to creamy Potage Germiny to the schav of Eastern Europe. A healthful green sauce made of sorrel and an assortment of other fresh herbs is favored in Germany. Sorrel tastes wonderful in a salad of early spring greens, when the palate craves something fresh and local. Another simple way to enjoy sorrel is to use its leaves in a cheese sandwich instead of lettuce. And of course you can nibble young leaves right in the garden. Note: When preparing sorrel, use stainless steel knives and enamel or stainless steel cookware, which will not react and turn black in contact with this acidic herb.

Medicinal uses: Traditionally, sorrel is valued as a spring tonic, to cleanse the system and provide abundant vitamins and minerals after the lean season. Folk wisdom also prescribed sorrel for scurvy prevention, and indeed the herb is so high in vitamin C that $1/2$ cup of chopped leaves provides 54 percent of an adult's daily requirements. It is also rich in vitamin A and calcium. Sorrel has mild diuretic and cooling properties, and helps bring down fevers not caused by infection. Due to its high oxalate content, however, sorrel should not be eaten in large amounts, and should be avoided by pregnant women and people with gout, rheumatism, or kidney problems.

Within the past few years, sheep sorrel has become widely known as one of the ingredients in the Essiac Herb formula. The formula was given by Cree Indians to a Canadian woman, Marie Cassie (Essiac spelled backwards), and is claimed to have cured or slowed cancer in many cases. The jury is still out on this one.

St. John's Wort

Common names: St. Joan's wort, Common St. John's wort, Perforate St. John's wort

Latin name: *Hypericum perforatum*

Latin and common family names: Hypericaceae (St. John's wort family)

Alternative spellings: St. Johns wort, St. John's Wort, St. Johnswort, St.-John's-wort

Related species: *H. calycinum*, Aaron's Beard, *H. hirsutum*, *H. puctatum*, and others

Description: The "herb of St. John" is a bushy plant 2 to 3 feet high, with erect branching stems and wiry, shallow, spreading roots. The leaves are smooth, oval, about 1 inch long, and form in opposite pairs or clusters up the stems. Hold one up to the light and you can see tiny dots that look like perforations but are actually oil sacs. Brilliant yellow flowers about an inch across have five petals with black dots along the margins that encircle a cluster of fine stamens. Both the flowers and the pointed buds contain the fluorescent red pigment hypericin, which leaves a red stain when you crush it between your fingertips. Myriad tiny brown seeds are held in clusters of stiff, upright oval pods.

Planting information and cultural directions: A rugged, hardy perennial, St. John's wort thrives in full sun and well-drained soils but can adapt to almost any situation except full shade. It is invasive and will soon take over an area if allowed. The plant dies back in late fall, leaving a skeleton of madrona-hued stems. It is hardy to 0°F or below.

Propagation: The steady spread of St. John's wort along roadsides from California to British Columbia attests to the plant's reproductive success. Translation: It's a weed! It is easy to grow from seed, sprinkled on top of the soil in a flat or on cultivated ground in late summer. Established plants reseed freely and the plants also spread by vigorous creeping roots. Divide the plants in spring or fall.

Year-round care: Little care is required for this plant; left on its own, it will happily grow and spread wherever it can. To keep it under control, cut back seed heads before they ripen, remove volunteer plants, and periodically prune back the root runners. In late autumn after the tops die back, cut plants to the ground and compost the brushy stems if you like a neat garden look, or leave them until spring cleanup time.

Pests and diseases: What pests? What diseases? This plant does not seem to have such problems.

Harvesting and preserving: The leafy flowering tops, harvested when the plants first come into bloom, contain the highest concentrations of medicinal constituents. For teas and tinctures, cut the entire leafy tops with the flowers. Use them fresh or hang them in small bunches where they can dry quickly and retain bright color. In about two weeks, when they are crisp to the touch, rub the leaves and flowers from the stems and store in glass jars. Harvest just the flower clusters or buds when making infused "red oil." Picking roadside plants for medicine making is not recommended; if there isn't room in your garden for this rampant grower, you can harvest wild stands of it in many out-of-the-way places.

Garden uses: *H. perforatum*, the medicinal St. John's wort, is attractive in its way but has limited use as an ornamental because of its spreading habit.

H. perforatum's more showy relative *H. calycinum* (Aaron's Beard, Creeping St. John's wort) is a popular and widely adaptable ground cover. With its golden yellow, 3-inch blossoms and dense evergreen foliage, it is an excellent plant for a wide range of problem areas such as hot, dry areas, shady spots under trees, or eroding sloping sites. In arid areas with cold winters, the plant does best in semishade with some extra watering, and may be deciduous. Aaron's Beard contains some of the medicinal constituents found in *H. perforatum*, but not the important red-pigmented glycoside, hypericin. *H. hirsutum* and *H. puctatum* are high in all active constituents.

Medicinal uses: Scientific studies have identified at least fifty constituents in this versatile medicinal herb, including hypericin and the closely related pseudohypericin. It also contains the flavonoids quercetin and rutin, plus choline, tannins, pectin, and volatile oil. This complex structure enables the herb to have a variety of seemingly unrelated effects on the body.

The use of St. John's wort as a folk remedy, primarily for inflammation, wound healing, and nervous conditions including depression and hysteria, dates back centuries. Currently, St. John's wort has received considerable attention for its antidepressive properties, which in some cases are as effective as prescription antidepressants, with fewer side effects. Hypericin, pseudohypericin, and related substances produce the same kinds of chemical changes in the brain (MAO inhibition) as some prescription mood-enhancing drugs. In fact, St. John's wort tea is often prescribed in Europe as an alternative medicine for treatment of nervous tension, anxiety, and sleep disturbances as well as depression. There is evidence that it is particularly helpful for bitchiness and other emotional problems during menopause.

As disease organisms become increasingly resistant to antibiotics and new viral diseases appear, the significant antibacterial and antiviral properties of St. John's wort are also being investigated. St. John's wort shows promise in treating flu, *Herpes simplex*, and even AIDS.

St. John's wort oil or "red oil" (for recipe, see Herbal Remedies in Chapter 4) is an excellent external remedy for nervous tissue damage, bruises, sore muscles, inflammation, burns, ulcers, and sores. I make a batch every summer and keep a bottle in my medicine cabinet and travel kit because it really works. Applied to bumps and bruises, strained backs, and sunburns, an infused oil of St. John's wort takes the pain away and speeds healing. Commercial preparations of St. John's wort oil mixed with arnica and lavender are a favorite of athletes and dancers.

Caution: There is some concern that sensitive persons may experience photoallergic reactions after taking hypericin internally or externally and then being exposed to bright sunlight.

Sweet Cicely

Common names: British myrrh, Great chervil, Sweet cis, Sweet fern

Latin name: *Myrrhis odorata*

Latin and common family names: Umbelliferae/Apiaceae (Carrot family)

Description: Though not widely appreciated, sweet cicely is an excellent herb for Northwest gardens. It is decorative, shade loving, and practically maintenance free. Its soft, downy leaves are made up of several pairs of finely cut, opposite leaflets that decrease in size toward the tips, much like the familiar bracken fern. They are often lightly mottled with white as though dusted with powdered sugar. Bees are attracted to sweet cicely's dense umbels of delicately fragrant white flowers, which bloom from May to June on hollow, branching stems. Tapering, ribbed seeds about 1 inch long turn from bright green to dark brown as they ripen.

Large fleshy taproots, light brown outside and creamy white within, reach deep into the soil. Mature plants are 2 to 3 feet tall and spread almost as wide. All parts of the plant have a pleasant licorice flavor. Plants are long-lived and among the hardiest of herbs, surviving temperatures as low as −40°F.

Planting information and cultural directions: Sweet cicely prefers a crumbly, moist soil with good drainage, the sort found around old fruit trees. Enrich a poor soil with compost or manure. Without shade at least part of the day, the leaves tend to wither in hot weather. At Silver Bay, a patch has grown and spread from seed on the shady north side of an outbuilding for nearly fifty years. Each spring a new generation expands its perimeter.

Propagation: The easiest way to get sweet cicely started is to buy a plant, which can most likely be found at your favorite herb farm. Starting plants from seed can be tricky, because seed does not remain viable for long unless conditions are perfect, yet it takes several months to germinate. For best success, mimic nature as closely as possible: sow the freshest seed available (preferably as soon as it ripens in June or July) in an outdoor seedbed and wait until spring. After winter chilling, seeds germinate readily in April or May. Seedlings are about 3 inches high, with a lacy, triangular true leaf between two long, narrow seed leaves.

Once plants are established, their roots can be dug and divided in fall or early spring. Make sure each division has an eye at the top. Don't worry if you slice a root with your shovel. It will probably heal up after transplanting and produce a fine plant.

Year-round care: After the plants bloom, the leaves turn yellow and shrivel up. Cut them back to the ground and they will put forth new leaves. Leaves die back in autumn; clean them up and cut off the seed heads or leave them to reseed on their own in spring.

Pests and diseases: Neither pests nor diseases have ever damaged the sweet cicely in my gardens.

Harvesting and preserving: The flavor of sweet cicely is too delicate to survive drying or freezing; the fresh herb is best. Pinch off tender leaflets by hand from February through September, or cut the stems with scissors or garden shears if a larger supply is needed.

Pick the sweet, anise-flavored unripe seeds when they are plump and fully grown but still bright green.

Nibble them as a snack, steep them in brandy or vodka for a warming cordial, or store them in the freezer in a glass jar. Harvest seeds for planting when they are dark and heavy. Sow them immediately, or, if that is not feasible, dry them on screens for a few days and store in the freezer to prolong their viability.

Garden uses: Sweet cicely offers a good solution for a shady problem area in the garden. Its lacy leaves and dainty flowers, while not showy, are quietly ornamental. They add textural interest in the back of a border, and act as a backdrop for nasturtiums and other low-growing herbs. Once established, plants can go rampant. Dig out volunteers while they're young to control spreading.

Culinary uses: This aptly named herb contains natural sweeteners that neutralize acids in tart fruits. If you add 1 tablespoon of chopped stems and leaves per cup of fruit in rhubarb cakes and pies, gooseberry compote, and similar dishes, you can cut the sugar by half.

Early herbalists extol the virtues of sweet cicely as a salad herb. Jean de la Quintinye, gardener to Louis XIV, believed that the herb gives a "perfuming relish" to salads and "ought never to be wanting in our sallets for it is exceeding wholesome and charming to the spirits." The root, boiled and dressed with "oile and vinegar," was also regarded as "most excellent in a sallade."

Sweet cicely is a readily available substitute for chervil, which also has a light licorice flavor but is a short-lived annual. Use chopped or small leaves to flavor carrots, parsnips, and sauces. Include them in a bouquet garni or sprinkle on soups as a garnish. Add 3 tablespoons to your favorite biscuit or shortbread recipe, and for a more noticeable anise flavor, mix in

1 to 2 teaspoons of chopped unripe seeds. Pick the young seeds to garnish a fruit salad or to chew as an herbal breath freshener.

Medicinal uses: Sweet cicely has health-promoting properties, though it is seldom used as a medicinal herb. Its essential oil contains anethol, the principal constituent of anise seed, as well as anisealdehyde, limonene, chavicolmethyl ether, and alpha-pinene. It is a digestive, carminative, and expectorant.

Culpeper pronounced this gentle herb "so harmless you can not use it amiss." While there are no health hazards or side effects associated with sweet cicely, a note of caution is in order. Be very sure that you do not mistake sweet cicely for some of its look-alike relatives such as water hemlock and fool's parsley, which are very poisonous.

Sweet Woodruff

Common names: Master of the Woods, Woodruff, May Bowl herb

Latin name: *Gallium odoratum* (previously *Asperula odorata*)

Latin and common family names: Rubiaceae (Madder family)

Description: Sweet woodruff is a charming herbal ground cover about 6 inches high that is covered with a froth of tiny white flowers from mid-April through May. Its glossy leaves, arranged in rufflike whorls of 6 to 9 on thin, brittle stems, are attractive almost year-round. Shallow, threadlike roots and weak-looking jointed rhizomes belie its effectiveness as a spreader. Fuzzy, round seeds are noticeable only on close inspection. The whole plant emits a fresh aroma variously described as vanilla, new-mown hay, or chypre, which becomes more pronounced when the herb is dried.

Planting information and cultural directions: Native to the forests of Germany and Northern Europe, sweet woodruff is ideally suited to Northwest gardens. It loves a woodland setting with loamy soil, and is one of only a few herbal ground covers that actually prefers full shade to full sun. It thrives in both situations, though the leaves take on a more yellowish hue in sun. Sweet woodruff is a long-lived, hardy perennial that withstands our coldest winters. The plant generally emerges from winter dormancy in March, and dies back to the ground in late winter.

Propagation: The best way to propagate sweet woodruff is by making plant divisions in early spring. Dig clumps with a sharp spade, and use a clipper to cut them apart rather than tearing the rootlets. Small plants set about 6 inches apart will grow together into solid mounds within a year or two. You can divide plants after flowering also, but be attentive to watering needs if rain is sparse. It is possible to collect ripe seed and plant it while fresh, but this method of propagation is recommended mainly to those who enjoy experimenting with plants.

Year-round care: Little care is required for this easy herb. Light weeding may be required until plants are established; after that it's a matter of pulling out a few grasses and other plants that compete halfheartedly with this sturdy creeper. You may want to rake the browned leaves away when you are in early spring cleanup mode, but it's not necessary.

Plants grown in very poor soil will benefit from applications of leaf mold or compost in the fall.

Pests and diseases: Sweet woodruff is blessedly free of insect and disease problems.

Harvesting and preserving: Gathering sweet woodruff leaves is much like pulling grass. A handful harvested now and then as needed requires no equipment and little effort. For larger amounts, grasp stems at the base and clip them close to the ground; to harvest a big patch, use a string trimmer and rake. Spread on racks or trays and dry out of the sun. Dry small amounts in the microwave, but avoid heat, which disperses the delicate scent. Or preserve your sweet woodruff in wine!

Garden uses: Sweet woodruff really shines in its role as a shade-loving herbal ground cover. Few herbs are so perfectly suited to grow under rhododendrons, azaleas, hydrangeas, and other shrubs. The shiny leaves fill in gaps and provide textural interest, and the go-with-anything white flowers are a bonus. Sweet woodruff can also help to hide the yellowing foliage of spent bulbs.

Keep in mind, however, that the creeping qualities that make this such a useful plant can also make it pesky. Overconfident of my vigilance, I once included sweet woodruff in a display garden of edible flowers. Three years later I was still trying to get every little rootlet out of that bed. So plant it where it can take over an area without annoying you, contain it in an enclosed bed, or confine it in planters or pots.

Culinary uses: Mai Bowle—a punch flavored with sweet woodruff—or May wine, made by steeping sprigs of the herb in sweet white wine, are the tradi-

tional beverages for celebrating the first of May in Germany. Sweet woodruff is approved for use in alcoholic beverages by the FDA; its coumarin flavor, reminiscent of vanilla, may be an acquired taste. For fans, a tea can be made by steeping the leaves and flowers in boiling water, and a few leaves added to jars of apple jelly impart a mysterious and unusual flavor. All foods containing coumarin should be ingested in moderation.

Craft and home uses: There are many ways to bring the intriguing scent of sweet woodruff into your home. Try scenting your house by putting a few stems in a barely warm oven with the door ajar, or stuff sachet bags or pillows with the dried herb and lay them in with linens, or toss one in the dryer with your clothes. To make a lightly aromatic wreath base, pack freshly cut sweet woodruff leaves and stems into a small ring mold. Allow to dry for two weeks, then unmold and decorate the wreath with dried flowers of your choice. The old custom of strewing herbs on the floor has passed out of fashion, but someday I'd love to try it with sweet woodruff in a woodland cabin. Sweet woodruff is in the same botanical family as madder, the famous dye plant. Its roots produce a red dye; its leaves a yellow dye.

Tarragon

Common names: French tarragon, Russian tarragon

Latin name: *Artemisia dracunculus* var. *sativa, A. dracunculoides*

Latin and common family names: Compositae/Asteraceae (Aster family)

Description: One of the great culinary herbs,

French tarragon is a hardy perennial that dies back to the ground in winter. Its Latin name and French nickname, meaning "little dragon," are thought to derive from its serpentine roots. In March or April, tarragon sends up numerous new shoots, which reach 12 to 15 inches. Its alternate leaves are bright green, narrow, flat, and shiny, rounded or pointed at the tips. They have a markedly anise flavor with a clovey, mouth-numbing aftertaste. The tiny green flowers that form along the tops of the stems are inconspicuous and do not produce viable seeds. Russian tarragon, a related herb, is very vigorous, often reaching 4 feet. It does set seed, but the flavor is so inferior that it is seldom grown.

Planting information and cultural directions: Tarragon, more particular than some other herbs, prefers a fairly rich soil with full sun and ample moisture. Good drainage is essential. The herb is very hardy, and the plants actually need a period of cold and dormancy every year. In cold, wet soil, however, the roots rot and the plants cannot survive. Occasionally, gardeners find that their tarragon plants fail to thrive. Try two or three different areas to see where the plants do best. After some experimentation, I find that growing tarragon in a raised bed, amply enriched with compost and all-purpose fertilizer, produces a splendid crop.

Indoor gardeners will find tarragon a suitable container herb, although it will not live long without a winter chilling period. Give it a well-lit position and avoid overwatering. Mist the leaves regularly.

Propagation: The easiest way to get started growing French tarragon is to purchase plants; three will suffice for most gardeners. To be sure you have the right plant, taste a leaf. French tarragon has that numbing licorice and clove bite; Russian tarragon is insipid by comparison.

Plant division is the most practical way to propagate French tarragon, since seed is unavailable and cuttings are fairly finicky about rooting. Dig three-year-old plants while they are dormant (October to February) and tease the roots apart, taking care not to break the brittle shoots. Make sure that there are at least two eyes or shoots on each piece. The new plants will be fully mature in about three years and should be replaced after the fourth.

Year-round care: Fertilize established plants in the spring and after major harvests by scratching ½ cup of All-Purpose Fertilizer Mix (see Chapter 1) around each plant. Keep them well weeded, since quack grass, sheep sorrel, and other pernicious weeds can overtake a bed of tarragon quickly. Leave the dead stems to mark the location of the plants during the winter if you like, but do clip them off in spring to make harvesting the new growth easier.

To prolong tarragon's growing season, lift a plant or two in September, pot in a rich mix, and transfer to a cool greenhouse. New growth will commence at least a month earlier than outdoors. Move the plants back outside in April or May.

Pests and diseases: Slugs like the tender emerging shoots of tarragon and can destroy young plants. Be vigilant, especially in early morning and on those damp feast days for slugs. Bait and other methods are helpful, but it also helps to keep the plants clear of weeds, which provide shady hiding places.

Harvesting and preserving: Pinch tarragon sprigs

at the base of the stems from early spring onward. When the plants have reached full growth and leaf tips begin to turn yellow, cut them back to about 2 inches from the ground. Fertilize the plants lightly with regular solution fish fertilizer, and they will produce a second and sometimes a third crop.

Preserving the bright green color and strong flavor of tarragon can be a challenge. Air-drying in bunches is often disappointing, but the additional heat provided by a dehydrator gives better results, as does microwaving. To freeze, tie sprigs into small bunches, blanch them in boiling water for 1 minute, then plunge into ice water for 2 minutes. Spread out on dish towels to dry, then freeze on a baking sheet and transfer to glass jars for freezer storage. Used straight from the freezer, frozen leaves taste almost as good as fresh.

Tarragon vinegar is an easy-to-make favorite (see recipe, page 66). To pickle tarragon sprigs in the French manner, wash them and pack them tightly into clean pint jars and fill with white wine vinegar. Steep for about a month. Use the preserved leaves as you would fresh ones; the concentrated vinegar is an excellent flavoring too.

Garden uses: Tarragon has a place in any kitchen and herb garden, and its vibrant green color and upright habit make it a fine choice for planter boxes. Harvest the plants regularly to keep them from becoming yellow and unattractive.

Culinary uses: Tarragon is one of the basic flavors of French cuisine. It is best used fresh; it's indispensable in true béarnaise, hollandaise, ravigote, verte, and tartar sauces, and excellent in mayonnaise and mus-

tards. It is also a wonderful herb in salads; a few whole leaves in a green, marinated vegetable, or chicken salad wake up the taste buds, or mince it and add it to salad dressings such as Green Goddess and tarragon vinaigrette.

This herb is delicious with chicken, steak, and meat or vegetable pâtés. It enhances fish and lobster, oysters, and other seafoods. It is often paired with eggs, in omelets, soufflés, and deviled eggs. Add chopped tarragon to asparagus spears, green beans, mushrooms, carrots, cauliflower, zucchini, and other vegetables. Use the herb to flavor pickled asparagus spears and the tiny, sour cucumber pickles known as cornichons.

Strip fresh leaves from the stems before using. If dried tarragon is your only alternative, look for a product that has a strong aroma and is green rather than brown. Steep it in a tablespoon of lemon juice or wine for a few minutes to bring out the flavor before adding it to your recipe.

Craft and home uses: Dried tarragon has an aroma sometimes likened to anise or new-mown hay. It adds a fresh herbaceous scent to potpourri and sachets. Essential oil of tarragon gives this quality to chypre or oak-moss–type perfumes such as Cabochard and L'Heure Bleue.

Medicinal uses: Tarragon's renown rests on its importance as a culinary herb. In traditional medicine, it is a minor herb that has been employed as an appetite stimulant and digestive, and, because of its numbing properties, to allay toothaches.

Aromatherapy: Estragon oil, or tarragon essential oil, distilled from the plant's leaves and stems, contains up to 70 percent estragole (methyl chavicrol). Other compounds include ocimene, narol, capillene, thujone, phellandrene, cineole, coumarins, tannins, and flavonoids. It is employed in aromatherapy to a limited extent for digestive irregularities, but caution must be exercised because of its high estragole content. Use of the oil is not recommended during pregnancy.

Thyme

Common names: Common, English, and French thyme

Latin name: *Thymus* spp.

Latin and common family names: Labiatae (Mint family)

Varieties and cultivars: Common thyme, *Thymus vulgaris;* 'Orange Balsam,' 'Porlock,' 'Wedgwood'

Silver thyme, *T.* 'Argenteus'

Lemon thyme, *T.* x *citriodorus*

Caraway thyme, *T. herba-barona*

'Pennsylvania Dutch Tea Thyme,' 'Oregano' or 'Oregano Scented,' *T. pulegioides* (mother of thyme)

T. praecox ssp. *arcticus* (eleven varieties, most listed below)

Woolly thyme, *T. pseudolanuginosis*

Golden thyme, *T.* 'Aureus,' 'Doone Valley,' 'Longwood,' 'Pinewood'

Description: Thyme is a culinary gem, a germ-killing antiseptic, a garden stalwart, a friend of bees, and a favorite of faeries. The earliest record of its use is a Sumerian tablet dating from 2750 B.C.; later the Egyptians used it in embalming, and medieval ladies embroidered scarves with bees and sprigs of thyme to proclaim their knights' courage. The herb has inspired writers and poets, including Kipling, who likened its scent to "dawn in Paradise." Most thymes are hardy perennials descended from plants that grow wild around the Mediterranean.

Confusion over botanical classification of this genus (and disagreement among experts) has been the status quo since Linnaeus described eight species in 1753. Some authors have suggested that there are three basic types of thyme—shrubby, mounding, and creeping. It's a handy way to think about them, if not strictly accurate botanically. The most important recent work on straightening out the names and identities of cultivated thymes in the United States was published by Harriet Flannery Phillips as her doctoral thesis at Cornell University in 1982. After growing and analyzing more than 400 specimens from herb growers all over the country, she divided them into about sixty species and cultivars. European researchers have identified seven distinct chemical forms, or chemotypes, of thyme, based on chemical analysis of their essential oils. Dr. Phillips determined that three of these forms are grown in this country, with thymol, carvacrol, and alpha-terpineol as their main oil components. The following classifications are based on her work.

The most popular and productive thyme for culinary purposes is *Thymus vulgaris,* usually known as common or English thyme. Dr. Phillips recommends "Narrow-leaf French" as a name to lessen confusion, but I'll stick with "common thyme" for now. While specimens vary in leaf color and growth habit, the elements they have in common include similar flowers, leaves that are rolled under and without hairs, and high thymol content. Common thyme is a hardy evergreen shrub that grows to about 12 inches tall. Its opposite, dark green, smooth-edged leaves are just ⅛ to ½ inch long, sharply pointed at the tips, and may bend backward. Masses of tiny pink flowers bloom on terminal whorls in April and May. Stems are thin, square, and wiry, sometimes red tinged, and woody at the base. Fibrous roots can reach 2 feet into the soil. Seeds are tiny, spherical, and brown to black. The plant is strongly aromatic. 'Porlock' is an improved variety with dark leaves and a dense habit; 'Wedgwood' is compact, with gold variegation. 'Orange Balsam' has very narrow leaves and a citrus aroma due to its alpha-terpineol content. Specimens with sparse gray leaves and a rangy habit, often called French thyme, are included in this classification.

Silver thyme (*T. argenteus*) has beautiful variegated leaves and blossoms, a growth habit similar to those above, but a more delicate flavor than common thyme. Golden thyme (*T. aureus*) is a chartreuse creeping variety that forms compact mounds about 6 inches high with inconspicuous white flowers; it looks good all year.

Lemon thymes vary in coloration, leaf size, and growth habit, but all have a fresh citrus flavor. *T. x citriodorus*, the standard lemon thyme, may be gold, green, or variegated, and is generally less vigorous and hardy than *T. vulgaris* types, with a fountainlike growth habit. The "x" in its Latin name means that lemon thyme is a hybrid and must be propagated vegetatively.

Caraway thyme (*T. herba-barona*) has small, dark green leaves and a low-to-the-ground, creeping habit. Native to Corsica and Sardinia, it has a pronounced

flavor of its namesake due to its high carvone content. 'Nutmeg' thyme is a variant. Stems of these thymes are hairy on all four sides.

T. praecox ssp. *arcticus* is characterized as prostrate, and often spreads extensively by creeping sterile shoots. It has hairs only on two opposite sides of the stems. (*T. serpyllum*, the "wild thyme" of Europe, has hairs on all four sides of the stem.) Among the eleven distinct cultivars of *T. praecox* ssp. *arcticus* are 'Albus,' 'Annie Hall,' 'Coccineus' (crimson thyme or creeping red thyme), 'Minor,' 'Pink Chintz,' 'White Moss,' 'Wild Garden Lavender,' and others.

T. pulegioides, known as mother of thyme, is described by Dr. Phillips as the "master of disguises" because of its many forms. It grows from 4 to 12 inches tall depending on conditions, and spreads via roots along the stems. Blossoms may be pink, white, red, or lavender. Leaves are egg-shaped to round, and ⅛ to ½ inch long. What distinguishes *pulegioides* varieties are their hairs, found only on the angles of the stems. Other thymes have prominent hairs either on all four sides or on two opposite sides. Some plants listed in catalogs or guidebooks as *T. serpyllum* or *T. praecox* are in fact *T. pulegioides*, according to Dr. Phillips. 'Oregano' and 'Pennsylvania Dutch Tea Thyme' are two fine varieties of *T. pulegioides*.

Some thymes of merit defied Dr. Phillips' attempts at classification. *T.* 'Doone Valley' has tiny, yellow-and-green leaves on the tips of the plants in spring and fall, lemon flavor, and a prostrate habit. *T.* 'Aureus,' or golden thyme, forms attractive golden mounds. The unspectacular *T.* 'Pinewood' has plain dark green leaves, but is tops for controlling erosion on a bank and looks good most of the year. *T.* 'Longwood' produces a handsome mat of gray, felted leaves, larger than the more common woolly thyme (often classified as *T. pseudolanuginosis*). This is the lowest-growing of all, a silvery ground-hugging carpet with minute downy leaves.

Though gardeners seldom have too much thyme on their hands (oops, couldn't resist), two or three varieties are enough for starters, and you can build up a nice collection without getting too carried away. If you get hooked and need more information, see Dr. Phillips's article, "The Best of Thymes," listed in the bibliography. Starts of Dr. Phillips's thymes were donated to the Herb Society of America and are maintained at the Inniswood Metro Gardens in Westerville, Ohio, for public enjoyment and study.

Planting information and cultural directions: One of the least demanding of herbs, thyme thrives in average to poor, well-limed soil with partial or full sun. This tough plant can cope with heat, drought, and cold, but good drainage and air circulation are essential. It may be necessary to amend a clay soil with sand since thyme can not tolerate heavy, waterlogged soil. Continuously damp foliage also creates problems, so make sure your thymes have some breathing room. Don't crowd them together or grow them in the shade of larger plants.

Propagation: Common thyme is easily grown from seed sown in flats or seedbeds early in the spring. The seedlings look like tiny sprigs of thyme and need careful weeding if grown outside. Potting two or three together produces sizable plants more quickly. The plants grow to about 8 inches in diameter the first season. Replace them after three or four years when the stems have become woody.

Commercially, most varieties of thyme are propagated by cuttings or root division, since seeds do not always duplicate the parent plant. Take cuttings from late spring through fall. Root them in propagating frames indoors, or outside in partially shaded beds. Be sure they are kept weeded. To divide plants, lift them with a garden fork or spade and tear rooted sections apart with your hands, or separate them with hand pruners or a sharp shovel.

For prostrate forms, I dig up sections, then cut them into squares with hand pruners or old scissors. Early spring is the best time to divide plants. Fall is okay too, provided that it's not too late for plants to become reestablished before cold weather sets in.

Year-round care: Prune upright-growing thyme plants lightly in February or March before new leaves appear, to stimulate new growth at the base of the stems. Cut plants back after they bloom to keep them shapely and vigorous. Many varieties become woody or sparse in the centers and need to be lifted and divided every three or four years as described above.

There is no need for mulching or other protection in the mild winters of the maritime Northwest. In colder areas, plants can be damaged by cold winds or frost heaving even though many species are hardy to −20°F. Blanket the plants with evergreen boughs to moderate temperatures, and keep melting snow from saturating soil around the roots. Remove the mulch in early spring.

Pests and diseases: Generally, all varieties of thyme are pest and disease free if grown well. There are a couple of caveats, however. Plants will rot when they lack good air circulation or are subject to high humidity or waterlogged soil. Also, hungry slugs can be a problem during a wet spring. I never imagined they would like such a strongly aromatic plant, but was amazed to find a horde of them methodically denuding a row of mulched common thyme plants at Silver Bay.

Harvesting and preserving: Cut or pinch sprigs year-round for kitchen use. As the plants begin budding, clip them back to 2 inches from the ground. New growth appears quickly. If rain or overhead sprinkling has caused dirt to splash up and cling to the leaves, rinse them well in running water, then blot with old towels and allow the sprigs to air-dry. Hang the thyme in bundles or spread it on screens until it is brittle. Hold the bundles over a sheet of newspaper and rub the leaves from the stems, then store in glass jars.

If you plan to use your thyme for wreaths or other ornamental purposes, harvest it in full bloom—the flowers dry to a rich shade of lavender.

Garden uses: The varying and harmonious forms, colors, and textures of thyme, with leaves and flowers shading from grays to greens and gold, pure white through pink and lavender to vibrant purple, present a multitude of possibilities. By choosing varieties with care, it is possible to have thyme in bloom for many months. Thyme's fragrance is an added bonus, as Sir Francis Bacon observed in his famous essay "On Gardening": "Those Plants which Perfume the Air most delightfully, being trodden upon and crushed are Three: that is Burnet, Wilde-Time and Water-mints, therefore you are to set whole Allies of them to have the Pleasure, when you walke or Tread."

The gently rounded *T. vulgaris* varieties are beautiful as edgings or interwoven among perennials in a border. They can also be clipped and used as elements in knot gardens and other formal designs. The soft look of silver thyme is particularly lovely when contrasted with bright flowers such as roses or plants with large dark leaves.

Creeping thymes are star performers in rockeries, cascading down steps or growing like a fragrant carpet among stepping stones. Medieval gardeners planted "thyme seats," dense cushions of fragrance perfect for dalliance, though challenging to maintain. Occasionally used in place of grass lawns, creeping thyme requires weeding, an activity that provides lessons in patience. A bank with an erosion-controlling species such as *T.* 'Pinewood' is marvelous but takes years to establish.

With a bit more effort, you can create a bower to attract bees and faeries, like the one described by Shakespeare's Puck: "I know a bank where the wild thyme blows / Where ox-lips, and the nodding violet grows; / Quite over-canopied with luscious woodbine, / With sweet musk-roses, and with eglantine." What sweeter place to lie and dream on a summer's day? Just thinking about it makes me want to go roll in the thyme.

Culinary uses: One of the most versatile of culinary herbs, thyme has a distinctive flavor that stands alone beautifully and blends equally well with other seasonings. Along with parsley and bay leaf, thyme is a constant in the French bouquet garni, and with summer savory in herbes de Provence. It is also an ingredient in poultry seasoning, Italian blends,

Jamaican jerk sauce, and Cajun blackening spices.

Thyme complements all kinds of meats, poultry, fish, and game. It retains its flavor when cooked and is especially good combined with wine, garlic, and onions in dishes that simmer long and slowly, such as coq au vin and boeuf bourguignon, as well as with ratatouille, oven-roasted vegetables, and vegetable stew. In cream of mushroom and French onion soups, clam chowder, and oyster stew, thyme adds depth of flavor. It is an important element of Caribbean cuisine, balancing the sweet spiciness of allspice, cinnamon, cloves, and nutmeg, and tempering the heat of chiles in Creole and Mexican dishes.

Try thyme with vegetables such as baked or fried onions, sautéed chanterelles, grilled portobellos, and roasted garlic. The herb also adds zest to carrots, tomatoes, and zucchini.

Lemon thyme sparks up chicken and fish dishes, whether placed inside the cavity, laid underneath, or used in a sauce or marinade. It is also refreshing in tea breads and fruit desserts such as applesauce, rhubarb compote, and berry cobblers.

The strong flavor of caraway thyme is good with roast beef and meat loaf, in breads or cream cheese spreads. Although edible, creeping thymes are seldom used for flavoring.

Craft and home uses: The ancient Greeks and Arabs burned thyme as incense and made perfumes based on it, and to "smell of thyme" was considered a compliment. Sachets and bags of thyme, laid in linen closets and drawers, impart a clean aroma while discouraging moths and mildew. Half a teaspoon of thyme oil added to a bucket of cleaning water is both disinfecting and aromatic—but wear gloves as you scrub.

Medicinal uses: Although thyme's stature as a culinary herb overshadows its medicinal use, it has many therapeutic applications. Thyme is valued as an antiseptic, antispasmodic, and expectorant.

Thyme has a reputation as a remedy for internal parasites such as roundworms and hookworms. Some pet owners slip a few fresh thyme leaves, along with garlic, into their animals' food for prevention. Diluted 1:10 with olive oil and rubbed on the scalp, thyme oil is also reputed to destroy head lice.

Products containing an extract of *T. vulgaris* may already be in your medicine cabinet. Thymol, the herb's major constituent, is a very effective germicide and is employed in well-known products such as mouthwash (Listerine), vapor rubs (Vicks), and various cough drops, ear drops, and ointments. A simple infusion of thyme makes an excellent lotion for acne, scabies, and for washing wounds of all kinds.

Thyme is also excellent for coughs. The *Physicians' Desk Reference for Herbal Medicine, British Herbal Pharmacopoeia,* and German Commission E all describe thyme as a bronchial antispasmodic and expectorant, helpful in acute bronchitis and whooping cough. A thyme infusion also clears up congestion due to head and sinus colds, coughs, and catarrhs. It is gargled for sore throats, laryngitis, and infected gums.

Thyme's antispasmodic and carminative properties are also beneficial to the digestive system, relaxing smooth muscles, easing cramps, and breaking down gas. The *British Herbal Pharmacopoeia* cites thyme for dyspepsia, chronic gastritis, and children's diarrhea.

Traditionally, warm thyme baths are taken after

strenuous physical exercise to soothe tired muscles, speed healing of bruises and sprains, and to ease rheumatic pains. A German friend swears by thyme footbaths in case of colds or flu.

Aromatherapy: The oil distilled from the leafy tops and tender stems of *Thymus vulgaris* as the plants come into flower is deep orange in color, with an intense herbal-medicinal odor, and is known as "red thyme oil." "White thyme oil," its redistilled form, is pale yellow and has a lighter aroma. According to British aromatherapist Julia Lawless, white thyme is not a "complete" oil because certain components are removed, and it is often adulterated, so be sure to purchase it from a reliable source.

Essential oil of thyme contains principally thymol (30 to 70 percent), carvacrol (2.5 to 14 percent), borneol, linalool, and cymene; antioxidants rosmarinic and ursolic acids; flavonoids; tannins; bitter principles; and other compounds. Its composition varies between the herb's seven chemotypes.

Because of its concentration of phenols, thymol, and carvacrol, thyme essential oil can be highly toxic. It must be used with caution and in diluted form. When colds and flu threaten, add a few drops of thyme oil to a pan of water and allow it to simmer on the stove or warm over a heat register. Its antiseptic vapors will kill germs and freshen the air throughout the house. Combine a small amount of thyme oil with water in a pump spray bottle to get rid of mildew. Diluted in salves, ointments, and vapor rubs, thyme essential oil is applied to the skin for coughs, athlete's foot, ringworm, and other ailments. Thyme oil is utilized in the cosmetic industry to scent soaps and toi-

letries, and is often paired with lavender to provide herbaceous notes in "green" and men's fragrances.

Caution: Both red and white thyme oil should be avoided by pregnant women and people with high blood pressure.

Valerian

Common names: Common valerian, American valerian

Latin name: *Valeriana officinalis*

Latin and common family names: Valerinaceae (Valerian family)

Related plants: Red valerian, *Centranthus ruber* (formerly *Valeriana rubra*)

Description: Valerian is a tall, stately perennial that grows from a 3-foot cluster of leaves, with 3- to 5-foot stems, and sweetly scented pinkish white flowers. The distinctive leaves are dark green with a maroon cast, smooth or notched, and arranged pinnately (in two rows) with six to twelve leaflets on opposite sides of the stems. Leaves along the flower stalks have irregular shapes and grow progressively smaller toward the top of the plant. Stems are erect, hollow, and notched. The tiny foamlike flowers in flat heads atop the stems have a cloyingly sweet aroma. Small seeds float from the plant on feathery pappi that are reminiscent of miniature dandelion puffs. The roots are stout rhizomes with many smaller runners and rootlets growing from them. They are light brown in color, cream-colored on the inside, and give off an earthy, penetrating odor that increases with drying. The red valerian commonly grown as a garden flower is *Centranthus ruber*, in the Valerian family.

Planting information and cultural directions: Give valerian a moist, rich soil in a sunny to mostly shaded location and it will grow lush and begin expanding outward with its steadily creeping roots. The foliage dies back each winter but plants live for many years. They are completely cold-hardy and easy to grow, requiring little maintenance.

Propagation: As with many perennial herbs, purchasing a small plant of valerian is the easiest way to begin. You can multiply your plant after three years by digging it up in early spring or fall and gently teasing the plantlets (root offsets) away from the mother root. If you allow plants to go to seed, tiny volunteers pop up near the mother plant, recognizable by their opposite leaves on arching stems. Valerian seed does not remain viable for long, but if you can find fresh seeds, press them into the surface of a sterile potting mix. Sift a thin layer of peat moss over the top, water them well from the bottom, and cover with plastic wrap. Watch over them, misting as necessary until germination occurs in about three weeks.

Year-round care: When planted in a moderately rich soil, valerian does not really need additional fertilizer to thrive. If you are going for maximum size and effect, enrich the soil with well-rotted manure before planting, scratch a cup or two of All-Purpose Fertilizer (see Chapter 1) around the plants in spring, keep plants weeded, and remove seed stalks in autumn. If you plan to harvest your valerian roots, you may wish to cut back emerging flower stalks to direct the plants' energy toward root development.

Pests and diseases: At times, aphids congregate on valerian flowers. Spray them with water or an insecticidal soap to remove them, or simply cut back the flower stalk and destroy it.

Harvesting and preserving: Harvest valerian roots in late autumn of their second year, when they are dormant and their medicinal constituents are most concentrated. Wait until frost has killed back the tops or, if this is not practical, cut them back. A garden fork works best to unearth the roots, being least likely to slice them, but a spade or shovel will do if used carefully. Dig up the entire root ball, pull off a few plantlets, and tuck them in the soil for future harvests. Swish the roots gently in a bucket of water, then spray them with a hose as you rub off any remaining dirt. Preserve the fresh roots in a tincture, or dry them in the shade at a low temperature. For drying, split or slice any roots larger than $\frac{3}{4}$ inch, and choose a location where their objectionable odor will not permeate your living space.

Garden uses: A full-size valerian is an imposing presence in the garden, especially when in bloom. Its height makes it a natural choice for the back of a border, growing beside other tall herbs such as angelica and copper fennel, or decorative perennials such as delphiniums and phlox. Late in the summer, its curious fragrance drifts through the air, inviting exploration.

Culinary uses: Although valerian was used to flavor food in medieval England when tropical spices were rare, it has fallen out of favor with modern cooks.

Craft and home uses: A few valerian flowers, in a vase by themselves or arranged with other herbs and flowers, can lend an air of mystery to your home. Keep it subtle or the fragrance will be too much. The blossoms tend to drop their petals quickly.

Medicinal uses: For more than 1,000 years, valerian has been esteemed as an herbal aid to relaxation and sleep, and abundant modern scientific research confirms that it acts as a central nervous system depressant. This action makes valerian one of the most reliable herbal sedatives, and it seems to be especially useful in cases where emotional stress results in nervous anxiety, headaches, stomach cramps, or insomnia. Clinical tests on human subjects with insomnia indicate that valerian shortens the time it takes to get to sleep, improves the quality of sleep, and does not cause a sleepy feeling in the morning or other adverse side effects of prescription sleep medications. It is also antispasmodic, and has been used to treat irritable bowel syndrome and menstrual cramps.

Valerian is usually taken in the form of a decoction (aqueous extract) or tincture, and is often combined with other herbs for a synergistic effect. Fresh or carefully dried roots are most effective. While some herbalists caution that taking large doses of this herb over an extended period of time can cause headaches or depression, others point out that no harmful side effects have been documented.

▌Viola

Common names: Wild pansy, Heartsease, Johnny Jump Up, Love in Idleness

Latin name: *Viola tricolor*

Latin and common family names: Violaceae (Violet family)

Varieties and cultivars: *V. hybrida* 'Helen Mount,' 'Cutie,' 'Sorbet' series (Lemon Chiffon, Blueberry Cream, Lavender Ice, French Vanilla), others

Description: Perky, delightful, and easy to grow, violas are a quintessential cottage-garden flower. They look like miniature pansies; each flower is just an inch or so across. The petals are velvety and scentless, with two above and three below, the lowest ending in a tapering spur. They come in a variety of colors, including white, yellow, and lavender, often with distinct color markings including veins that radiate from a bright yellow center. 'Helen Mount' is the classic tricolor form, in purple, yellow, and white. The petals drop to reveal a plump green ovary, which splits open into three sections, each filled with rows of tiny orange-brown seeds. Leaves are oval, 1 to 2 inches long, lightly notched or jagged at the edges, and grow in tufts. Plants ordinarily grow 6 to 12 inches tall, and their many-branching stems form bushy plants that can spread to 12 inches.

Planting information and cultural directions: Violas are annuals or short-lived perennials, springing up in the early months of the year and blooming into autumn if conditions are right. They do best in cool temperatures and ordinary to rich soil with good drainage and ample moisture. I once transplanted seedlings into a bed heavily enriched with composted horse manure, and was amazed to see viola plants grow over 2 feet tall! When temperatures are moderate they thrive in full sun or partial shade, but in hot weather they burn up unless shaded. Often a self-sown second generation is blooming by fall. Violas' compact growth habit and long-lasting show of color make them excellent container plants.

Propagation: For an early start, sow seeds indoors

in February or March, pressing them into the surface of a fine potting mix. Or keep it simple and sow seed directly in the garden as soon as the ground can be worked. Violas will often reseed and sometimes hybridize with related plants, providing a profusion of bright blossoms. Why not collect the seed and share it with friends or plant it the next season?

Year-round care: Violas are easy to grow and care for. A shot of liquid fertilizer as flower buds are forming and biweekly applications thereafter will keep your plants at their peak, though if the soil provides adequate nutrients this is not required. When the flowers are blooming, keep them picked or deadhead the plants regularly to extend the flowering period. In hot weather, move container plantings into the shade and check their watering needs daily.

Pests and diseases: In my experience, these sturdy descendants of wild pansies that grow throughout Europe are untroubled by insects or disease.

Harvesting and preserving: For edible flowers, pick violas when the flowers are fully open. Choose fresh-looking blossoms, free of spots or holes. Although they are most often used fresh, it's fun to preserve some flowers to decorate cakes and tea sandwiches by candying them. For medicinal use, cut the entire plant as it comes into bloom and dry it quickly in a microwave or dehydrator.

Garden uses: Floriferous violas brighten up a sunny spot all spring; in shade they carry on through summer. Grow them along the approach to your door or in pots on the front step and they will offer a perky greeting to you and your visitors. Or situate them where they will be seen often and are handy for pick-ing, perhaps a hanging basket or window box just outside the kitchen. These low-growing flowers are great for filling in shady areas, and give a simple charm to edgings and borders. Children love them, and their ease of cultivation makes them a natural choice for a child's garden.

Culinary uses: Like pansies, violas have a sweet, mild flavor and can be used to decorate tea cakes and sandwiches, salads, and other dishes. They are popular on wedding cakes, not only for their color and daintiness, but also because they carry a message of "loving thoughts" in the language of flowers. Try freezing them in ice cubes or a ring mold to float in a punch bowl on festive occasions.

Craft and home uses: Violas make charming pressed flowers for craft projects such as greeting cards, handmade paper, and pressed flower pictures. Use a flower press with special absorbent paper, or just place the flowers between the pages of a fat telephone book for about two weeks.

Medicinal uses: In Shakespeare's day, the little plant he called Love in Idleness was considered an aphrodisiac, and it was the juice of this flower that Puck squeezed into the eyes of the hapless faerie queen Titania in *A Midsummer Night's Dream*. The herb has a long folk-medicine tradition in Europe; in fact, some species, including the Yellow Mountain Viola, have been so overharvested that they are now protected by law. An infusion of the flowering tops is taken internally for lung conditions such as bronchitis and urinary tract infections, and internally and externally (by compress) for eczema.

Watercress

Common name: American cress

Latin name: *Nasturtium officinale*

Latin and common family names: Cruciferae/
Brassicaceae (Mustard family)

Description: Native to Europe, watercress is
grown around the world, especially in areas with
limestone soils. It is a succulent plant with a spreading root system, forming 12-inch mounds of dark
green, ovate leaves opposite on branching hollow
stems. Clusters of small white flowers appear in summer, followed by long seedpods that split open when
seeds are ripe. In late autumn the seeds germinate and
a new crop of watercress begins to grow.

Planting information and cultural directions:
Watercress requires both sunlight and ample water to
flourish. It grows best in gently flowing streams and is
commonly seen growing untended in city parks and
roadside ditches. Commercially it is grown in tanks
with a base of soil and water enough to float its
crowns. Home gardeners can grow it successfully in
specially created tubs with moving water, or even in
moist garden spots, where rampant spreading is seldom a problem.

Propagation: The easiest way to start watercress is
to transfer rooted branches from an outdoor planting
to your chosen site. If this is not possible, it's easy to
root sprigs from the grocery store in a glass of water,
then transfer them to a moist spot in the garden. Or
start watercress from seed, pressing the seed into
moist soil. It germinates easily at about 55°F and
grows quickly to harvestable size.

Year-round care: Lucky is the gardener with a
small stream for watercress—or is it such a good
thing? Watercress grows almost year-round in mild
areas and can become a stream-choking nuisance. My
friends at Bangor Manor near Silverdale expend a lot
of energy clearing the overabundant watercress out of
their creek every year—fortunately it makes good
compost. It's something to consider as you decide
whether to introduce watercress into your streambed
or to keep it under control in a more confined area.
Either way, you'll probably want to trim plants back to
the base of the stems when they start turning yellow
as summer's heat sets in.

Pests and diseases: Because it readily absorbs pol-
lutants and takes up waterborne parasites from grazing animals, watercress should not be gathered in the
wild unless you are certain the stream is clean. The
plants can look wonderfully healthy, but when in
doubt, don't—it's easy to find watercress in grocery
stores and markets.

Harvesting and preserving: Frequent cutting keeps
watercress plants bushy and delays flowering. You can
begin harvesting sprigs of watercress when they are
just a few inches long, and grasp great handfuls of
stems when the season is at its peak. Quality is highest in spring and fall when the weather is cool, since
rising temperatures bring on unpalatable blossoms,
tough stems, and an unpleasantly hot and bitter flavor.
Watercress does not dry well, but it can be steamed,
puréed or chopped, and frozen as a base for soups
when the fresh herb is not available.

Garden uses: Shiny green watercress leaves give
the impression of vitality, and the white flowers are
certainly not unattractive, yet because of its growth

habits watercress does not really possess the attributes of a choice ornamental plant. It deserves a place in the garden mainly as a tasty edible herb.

Culinary uses: High in vitamin C and iron, watercress also has a fresh, peppery flavor that makes it a popular culinary herb. It is great in salads, lending piquancy when combined with blue cheese and pears or apples, mixed wild greens, or in Asian-inspired recipes. It is more flavorful than lettuce in sandwiches, whether delicate tea sandwiches or hearty heroes and subs. Watercress is also good in a variety of soups such as creamy French *Potage au Cresson* or lighter broths and egg-drop–style soups. Stir-fried with tofu and served with rice, watercress takes on the role of a nutritious leafy green.

▌Wild Ginger

Common names: Canadian snakeroot, False coltsfoot, Indian ginger, Wild ginger

Latin name: *Asarum* or *A. caudatum*

Latin and common family names: Aristolochiaceae (Birthwort family)

Related species: Asarabacca, Hazelwort, Wild Nard, *Asarum canadense*, *A. europaeum*

Description: Wild ginger is an elusive woodland perennial that forms a carpet of shiny, heart-shaped leaves. The plants creep via shallow, fleshy, branched rhizomes, yellowish in color, with slender rootlets that inspire one of the plant's common names, snakeroot. Two leaves, each on a thin stem 2 to 8 inches long, grow from each node. The leaves are dark green with intricate veining; their undersides are light green and slightly woolly. The leaves, stem, and

especially the roots are aromatic when bruised and have a distinctive spicy flavor.

Single maroon flowers grow on short stems from the leaf junctions and hide near the ground. Reach down among the leaves to find these helmet-shaped blossoms with three tapering tails (sepals). Their unusual appearance gives them an aura of mystery. Wild ginger is native to North America. Its range extends from northern California to British Columbia and Idaho; the related *A. canadense* is also found in several eastern states and provinces.

Planting information and cultural directions: It is not always easy to establish wild ginger in a garden setting. Success is most likely where conditions duplicate the moist, humusy soil, rich in leaf mold, of the herb's natural habitat. Dappled to nearly full shade is ideal. In such situations, clumps grow thick and lush, spreading quickly. Plants are hardy and require little maintenance.

Propagation: Starts of wild ginger are not easy to come by, but occasionally you can find one at a plant sale or nursery. It is possible to dig starts in the woods, but development pressures have shrunk the once-large stands. If you do find wild plants and take starts, make sure that you leave plenty of roots to regenerate. Once you have your own patch established, it is easy to divide plants in the fall and increase its size.

Pests and diseases: Slugs and snails have a taste for wild ginger, darn it. Their appetites are often the cause of cultivated plants' demise. Check regularly, and if you find evidence of slug or snail attacks, take steps immediately to protect your plants.

Harvesting and preserving: Wild ginger roots are

at their best in autumn. The roots are shallow and easy to dig, especially in the loose, woodsy soil they favor. If you are careful, you can harvest pieces that connect rooted sections, hardly disturbing the plants. Wash them thoroughly, changing the water several times. They do not require peeling. Snip the roots into small pieces and dry them at room temperature or in a slow oven. With proper storage, dried wild ginger keeps indefinitely.

Wild ginger is a choice garden ornament for shady areas. The dark, beautifully shaped leaves are excellent in naturalistic and foliage gardens, perhaps in contrast with lacy ferns or sweet woodruff.

Culinary uses: This herb's zingy flavor is definitely reminiscent of tropical root ginger (no relation), though milder and slightly bitter. Early settlers used it as a ginger substitute, doubling the quantity in their "receipts." To candy the root, first cook it until tender, drain, then simmer it in a sugar syrup. For a flavorful tea, simmer roots in water for 20 minutes. Some hikers like to chew on the fresh root. A piece an inch long or less, tucked under the lip like snoose and chewed intermittently, retains its flavor for a long time.

Medicinal uses: Native Americans and early settlers used the roots of wild ginger for medicine. In *Ethnobotany of Western Washington,* Erna Gunther reported that the Native people of the Skagit boiled it as a tonic tea and ate the leaves to stimulate the appetite. They called it *tuxop'bida'libut* or *toxop* (pheasant), because pheasants eat the plant. Tribes of the eastern states are reported to have used *A. canadense* as a general tonic, for sore throats, stomach cramps, and as a contraceptive. Pioneers treated kidney ailments, stomach problems,

and delayed menstruation with wild ginger root.

Essential oil distilled from wild ginger roots contains asarene, azulene, pinenes, linalool, borneol, terpineol, geraniol, eugenol, and other substances. It has antibacterial properties. The roots also contain sugars, resin, mucilage, alkaloid, and aristolochic acid, thought to be an antitumor compound. Wild ginger has limited use in modern herbal medicine as a digestive herb that relieves indigestion, cramps, and gas.

Caution: Large doses cause nausea.

monthly

planner

Part of the pleasure of gardening is
working in harmony with the seasons. Gardeners
learn to submit to nature's timetable, as each
season flows inexorably into the next,
bringing its own tasks and rewards.

Still, the dozens of chores that await
the gardener, whatever the season or the weather,
can be daunting. Before the busy growing season begins,
start a garden journal for keeping daily or weekly records,
taking notes, and making diagrams of your plantings.
Mine has been invaluable to me as both a record and a
reference. Use your time productively—if it's too soggy
to work outdoors, clean seeds or tidy the shed. By keeping up steadily, even working just an hour a week,
you'll be rewarded with better results.

Spring is
one of the busiest
seasons in the
garden, when the
earth awakens and
new life stirs.

spring

Spring work, as it is called, means sowing, watering, and tending seeds in the greenhouse, then hardening off and transplanting seedlings to the garden. It also means getting the garden in shape—digging, tilling, fertilizing, making beds, mulching paths—and sowing seeds or transplanting herbs. This work continues throughout the entire season.

March

This can be a fine wild month, due to the vernal equinox. As the days warm up, gardening possibilities increase. It is prime time for harvesting wild nettles, dandelions, and other spring greens.

Garden checklist: Construct beds and paths if the weather allows. Till or dig over existing beds as soon as possible to dry out soggy soil and give green

manures time to break down. Work on the compost pile and worm bin; apply finished compost, worm castings, and all-purpose fertilizer to beds and fast-growing plants. Remove mulches covering your plants to allow air and sunlight to reach them; start a new compost pile with appropriate mulching materials. Look out for slugs and snails that weaken plants by eating tender shoots.

Plant checklist: March is an excellent time to divide or transplant perennials and rearrange your garden. Divide perennials such as chives, echinacea, monarda, lovage, oregano, thyme, mint, and valerian before they begin fast growth. Dig up and divide tarragon early, before the brittle pinkish shoots grow long. Tease invasive grass roots out of these perennials, taking care not to let them break.

Prune roses and sage. Dig up starts of hops. Plant starts of horseradish. Pot up overwintered geranium cuttings. Put a bucket over dandelion clumps to blanch the leaves.

Many kinds of seed can be planted safely indoors and out. Seed packets often instruct you to sow a certain number of weeks from the date of the last expected frost. In the maritime Northwest, calculate back from April 30; in colder areas, wait another two weeks or longer. Plant seeds of angelica, arugula, borage, calendula, chevil, cilantro, fennel, and violas directly into the soil. Indoors, sow anise hyssop, basil, lavender, marjoram, nasturtium, oregano, sage, salad burnet, summer and winter savory, thyme, and others. Keep track of sowing dates in your journal.

April

Gardening fever strikes! Spring is definitely here, but the weather is changeable. April showers usually make watering even seedling beds unnecessary. Remember that tender plants may be nipped by frost if set out too soon. Coax an earlier harvest of many herbs either by covering individual plants with mini-greenhouses made of plastic milk jugs, or protecting entire rows with spun-bonded polyester covers. Wait to set out basil until the soil is warmer, unless you are a gambler willing to risk your first planting.

Garden checklist: Outdoors, keep working on garden beds and other structural elements. Try to finish planting annual and perennial herbs. Control slugs, which can do tremendous damage to seedlings. Hoe weeds while they are still young and put them on the compost pile along with grass clippings, com-

frey leaves, and straw or dried material. Weed perennials regularly to avoid more tedious work later. Sidedress them with compost, worm castings, or all-purpose fertilizer by scratching it into the ground around the plants. Plant herbs in containers and situate them in sheltered locations; rejuvenate established containers with compost and fertilizer. Replace annuals that have died over the winter.

Plant checklist: Sow arugula, chervil, dill, cilantro, nasturtium, and summer savory directly in the ground. Harvest perennial herbs that have overwintered: young leaves of chives, fennel, lemon balm, lovage, salad burnet, sweet cicely, parsley, salad burnet, and tarragon are delicious additions to spring salads. Borage and chive flowers may be available for garnishing. Fresh watercress and sorrel are great in soups and salads. Prune scented geraniums and add the leaves to teas, cakes, and syrups.

Late in the month, set out bay trees, lemon verbena, pineapple sage, scented geraniums, and other plants that were wintered indoors. Set out sweet marjoram. Cold weather may check growth of these herbs; if the weather seems uncooperative, wait until mid-May to be on the safe side.

In the greenhouse, make a second sowing of basil early in the month. Keep a watchful eye on seedlings, watering regularly and transplanting them to larger pots if necessary to encourage steady growth. Harden off plants that are ready to go outside.

May

If you are going to plant a small herb garden in a day or a weekend, the last weeks of this month are the time to do it. "The weather is settled," as the seed catalogs say, and "the soil has warmed." In all but the coldest Northwest locations, frost is no longer a worry. Although there may be unseasonal hailstorms, it is generally safe to transplant all your seedlings or purchased plants outdoors. It's also a great time to fill containers, window boxes, and hanging baskets.

Garden checklist: Transplant, sow, thin, stake, and weed. If possible, choose a calm, cloudy day to transplant basil and other seedlings. Harden plants off properly so bright sunlight won't scald their leaves. Fertilize transplants with Regular Solution Fish Fertilizer and they will perk up quickly. Keep feeding fast-growing plants.

Do not allow seedbeds to dry out, even if this means watering two or three times a day with a watering can. Or, to save labor, soak a burlap bag and place it over the bed until the seeds germinate.

Plant checklist: Celebrate spring with sweet woodruff in a Mai Bowle; pick and dry the flowers for potpourri. Tarragon, fennel, mints, oregano, sage, sweet cicely, and other perennials are also sizable enough to harvest. Fertilize plants that are growing fast with applications of Regular Solution Fish Fertilizer or All-Purpose Fertilizer Mix. Volunteer (self-sown) seedlings of anise hyssop, calendula, summer savory, dill, fennel, nasturtium, parsley, chives, thyme, oregano, and other herbs from last year's garden may have appeared by now, too. Leave them to grow on the spot, transplant them to more appropriate places, or weed them out without mercy as you choose.

Thyme and chives are among the earliest herbs to

bloom. Cut upright thymes back almost to the ground and hang the aromatic bunches to dry. Enjoy the multihued carpet of creeping thymes in flower. Cut back the chives, or harvest individual stems, strip off the leaves, and hang the bunches to dry. This year's seedlings of quick-growing arugula, cilantro, dill, savory, and other greens can be thinned and used in the kitchen. Make a second or third sowing of these herbs for continuous harvests. Water, weed, top-dress, and mulch garlic.

summer

Ah, salad days! This is the season to really enjoy your garden. Lavish your meals with an abundance of fresh herbs, and pick bouquets of fragrant herb blossoms for centerpieces and home decoration. If possible, set a couple of chairs or a picnic table near your herb patch, and take advantage of the fragrant atmosphere for pleasant conversation and dining with family and guests.

June

The weather may be cool and cloudy this month, though warm spells are not uncommon. Once your direct-sown seedlings are up and transplants are getting established, maintenance is the key. Aphids and other pests may show up now. Review your watering system; check hoses and sprinklers and consider investing in a timer or a drip system.

Garden checklist: Continue fertilizing annuals and perennials. Trim bay trees, topiaries, formal edgings, and knot gardens while plants are in fast growth. Water and weed young plants steadily to maintain optimum growth. Larger plants can successfully compete with weeds, but go over the beds thoroughly at least once to clean them up. Then mulch with grass clippings, straw, shredded newspaper, or other organic material to suppress new weeds—if the weather is dry and slug populations are low.

Plant checklist: June is the month of roses, especially the old-fashioned varieties that bloom only once; make the most of it by harvesting plenty of petals. Lemon verbenas should be leafing out, and early lavenders may begin flowering. If winter-damaged rosemary plants are not putting out new growth by now, give up on them. Gather elder blossoms and make at least one batch of Elderflower Fizz. Begin picking basil tips! Harvest calendula flowers, green sweet cicely seeds, and catnip and feverfew leaves. Cut back watercress flowers. Sow more arugula, cilantro, and dill.

July

Take a walk around your garden regularly, observing the growth, needs, and problems of your plants. It is time well spent. As you become intimately familiar with them, garden priorities will become clear. In your journal, note observations about maturity dates, productivity, and any special characteristics of your plants. During this lush month, rewards are all around you.

Start making herbal jellies, vinegars, butters, seasoning blends, oils, and tinctures to last through the winter months. Put up extras for gifts. Sip teas made from lemon verbena, monarda, anise hyssop, mint,

lemon balm, and other herbs through lovage straws in the shade of your hop-covered arbor.

Garden checklist: When the weather is hot, do watering and other gardening tasks in the coolness of morning. Harvest herbs before they flower, go to seed, and look unattractive. Conditions are ideal at midmorning on hot days. Remove spent blooms of ornamental herbs regularly. Keep feeding plants in rapid growth. Most plants will put on new growth and yield a second harvest.

Plant checklist: Lavender is glorious this month. Gather bouquets and bunches; make lavender wands and potpourri. Immerse yourself in the lavender festival in Sequim, Washington, on the third weekend of the month. Harvest buds and flowering tops of St. John's wort for tinctures, teas, and oils; echinacea flowering tops for teas and tinctures. Observe bay trees—yellow leaves indicate lack of water; brown leaves may be sun scorched; small flat discs on the undersides are scale insects. Sow parsley and chervil seed toward the end of the month for a winter crop.

August

As the herb garden reaches a crescendo, the supply seems endless. A hot spell when you can hear your basil growing is almost predictable. Drought-resistant herbs show off their advantages now. Irrigate roses, basil, parsley, mint, and other moisture lovers regularly. Container-grown herbs may need daily watering. Watch for anything that begins to droop, including rosemary, and give it a good soaking. For mildew on hops, monarda, sage, or other plants, spray with a baking-soda solution.

Take softwood cuttings of bay trees, lavender, rosemary, tarragon, thyme, sage, rose geraniums, winter savory, and other herbs. Keep them moist and semishaded until rooted.

Preserve a good supply of herbs by freezing, drying, and making flavored vinegars—already the days are growing shorter and the nights are cooling off.

Throughout the month, reward yourself by enjoying your garden. It's the perfect time for outdoor meals, garden parties, and relaxing amid all the lovely herbs.

Garden checklist: Early in the month, make one last sowing of dill and cilantro. Keep seedlings moist until germination takes place. Seed heads are ripening; gather dill for making pickles, and borage, calendula, chamomile, cilantro, rosemary, sweet cicely, and other seeds to dry. Sow green-manure seeds such as crimson clover, vetch, or small-seeded fava beans for a cover crop in empty beds or underneath annuals such as basil and summer savory. Started while the weather is warm, green-manure plants will blanket the ground with green in winter.

Plant checklist: Basil is now at its peak. Pinch back the plants every two or three days to keep them productive. Hang bunches of basil to dry, make pesto to freeze, and eat plenty of the king of herbs. Harvest, dry, and braid garlic. Cut comfrey and lemon balm back; dry or compost the leaves. Shear thymes that have flowered; cut back tarragon that is yellowing. Pinch off St. John's wort seed heads to prevent mass invasion later. Harvest bouquets of echinacea; dry the flowering tops for tea or make tinctures.

autumn

As late-season splendors grace the autumn garden, finish harvesting and start putting the garden to bed.

September

This month often brings our most beautiful weather, so treat yourself to a picnic in the garden while you can. Many fruits and vegetables reach their peak harvest, and herbs are still in good supply to preserve for later use.

Garden checklist: Early in the month, sow annual winter rye for green manure. Rake and shred falling leaves and start a new compost heap. Test your soil and apply dolomite lime as needed. Lay out and prepare new beds to get a head start on spring.

Plant checklist: Pick basil as long as you can. Make a last sowing of arugula. Harvest hops when the strobiles begin to turn gold. Pickle cucumbers with dill, shallots with rosemary, beans with tarragon. I like to make up giant batches of tomato sauce and minestrone soup with lots of herbs and freeze them for winter meals. Pick elderberries and preserve them for winter.

Keep harvesting ripe herb seeds such as arugula, cilantro, dill, nasturtium, sage, lovage, chives, fennel, sweet cicely, calendula, summer and winter savory, lemon balm, and others. Transplant parsley and chervil plants sown in July. Gather reinvigorated watercress for autumn salads. Garnish drinks and salads with the brilliant red blossoms of pineapple sage, or just admire them in the garden. Gather rose hips.

October

Harvesting is slowing down, the growing season is nearly over, and putting the garden to rest before heavy rains and cold weather arrive is now a priority. This can be one of the most productive months in the garden, since much of the work you accomplish in October will pay dividends in labor saved during the spring. Light frosts, expected this month, gradually become sharper until a killing frost zaps tender plants.

Garden checklist: Continue to work on new and established beds. Sprinkle open beds with long-term soil amendments such as dolomite lime and rock phosphate before digging or tilling them. Try to rid your perennials of pernicious weeds, especially grasses, which will otherwise resume their growth as early as January. Cover beds with a layer of straw, lawn clippings, or shredded leaves. Like green manures, these mulches help keep down weeds and prevent nutrients from leaching from your soil. By spring the mulch will turn into rich, crumbly humus.

Plant checklist: Dig scented geraniums, pot them in damp peat moss, and bring them into the greenhouse, garage, or porch for the winter. Bring in bay trees potted in a rich soil mix (check leaves for scale insects). Bring in French lavender plants to bloom during the holidays. Take in lemon verbenas, pineapple sage, and one-year-old rosemaries to be sure they will survive the winter. Water these plants sparingly and watch for aphids and other bugs.

Plant garlic. Cut down the stalks and seed heads of perennials such as fennel and lovage. Pull out arugula, basil, calendula, dill, summer savory and other spent annuals after frost, or shear them with a lawn mower and add the clippings to your compost bin. Once the ground has been deeply moistened by autumn rains, divide and move perennials.

Prolong harvests of baby dill, chervil, cilantro, summer savory, and sweet marjoram by covering plants with row covers. Sow echinacea and rose seeds in flats outside to stratify over the winter. Take hardwood cuttings of rose and elder.

November

Rain and cold weather set in, but there is still time to do some of the tasks you couldn't get to earlier. Tidy the garden; add to the compost heap; dig over the ground for a new herb bed or garden. If it is too wet or frosty to garden, keep warm indoors and catch up your gardening journal while the past season is still fresh in your mind. Strip the leaves from bunches of dried herbs and store in glass jars. Make potpourri, teas, and seasoning blends.

Garden checklist: Dig finished compost and spread it 2 inches thick around the base of perennials such as rosemary—not only will it protect them from winter cold, but it will also nourish them when spring growth begins. Finish moving and dividing perennials; mulch your garlic with straw or leaf mold. Start ordering catalogs.

Plant checklist: Dig and pot one or two parsley, chervil, chive, mint, tarragon, and winter savory plants in good potting soil. Water well with Regular Solution Fish Fertilizer and keep them indoors or in the greenhouse. You can enjoy a harvest of fresh herbs before your outdoor garden is producing.

Dandelion roots are prime now, plump and high in inulin after light frosts. Roots of comfrey, valerian, and wild ginger are also ready to harvest. Dry the roots or make tinctures. Dig horseradish and store it in damp sand for easy harvesting all winter. Plant bare-root roses.

winter

Seasoned gardeners know that the quiet days of winter are ideal for planning and preparing next year's garden. Rest is also important.

December

Your dried and preserved herbs now add a personal touch to holiday meals and gifts. Garlic braids, herb vinegars, dream pillows, and bundles or wreaths of dried herbs are always appreciated. Seed catalogs begin arriving for your perusal. Harvest, groom, and fertilize your indoor herb garden; make sure its lighting is adequate, check regularly for bugs, and don't overwater.

Garden checklist: Take a break. If the weather is mild, you may have a chance to do a little weeding and mulching.

Plant checklist: Rosemary and bay trees make lovely Christmas trees, and French lavenders, scented geraniums, and other plants you have taken in can make a beautiful display indoors. You can also harvest fresh sage, rosemary, winter savory, and thyme from your garden.

January

This is the month for resting, dreaming, planning, and laying the foundation for the coming year. The preparation you do even when the garden is frozen will make everything go more smoothly later. Begin a fresh garden journal for keeping daily or weekly records, taking notes, making maps with the names of things you plant, and jotting down other information. A three-year format allows quick visual comparisons of planting and germination dates, weather patterns, and the like. It is a learning tool that can help you become a more organized and accomplished gardener.

It's a great time to read herb and gardening books and store up ideas for future reference. Many seed catalogs are informative sources about growing classic herbs and new varieties. Go through and organize seeds you purchased or collected last year. Get started ordering new seeds before the spring rush. Plan and organize, write out labels, mend tools, and get little jobs done before the busy time of sowing, transplanting, and then weeding and harvesting arrives.

Garden checklist: Check the straw mulch on your garlic and apply more if necessary. Plant garlic if you didn't do it earlier. Prune roses after their leaves drop. Wheel out manure and compost and place it in heaps while the ground is frozen. If there is a break in the weather, dig over beds and begin preparation for planting, but avoid packing down wet soil.

Clean out your greenhouse, sterilize used pots in a solution of 1 tablespoon of bleach per gallon of water, or set up an area indoors for seedlings. Write out plant markers when you have time.

Plant checklist: Keep an eye on any herbs you've

taken indoors; water them sparingly. Spray scented geraniums, bay trees, and other tender plants in the greenhouse with insecticidal soap for aphids. In case of a serious cold snap, throw an old blanket over your rosemary plants at night and bring your most cherished semi-hardy plants indoors temporarily. Knock heavy snow off your perennials, especially lavenders, to keep the branches from splaying or breaking.

February

It is always a pleasure to watch the stirrings of spring in February. The Northwest Flower and Garden Show, held in Seattle in midmonth, is an extravaganza not to be missed. Attend excellent seminars, discover dozens of garden-related businesses and organizations, and be inspired by the beautiful gardens that give you a preview of spring. Finish up seed orders this month to be sure choice varieties are still available and that the seeds arrive before you need them.

Garden checklist: If the weather is fine, begin winter cleanup—rake leaves, pick up fallen branches, pile plant debris on the compost heap. This is your last chance to plant that garlic!

Get a head start on pulling weeds, the earlier the better before they get ahead of you. If quack grass and other harmful weeds are invading chives, tarragon, or other perennials, dig the plants up and gently tease the grass roots out. If the problem is really severe, plan to start new, weed-free plants in a different location soon. In cold areas, some of these tasks will have to wait.

Plant checklist: Cut back dead stalks of lemon balm, mint, oregano, tarragon, and other perennials

with pruning shears or a string trimmer. Prune back woody sage plants and spread a handful of all-purpose fertilizer beneath each plant—they will bush out beautifully later.

Purchase or mix your potting soil. Indoors, sow seeds of parsley, chives and garlic chives, lovage, thyme, lemon balm, and other herbs you can move outside while the weather is still cool. Cut back scented geraniums by half to keep them from getting spindly. Harvest the herbs wintering over indoors. For commercial greenhouses, February is peak season as seedlings of all kinds are readied for marketing to your garden.

Extending the Season

My idea of luxury is a salad spiked with homegrown herbs in March, and fresh tarragon to go with early spring asparagus. I admit to feeling smug about picking basil in October, and I get a certain thrill when my French lavender blooms in February. And as a market gardener I learned that early produce brings a premium price, because people are hungry for a taste of something fresh and local. For herb lovers like me, the reward is worth the effort.

Most herbs start growing when spring temperatures reach about 43°F, and stop when temperatures drop to that point in the fall. Given adequate moisture and nutrients, they grow faster as temperatures rise. The number of days within this temperature range each year is called the growing season. As you become a more proficient gardener who uses herbs frequently, you too will probably want to make the most of your plants by learning to extend the growing season.

This is nothing new. Gardeners have always manipulated nature in order to grow desired plants in a particular location, sometimes tricking and coaxing, sometimes pushing the limits. The walled gardens of medieval monasteries kept out cold winds as well as grazing animals. Victorian gardeners developed "hot beds" by burying fresh manure beneath a layer of soil in cold frames. The extra heat enabled them to produce out-of-season delicacies. What's changed since then is the array of materials and devices designed to help gardeners prolong their harvests.

We're not talking about creating an artificial climate in order to grow plants that would not otherwise survive in the Northwest. Vanilla beans, clove trees, black pepper vines, and other fascinating tropicals require a heated greenhouse with precise temperature and humidity controls to grow here. In my years of gardening I've tried growing all sorts of things in a simple solar-heated greenhouse, from cardamom and ginger to loofah gourds and passion vines. It was fun, but eventually they all died because providing one or another of their requirements was not high enough on my priority list. I've become content with the many things that grow easily in our climate, plus a few favorites among the borderline hardy that need help to survive the cold winters. Because I love to use aloe vera, scented geraniums, lemon verbena, bay leaf, and certain others, I'm willing to make a little extra effort to keep them alive and near at hand.

The question is, how much time and effort is involved? The answer depends on decisions you make, based on your lifestyle. The catalogs of major seed companies offer various supplies and devices for protecting plants at every stage of their existence. General gardening books and magazines feature diagrams and plans for do-it-yourselfers. It may all sound great, but if you take on more than is realistic, you won't be able to keep it up. Here are some choices to consider.

The simplest thing is to make an early start in the garden. Like staying in bed a little longer in the morning, it's tempting to procrastinate the early spring work. Many herb seeds can be planted "as early as the ground can be worked," and if you get with it, you can enjoy two or three extra weeks of delicious fresh herbs. There may be a sunny spell in February when the ground dries up enough to pass the squeeze test. Squeeze a handful of soil in your hand, then tap it lightly. If it holds its shape until you tap it, then falls apart, the ground is ready for you to get going with arugula, chervil, fennel, and other cold-tolerant seeds.

Starting seeds indoors as described in Chapter 1 is an excellent way to extend your harvest, especially with heat-loving herbs such as basil. Minimize transplanting shock to seedlings by hardening plants off, handling them carefully, and providing some form of initial protection from the elements.

In Victorian times, the term *cloche*, derived from a French word meaning "bell", referred to special glass jars that were open at the bottom and had a knob on top for a handle. These were placed over individual plants and removed when the temperature inside became too hot. What a sight a row of these graceful bell jars must have made in the garden, even if the knobs were knocked off to prevent a magnifying-glass effect. Glass bell jars are once again available in specialty garden shops, but—alas for romance— recycled plastic milk jugs or soft-drink containers with the bottoms cut out are readily available substitutes. These act like mini-greenhouses and provide protection from chilling winds, and you can leave the tops off for ventilation, keeping in mind that slugs are quite capable of crawling in to devour your plants.

Cloche has now become a collective term used to describe many styles of portable protective devices. For a very basic cloche, bend coat-hanger wires into A-frames and cover them with a large, clear plastic bag, fastening it with clothespins. To form low tunnels that cover several plants in a row, stretch plastic sheeting over metal hoops, leaving enough extra plastic at either end to gather it together and peg it down. More elaborate plastic tunnels are available commercially. For an excellent overview of cloches, frames, and the whole subject of what's called protective cropping from an English viewpoint, I recommend Joy Larkcomb's excellent book, *The Salad Garden.*

Spun-bonded polyester, a filmy, gossamer fabric that lets in light and water but keeps out wind and insects, is a marvelous innovation. Known to the trade as row cover or floating row covers, the fabric comes in rolls or sheets of various sizes, and can be laid over garden beds with the edges held in place by being buried with soil and weighted down by rocks or bricks. I became a fan when an unseasonal hailstorm hit my garden one June, and row covers saved the basil transplants from being shredded. If used with care and stored indoors over the winter, the fabric can last two or three seasons.

Cold frames are boxes, usually with angled sides, covered with glass or plastic and hinged at the top to allow easy access and ventilation. Recycled aluminum windows that slide open and shut are great for cold frames, and automatic openers, available through the mail, eliminate the need to be in constant attendance. Plastic lean-tos, tents, awnings, and similar structures are also considered cold frames and can be a big help toward more productive gardening.

By the time you're wishing for a greenhouse, you are probably a fairly serious gardener. When you finally make the investment and start using your greenhouse, you may wonder why you waited so long. A greenhouse is multifunctional and makes it easier to start seeds, grow heat-loving plants, and overwinter tender perennials. Commercial options range from collapsible plastic Germinators to models in glass or various plastics. Managing a greenhouse involves organization and equipment, watering, temperature and humidity controls, air circulation, sanitation procedures, and more. Scheduling plantings to maximize space is very important in commercial greenhouse operations; your own well-kept records will provide invaluable information over time. For tips on greenhouse management, consult a good book on the subject and look for information at home and garden shows. *Building and Using Our Sun Heated Greenhouse,* by Scott and Helen Nearing, is written from a self-sufficient homesteader's perspective.

resources

index

Resources
Index

GARDENS

Northwest gardeners can gain information and inspiration from many public and private herb gardens. You can learn a great deal by observing the ways that knowledgeable herb growers bring their experience to their gardens to solve design challenges and combine or highlight certain herbs.

The gardens mentioned here are by no means limited in scope to the 50 herbs described in this book. Each has its own character and focus. The display gardens of various institutions, estates, and businesses are intended for public enjoyment and education. Generally, the larger ones are most accessible, but smaller gardens, that may be open fewer hours, are also rewarding to visit. Other interesting gardens are located at restaurants and inns, providing fresh herbs and greens for the kitchen and a pleasant scene for guests. There is also something very appealing in community gardens, which combine the resources and styles of many people. The herb farms listed all specialize in herbs and herbal products. Many offer books, classes, and other educational opportunities, as well as plants and seeds.

Abundant Life Seed Gardens. 411 Discovery Road (look across the street), Port Townsend, WA 98368; 360-385-5660.

Anna B. Smith Park, Children's Garden. Tracyton Blvd, Bremerton, WA 98311. Master Gardeners, 360-337-7158.

Barn Owl Nursery. Chris and Ed Mulder. 22999 SW Newland Rd, Wilsonville, OR 97070; 503-638-0387.

Cedarbrook Herb Farm. Toni Anderson. 1345 S. Sequim Ave, Sequim, WA 98382; 360-683-7733.

The Cloisters, The Metropolitan Museum of Art Medieval Herb Garden, Fort Tyron Park, NY 10040; 212-233-3700.

Dutchmill Herbfarm. Barbara Remington. 6640 NW Marsh Rd, Forest Grove, OR 97116; 503-357-0924.

Elderflower Farm. John and Kelly Stelzer. 501 Callahan Rd., Roseburg, OR 97470; 541-672-7766.

Foxglove Herb Farm. Michael Burkhart, Nancy Andrews, and Jane Cooper. 6617 Rosedale St, Gig Harbor, WA 98335; 253-853-4878.

Fairie Herb Gardens. Dave Baird and Steve Taylor. 6236 Elm St SE, Tumwater, WA 98501; 360-754-9249.

Fairlight Gardens. Judy and Don Jensen. 30904 164 SE, Auburn, WA 98002; 253-631-8932.

Gardenscapes. Susan Dearth and Marilyn Hepner. 4556 Terrace Way SE, Port Orchard, WA 98366; 360-871-7245.

Happy Valley Herbs. Lynda and Mike Dowling. 3505 Happy Valley Rd, Victoria, BC V9C 2Y2; 250-474-5767. Open by appointment.

Hazelwood Herb Farm. Richard White and Jacynthe Dugas. 13576 Adshead Rd, Ladysmith, BC V9G1H6; 250-245-8007.

Herban Renewal. Janice Peltier. 18915 Marine View Dr SW, Normandy Park, WA 98166; 206-243-8821. Organic herbs, worms, and garden consulting; by appointment only.

Heronswood. Dan Hinkley. 7530 288th St, Kingston, WA 98346; 360-297-4172.

Hummingbird Farm. Ward Beebee and Leslie Johnson. 2319 N. Zylstra Rd, Oak Harbor, WA 98277; 360-679-5044.

Lakewold Gardens. Friends of Lakewold, 12317 Gravelly Lake Dr SW, Lakewood, WA 98499; 253-584-3360, 1-888-858-4106.

The National Herb Garden. US National Arboretum, 3501 New York Ave NE, Washington, DC 20002. Historic Rose Garden and 10 specialty herb gardens.

Raven Hill Herb Farm. Noel Richardson and Andrew Yeoman. 1330 Mt. Newton Crossing Rd, Sannichton, BC V8M 1S1; 250-652-4024.

Seattle Tilth. 4649 Sunnyside Ave N, Seattle, WA 98103; 206-633-0451.

Sooke Harbour House. Sinclair and Fredricka Phillip. 1528 Whiffen Spit Rd, Sooke, BC V0S 1N0; 250-642-3421. Contact Byron Cook, head gardener for herb garden info.

University of Washington Medicinal Herb Garden. University of Washington Botany Department, Seattle, WA 98195; 206-543-1126. Free tours are available the second and fourth Sunday of the month from 12–1 pm.

University of British Columbia Physic Garden. At the UBC Botanical Garden, 6804 SW Marine Dr, Vancouver, BC V6T 1Z4; 604-822-9666 general information.

Van Dusen Botanical Garden. 5251 Oak Street, Vancouver, BC V6M 4H1; 604-878-9274. 55 acres including an Elizabethan maze.

SOURCES

Abundant Life Seed Foundation. PO Box 772, Port Townsend, WA 98368; 360-385-5660, Fax 360-385-7455. Open pollinated, rare and heirloom seeds.

Goodwin Creek Gardens. Jim and Dotti Becker. Box 83, Williams, OR 97544; Phone/Fax 541-846-7357; www.goodwincreekgardens.com. Catalog $1. Herb and everlasting flower plants, seeds.

Hazelwood Herb Farm. 13576 Adshead Rd, Ladysmith BC V9G 1H6, 250-245-8007.

The Herbalist. Tierny Salter. 2106 NE 65th, Seattle, WA 98115; 206-523-2600; www.theherbalist.com. Herbal medicines, books.

Herban Pottery. 3220 First Ave S, Seattle, WA 98134; 206-621-8601. Imported pots, plants, books.

Heirloom Old Garden Roses. Louise Clements. 24062 NE Riverside Dr, St Paul, OR 97137; 503-538-1576; www. heirloomroses.com.

Horizon Herbs. Richo Cech. PO Box 69, Williams, OR 97544; 541-846-6704; www.chatlink.com/~herbseed. Medicinal herb seeds.

Nichols Garden Nursery. 1190 Old Salem Rd NE, Albany, OR 97321; 541-928-9280, Fax 800-231-5306; www. gardennursery.com. Retail store and mail order catalog

Pacific Botanicals. 4350 Fish Hatchery Road, Grants Pass, OR 97527; 541-479-7777, Fax 541-5271. High quality dried medicinal herbs.

Raintree Nursery. 391 Butts Rd, Morton, WA 98356; 360-496-6400, 1-888-770-8358. Elder trees, fruit trees, berries, and more.

Renee's Garden. 7389 West Zayante Road, Felton, CA 95018. 1-888-880-7228.

Richter and Sons, Ltd. Box 26, Goodwood, ON L0C 1A0; 905-640-6677, Fax 905-640-6641, www.richters.com. Huge selection of herb plants, seeds, and books.

Trout Lake Farms. 149 Little Mountain Rd, PO Box 181, Trout Lake, WA 98650; 509-395-2025, Fax 509-395-2645.

Territorial Seed Company. PO Box 157, Cottage Grove, OR 97424; 541-942-9547; www.territorial-seed.com. Herb, vegetable, and flower seeds adapted to Northwest conditions. Gardening equipment and books also.

PUBLICATIONS

American Herb Association. PO Box 1673, Nevada City, CA 95959. Quarterly newsletter.

American Herbal Pharmacopoeia. Box 5159, Santa Cruz, CA 95063; 408-461-6317; www.herbal-ahp.org.

Herb Companion Magazine. 201 E Fourth St, Loveland, CO 80537.

Herbal Gram. PO Box 201660 Austin, TX 78720.

Herbs for Health Magazine. 741 Corporate Circle, Suite A, Box 4101, Golden, CO 80401.

Medical Herbalism. PO Box 33080, Portland, OR 97233.

SOCIETIES AND ORGANIZATIONS

American Herb Association. PO Box 1673, Nevada City, CA 95959.

Canadian Herb Society. 5251 Oak St, Vancouver, BC 76M 4H1; www.herbsociety.ca.

Center for Wild Vegetable Research and Education. Goosefoot Acres, Inc, PO Box 18016, Cleveland Heights, OH 44118; 216-932-2145.

Herb Society of America. 2 Independence Court, Concord, MA 01742.

Herb Research Foundation. 1007 Pearl St, Suite 200, Boulder, CO 803023; www.herbs.org.

International Herb Association. PO Box 317, Mundelein, IL 60060; 847-949-4372, Fax 847-949-5896; www. herb-pros.com.

King County Solid Waste Division, Department of Natural Resources. 400 Yesler Way, Room 600, Seattle, WA 98104. Guide to yard waste compost bins, other materials and source lists. Recycling and Composting Information Line 206-294-4466; 1-800-325-6165; www.metrokc.gov/dnr/swd/index.htm.

National Center for the Preservation of Medicinal Herbs, Frontier Natural Products Co-op. 33560 Beechwood Grove Rd, Rutland, OH 45775; 740-742-4401, Fax 740-742-4401 (Frontier: 1-800-669-3275).

Seattle Tilth Association. 4649 Sunnyside Ave N, Room 1, Seattle, WA 98103; 206-633-0451, Fax 206-633-0450.

BIBLIOGRAPHY

Applehoff, Mary. *Worms Eat My Garbage.* Kalamazoo, MI: Flower Press, 1982.

Bayard, Tania. *Sweet Herbs and Sundry Flowers: Medieval Gardens and the Gardens of the Cloisters.* New York: The Metropolitan Museum of Art, 1985.

Becker, Jim and Brawner, Faye. *Scented Geraniums: Knowing, Growing and Enjoying Scented Pelargoniums.* Loveland, CO: Interweave Press, 1996.

Bown, Deni. *The Herb Society of America Encyclopedia of Herbs and Their Uses.* New York: Dorling Kindersley Publications, Inc., 1995.

Brenzel, Kathleen N., editor. *Sunset Western Garden Book Sixth Edition.* Menlo Park, CA: Sunset Publishing Corporation, 1995.

Bubel, Nancy. *The Seed Starter's Handbook.* Emmaus, PA: Rodale Press, 1978.

Campbell, Stu. *Let it Rot.* Pownal, VT: Storey Books, 1990.

Clarkson, Rosetta E. *The Golden Age of Herbs & Herbalists.* New York: Dover Publications Inc., 1972.

Engeland, Ron L. *Growing Great Garlic: The Definitive Guide for Organic Gardeners and Small Farmers.* Okanogan, WA: Filaree Productions, 1992.

Facetti, Aldo. *Natural Beauty.* New York: Simon & Schuster, 1990.

Foster, Gertrude B., and Louden, Rosemary F. *Park's Success with Herbs.* Greenwood, SC: Geo. W. Park. Seed Co. Inc., 1980.

Foster, Steven. *Herbal Renaissance.* Salt Lake City: Gibbs-Smith Publisher, 1997.

————. "Comfrey, A Fading Romance." *The Herb Companion,* Feb/Mar 1992.

Gail, Peter. *On the Trail of the Yellow Flowered Earth Nail: A Dandelion Sampler.* Cleveland Heights, OH: Goosefoot Acres Press, 1989.

Gladstar, Rosemary. *Herbal Healing for Women.* New York: Simon and Schuster, 1993.

Gordon, Lesley. *A Country Herbal.* New York: W. H. Smith Publishers Inc., 1980.

Grieve, Maude. *A Modern Herbal.* New York: Barnes & Noble Books, 1996 (reprinted from 1931 edition).

Groom, Nigel. *The Perfume Handbook.* London: Chapman & Hall, 1992.

Gunther, Erna. *Ethnobotany of Western Washington.* Seattle: University of Washington Press, 1974.

Hartman, H. T., and Kester, Dale E. *Plant Propagation: Principles and Practices.* New York: Universe Books, 1976.

Hills, Lawrence D. *Comfrey: Fodder, Food and Remedy.* New York: Universe Books, 1976.

Hitchcock, Leo J., and Cronquist, Arthur. *Flora of the Pacific Northwest.* Seattle: University of Washington Press, 1973.

Hobbs, Christopher. *Echinacea: the Immune Herb.* Soquel, CA: Botanica Press, 1990.

Hoffmann, David. *The New Holistic Herbal.* New York: Barnes & Noble Books, 1991.

Huxley, Anthony, Griffiths, Mark, and Levy, Margot, editors. *New Royal Horticultural Society Dictionary of Gardening.* London: MacMillan Press, Ltd, and New York: Stockton Press, 1992.

Keville, Kathi. *The Illustrated Herb Encyclopedia.* New York: Michael Friedman Publishing Group Inc., 1991.

Larkcom, Joy. *The Salad Garden.* New York: The Viking Press, 1984.

Lawless, Julia. *The Illustrated Encyclopedia of Essential Oils.* New York: Barnes & Noble Books, 1995.

MacNicol, Mary. *Flower Cookery.* New York: Fleet Press Corporation (The Macmillan Company), 1967.

Maury, Marguerite. *Marguerite Maury's Guide to Aromatherapy,* C. W. Daniel, 1989.

McIntyre, Anne. *The Complete Woman's Herbal.* New York: Henry Holt and Company Inc., 1995.

McLeod, Judyth A. *Lavender, Sweet Lavender.* Kenthurst NSW: Kangaroo Press Ltd, 1993.

Muenscher, Walter C., and Rice, Myron A. *Garden Spice and Wild Pot-Herbs.* Ithaca, NY: Cornell University Press, 1955.

Murray, Michael T., and Pizzorno, Joseph E. *Encyclopedia of Natural Medicine.* Rocklin, CA: Prima Publishing, 1991.

Nearing, Scott and Helen. *Building and Using our Sun Heated Greenhouse.* Charlotte, VT: Garden Way Publishing, 1977.

Phillips, Harriett F. "What Thyme Is It: A Guide to the Thyme Taxa Cultivated in the United States." In *Proceedings of the Fourth National Herb Growing and Marketing Conference,* ed.

J.E. Simon, 44–50. Silver Spring, PA: International Herb Association, 1989.

———,"The Best of Thymes." *The Herb Companion*, Apr/May 1991.

Preus, Mary E. *Growing Herbs*. Seattle: Sasquatch Books, 1994.

Phillips, Roger. *Wild Food*. Boston: Little, Brown & Company, 1986.

Rohde, Eleanour S. *Rose Recipes from Olden Times*. New York: Dover Publications Inc, 1973.

Shepherd, Renee, and Raboff, Fran. *Recipes from a Kitchen Garden*. Berkeley: 10 Speed Press, 1993.

Stary, Frantisek. *The Natural Guide to Medicinal Herbs and Plants*. New York: Barnes & Noble Books, 1994.

Stobart, Tom. *Herbs Spices and Flavorings*. Woodstock, NY: The Overlook Press, 1982.

Stuart, Malcolm, ed. *The Encyclopedia of Herbs and Herbalism*. New York: Crescent Books, 1979.

Sturdivant, Lee, and Blakley, Tim. *Medicinal Herbs in the Garden, Field, and Marketplace*. Friday Harbor, WA: San Juan Naturals, 1999.

Tisserand, Robert. *Aromatherapy: To Heal And Tend The Body*. Wilmot, WI: Lotus Press, 1988.

Tucker, Arthur O. "Will the Real Oregano Please Stand Up?" *The Herb Companion*, Feb/Mar 1992.

Turner, Nancy J. *Food Plants of Interior First Peoples*. Vancouver, BC: University of British Columbia Press, 1997.

Tyler, Varro E. *Herbs of Choice*. New York: The Haworth Press, Inc., 1994.

Vilmorin-Andrieux, Mm. *The Vegetable Garden*. Palo Alto, CA: The Jeavons-Leler Press, 1976 (reprinted from 1885 edition).

Weed, Susun S. *Healing Wise*. Woodstock, NY: The Ash Tree Press, 1989.

Weiss, Rudolf F. *Herbal Medicine*. Translated from 6th German ed. of Lehrbuch der Phytotherepie. A. R. Meuss, Beaconsfield, England: Beaconsfield Publishers Ltd., 1988.

Worwood, Valerie Ann. *The Complete Book of Essential Oils and Aromatherapy*. Novato, CA: New World Library, 1991.

INDEX